To:

_____

From:

_____

Date:

_____

Be still, and know that I am God.

PSALM 46:10

The Beauty
of the
LORD

A 365 Daily Devotional Journal

summerside
PRESS

Summerside Press™
Minneapolis 55337
www.summersidepress.com

The Beauty of the Lord
A 365 Devotional Journal
© 2011 by Summerside Press

ISBN 978-1-60936-222-5

Stock or custom editions of Summerside Press titles may be purchased in bulk for educational, business, ministry,
fundraising, or sales promotional use. For information, please e-mail specialmarkets@summersidepress.com.

Devotional writing by Vicki J. Kuyper and Patricia Mitchell in association with Snapdragon Group℠, Tulsa, OK, USA.

The "Plan for Bible Reading" was created by Scottish minister Robert Murray M'Cheyne (1813–1843).

For Bible version information, see appendix after December 31.

Cover design by faceoutstudio | www.faceoutstudio.com.
Interior design and typesetting by Thinkpen Design | www.thinkpende sign.com

Summerside Press is an inspirational publisher offering fresh, irresistible books to uplift the heart and engage the mind.

Printed in China.

Women have always had a special place in God's heart. The Bible is filled with stories extolling their beauty, wisdom, and courage. Esther's beauty placed her in a position to boldly expose the treachery of an evil man intent on destroying her people. Deborah's wisdom led her into a position of authority as a greatly respected judge over a nation. Mary the mother of Jesus courageously submitted herself to God's will and thus became the mother of the long-awaited Messiah and Savior of the world. Again and again, God has placed His confidence in women, and they have not failed Him.

God also desires to use the women of today—like you—as chosen vessels integral to His established plan. That might be in a place of notoriety visible to all the world, or it could be in a place of quiet constancy for an unseen and unsung task. Regardless of which path your life might take, He is waiting, ready to show you the amazing possibilities He has for you.

The Beauty of the Lord has 365 stirring devotions—one for each day of the year. We hope you will see each as an opportunity to draw closer to God and discover who He has created you to be. We have included a "Plan for Bible Reading" with a suggested daily reading as well. It is our prayer that these encouraging and insightful devotions will help you grow strong in your relationship with God and become more familiar with His Word.

May you be blessed with a great adventure as you discover who you truly are in God.

The Authors

Starting Fresh

The Lord's love never ends; his mercies never stop. They are new every morning.
LAMENTATIONS 3:22–23 NCV

A brand-new year feels like a fresh, new start. Those temporarily blank calendar pages invite you to fill them with appointments, birthday reminders, and vacation plans. But some things never make it onto a calendar page. They just show up, unexpectedly, for better or for worse.

Though you don't know what your future holds, there's someone who does. God knows your future, as well as your past—and He promises He can bring something good out of each day regardless of your circumstances, personal history, or hormonal ups and downs. Through Him you can daily have the hope of New Year's Day.

Begin afresh with God each morning. Though you cannot see Him, He's always near. Put yesterday into His hands. Allow His forgiveness to cleanse away any bad choices you've made. Then ask Him to fill you with the wisdom and power you need to head in a new direction, one that leads you closer to Him. Once yesterday is truly behind you, you're ready to give your heart more fully to today.

Dear God, guide my steps as I...

The Beauty of the Lord

*The Lord appeared to us in the past, saying: "I have loved you
with an everlasting love; I have drawn you with loving-kindness."*

JEREMIAH 31:3

Why does every mother believe she's given birth to the most beautiful child the world has ever seen? Because the more you love someone, the more beautiful they become in your eyes. The same is true with God.

Loving a God you cannot see can be tricky at times. That's because it's unlike any other relationship you'll ever have. You can't experience God with your five senses, like you do everyone else. But you can experience the effects of His love.

As you become more familiar with God by reading the Bible and spending time in prayer, you become more aware of God's hand at work in your life. You notice peace beginning to replace fear and worry. You find joy, even in difficult circumstances. You feel valued, even when you fail. You find forgiveness erasing your guilt and shame. You discover firsthand the true beauty of the Lord.

Draw closer to God. Celebrate the fact that He's near. Take time to bask in the beauty of loving and being loved.

God, the thing I find most beautiful about You is...

A Beautiful Reflection

When God created the human race, he made it godlike,
with a nature akin to God. He created both male
and female and blessed them.

GENESIS 5:1 MSG

"Mirror, mirror on the wall, I'm more than my appearance, after all...." Do you believe that? Or does the mirror play a larger part than you would like in your self-image? Television, movies, and modern culture try to convince you that image is everything, that youth, killer abs, and maintaining the same weight now that you had as a preteen girl are not only desirable, but expected.

God disagrees. He says your image is a reflection of His own. But you can't see this kind of image in the mirror. God is spirit, something you can't see. It's true; Jesus walked this earth dressed in a human body for a time. But God's image isn't even found in the face of Christ. God's image is more like a picture of His heart.

You were created in that image, created to reflect love, mercy, forgiveness, and grace. You'll never find these in your bathroom mirror. Instead, look at the reflection your life casts on those around you. That's where God's image can most clearly be seen.

Lord, I see Your image reflected when I...

God's Amazing Grace

How rich is God's grace, which he has given to us so fully and freely.
EPHESIANS 1:7–8 NCV

Whether you're on the dance floor, holding a yoga position, or trying out a new pair of heels, hearing the words, "You're so graceful!" can really boost your spirits. After all, there's beauty in someone who moves through life with physical grace.

But being "grace-full" is even more beautiful than being "graceful." God's love lavishes you with an endless supply of this kind of grace. His forgiveness is offered without limit. His acceptance is yours without condition. Because of God's grace, you can trust He'll always love you, no matter what.

God's grace is a gift. That means it can't be earned. When you accept it, you get a bonus gift, as well: the ability to see who you really are—a woman whose worth is beyond price.

Once you see yourself this way, you begin to recognize the worth of those around you, people just like you, wholly loved and accepted by a grace-full God. That's when God's gift of grace overflows from you into the lives of those around you. What could be more beautiful?

Dear God, I'm amazed at the grace of...

Twinkle, Twinkle, Awesome Star

[God] has made everything beautiful in its time.
He has also set eternity in the hearts of men; yet they cannot fathom
what God has done from beginning to end.
ECCLESIASTES 3:11

Suppose the stars didn't come out at night. At the end of each day a black shade is drawn across the universe, hiding its wonders from view. Then one night, God pulls back the shade. The world sees the heavens for the very first time. The Milky Way spills across the sky. Orion's belt twinkles like Christmas lights. Even those who'd never given God much thought would ask, "What—or who—has made something so grand as this?"

We walk past miracles every day. Towering trees, fragile flowers, and countless stars beckon us to explore a universe so vast we can't even begin to comprehend its size. But familiarity with the world can dim its true glory.

Take a fresh look at the world around you. Consider the power and artistry behind creation like a child who's seeing it for the very first time. Then, take joy in the fact that even though God calls every star by name, He considers you more glorious than all of them.

Open my eyes, Lord, to the glory of...

_____

_____

_____

_____

_____

_____

_____

_____

Face Your Goliath

Every child of God defeats this evil world, and we achieve this victory through our faith.
1 JOHN 5:4 NLT

Every woman faces giants during her lifetime—giants like physical illness, marital struggles, or unfulfilled dreams. When you're struggling against what feels like insurmountable odds, victory seems improbable, if not impossible. But the battle you're fighting isn't yours alone. It's also God's.

In the same way a mother would fight for her beloved child, your heavenly Father will fight for you. He's right by your side, right here, right now. He can provide the strength, wisdom, and perseverance you need to conquer any giant that comes your way. Simply put your trust in Him.

That's what David did. When this biblical hero was young, he stood up to Goliath. Too small to wear the king's armor and too weak to wield his sword, David trusted that God could use a simple shepherd armed with a slingshot to bring down a giant. He was right.

There's no Goliath in your life so big that God is not bigger still. Lean on Him. You'll not only stand up to the giants in your life but watch them fall as well.

God, one giant I need Your help in overcoming is...

_____

_____

_____

_____

_____

_____

_____

_____

Sole Mate or Soul Mate?

There are different kinds of gifts, but the same Spirit.
There are different kinds of service, but the same Lord.
1 CORINTHIANS 12:4–5

Some people view finding a spouse like matching a pair of socks. After carefully sorting through a world-sized mountain of potential mates, they find the one who matches their own fabric and design: their "sole" mate. Separately they were of little worth, just a random sock minus its corresponding mate. Now they're complete.

God's design for marriage is more like a teacup and saucer than a pair of socks. The cup and saucer may have a matching motif—or not. They complement each other in purpose and design, but they're not interchangeable. They need to be cleaned regularly and handled with care to prevent chips and cracks. Though they're in and out of hot water, they stand up to the task at hand, year after year. They're "soul" mates.

If you're married, consider how your spouse's God-given strengths complement your own. Celebrate who you are as a couple and as individuals. If you're not married, thank God that you're complete just the way you are. Married or single, wholeness is found not in other people but only in God's love.

Dear God, make me a soul mate who....

_____

_____

_____

_____

_____

_____

_____

_____

Resting in God's Love

*The beloved of the LORD rests in safety—the High God surrounds him
all day long—the beloved rests between his shoulders.*
DEUTERONOMY 33:12 NRSV

Rest...what a wonderful word. It brings to mind afternoon naps, gently swaying hammocks, or slowing your heart rate after finishing a run. Your body can't survive without rest.

God created you as a spiritual being, as well as a physical one. A well-rested soul is like a well-rested body. It has the energy it needs to face the day ahead. Are you in need of some down time with God?

It's kind of like climbing into a spiritual hammock, where you allow your entire weight to rest fully on God. There's a time to learn more about God, to read the Bible, to allow God's love to work through you as you reach out to others. This is simply a time to enjoy being close to Him.

Wherever you are, close your eyes for a moment and relax. Consider the depth of God's love for you, His absolute acceptance of who you are, His delight in your love for Him. Rest in knowing that even while you sleep, God's wide-awake, watching over you.

Help me, dear God, to rest in Your presence, especially when...

Let the Winds Blow

He who dwells in the shelter of the Most High will rest in the shadow of the Almighty.

PSALM 91:1

There's beauty in the power of a storm. But it's easier to appreciate that beauty when you're safe and warm, sheltered from what's going on outside. The same holds true when stormy circumstances blow into your life.

When tears fall like rain, tragedy blows harshly against your heart, or angry words crack like thunder through your life, don't lose hope. God promises He'll be your shelter. What He doesn't promise is perpetual blue skies. There'll always be gusts and gales, both figuratively and metaphorically, in this world. But if you turn to God when the winds begin to blow, He'll offer you protection and perspective.

God doesn't cover your eyes so you can't see what's happening. Instead, He broadens your outlook. With His help, you may notice hidden strengths revealed by the storm or rejoice in nonessential things it's washed away. He'll help you focus on what really matters.

Every storm comes to an end. But thanks to God, His plan for your life keeps moving straight ahead. Nothing can blow you off course.

God, thank You for the storms and for letting me see...

Justice Is Served

Speak up for those who cannot speak for themselves,
for the rights of all who are destitute. Speak up and judge fairly.

PROVERBS 31:8–9

There's something inside us all that cries out for justice. We want the good guys to win and the bad guys to get what they deserve. We long for heroes. We cheer for Robin Hood, fairly certain that taking from the rich and giving to the poor really is the right thing to do. The *just* thing to do.

From what we read in the Bible, it seems as though God feels the same way. He doesn't just demand justice, He promises to bring it about. Then why do murders go unsolved? Scams to rob the elderly succeed? The poor die of malnutrition while the rich continue to live in luxury?

God's vantage point is the only one broad enough to see every detail of this life—and beyond. He's also the only one wise enough to know how to administer true justice. When injustice upsets you, talk to God about it. He'll calm your anxious heart. You can trust He's already at work behind the scenes, doing the right thing. The *just* thing.

Dear Lord, I'm burdened by the injustice of...

_____

_____

_____

_____

_____

_____

_____

_____

_____

_____

_____

_____

The Gift of You

The LORD your God is with you, he is mighty to save. He will take great delight in you, he will quiet you with his love, he will rejoice over you with singing.

ZEPHANIAH 3:17

You're a gift to this world, a unique blend of family history, personality, talents, and experiences. But there's more. God's wrapped this perfect package in His love and power. That means you don't need to fear opening yourself up to others. Whether they accept the gift of you or foolishly reject such a priceless treasure, you're enough just the way you are.

Some days, holding on to this truth may be difficult. Your expectations of what a gift looks like may differ from the picture reality has painted. When this happens, allow God to remind you of who you are—instead of focusing on who you're not. You're growing and changing, continually maturing into a gift that grows more beautiful with every passing year. As you rely on God day by day, you'll find the power you need to meet the potential you hold.

Risk giving away the gift of yourself to others. There's a wonderful place in this world only you can fill.

Enable me, Lord, to share with others my gifts of...

_____

_____

_____

_____

_____

_____

_____

_____

_____

_____

_____

Longing for Beauty

Give unto the Lord the glory due unto his name;
worship the Lord in the beauty of holiness.
PSALM 29:2 KJV

Whether it's a sunset, a field of wildflowers, or the toothless grin of a newborn child, our eyes are drawn to beauty. But it's not just the exquisite nature of God's creation that catches our eye— we're drawn to many different kinds of beauty.

What we define as beautiful may differ from woman to woman. For some it's a diamond's sparkle. Others fancy impressionistic art. But even something as ordinary as a pair of socks at the mall can make us whip out our credit card so we can take a bit of beauty home with us.

Beauty is one aspect of who God is. That's why we're drawn to it. Owning something beautiful is a way of surrounding ourselves with a dim reflection of God's character. But it's a poor substitute for the real thing.

When your heart craves beauty, don't automatically head to the mall. Bask in the beauty of creation and its Creator. Each masterpiece of nature provides more than enough beauty to satisfy a hungry heart.

Lord, I think one of Your most beautiful creations is...

_____

_____

_____

_____

_____

_____

_____

_____

Emotion vs. Truth

This then is how we know that we belong to the truth...
God is greater than our hearts, and he knows everything.

1 JOHN 3:19–20

Do you feel God's presence? Is your heart resting in the assurance that God's not only watching over you but actively involved in your life? If so, celebrate.

If not, there's still cause for celebration. That's because emotions cannot be trusted to give an accurate account of the truth. Think back on your life. Has there ever been a time when you were angry over something and later realized it was simply a misunderstanding? Or perhaps you've woken up on the proverbial "wrong side of the bed," knowing there was nothing really wrong, but just feeling out of sorts?

God knows the role emotions play in your life. He wove them deeply into your feminine frame. They're a physical response to what's happening both inside and outside of you. They don't evaluate. They simply react. Right or wrong.

Regardless of what you are feeling, God is near. His love for you is based on truth, rather than emotions. You're His daughter, His delight. Like a good father, God will never abandon His children.

Dear God, today I feel...

Common Ground for Uncommon Love

If we are living in the light, as God is in the light, then we have fellowship with each other.

1 JOHN 1:7 NLT

God loves diversity. New species are still being discovered. His world is a mosaic of landscapes. He created generations of people of different sizes, shapes, colors, and personalities. Every face, fingerprint, and life story is a one-of-a-kind wonder.

Though God loves diversity, His children seem to have a harder time embracing it. In general, we like to hang out with people like us. They usually live in the same area of town, fall into the same income bracket, and have a similar educational background. Their nationality, race, and religious beliefs commonly bear a striking resemblance to our own.

The world's so much bigger than our own backyard. Inviting those who see things from a different point of view into our circle of relationships can teach us a lot about life, love, and God.

Instead of allowing differences to come between you, focus on what you have in common with the rest of the world. The same God who loves you loves each and every person you meet.

Lord, someone I'd like to get to know better is...

_____

_____

_____

_____

_____

_____

_____

_____

_____

From Ordinary to Extraordinary

Before they call I will answer, while they are yet speaking I will hear.

ISAIAH 65:24 NRSV

It would be nice if God had human arms, so you could find comfort in His embrace. There's one way you can. God's Spirit works through the lives of every person who chooses to follow Him. That means the answer to your prayers may come to you through human hands.

Throughout history, God has worked through people to fulfill His plans. The Red Sea parted when Moses stretched out his arms, allowing God's people to escape. The walls of Jericho fell after Joshua obeyed God's direction to walk and then blow trumpets. A young girl gave birth to the Savior of the world by saying yes to God. In each case, God's power worked through ordinary people to accomplish extraordinary things.

As you look for God's answers to your prayers for help, don't overlook God's gift of those around you. God can inspire them to speak the words you need to hear or to act in ways that fill your needs. Who knows? The very next hug you receive may be an embrace from the Lord.

Lord, You answered my prayer through another person when...

The Goodness of God's Character

Love the LORD your God,
listen to his voice, and hold fast to him.
For the LORD is your life.
DEUTERONOMY 30:20

Forrest Gump said, "Life is like a box of chocolates." Sometimes we act as though God's a box of chocolates. We choose what we like about His character. We select what suits our own personal taste and lifestyle. What we don't care for, we put back in the box.

Like people, God's a complex being. It takes time to get to know Him on a deeply intimate level. His love and mercy may appeal to us right away. But attributes such as power and purity may take longer to appreciate.

Savor the time you spend getting to know God as you would a box of fine chocolates. You probably wouldn't wolf down a box of Godiva in one sitting. You would slowly consider the qualities of each individual piece. At first, you'd most likely reach for your favorites. But over time, chances are you'd work your way through the whole box. You'd accept that at the right time, goodness can even be found in a coconut cream.

Lord, a quality of Your character I need to digest more slowly is...

_____

_____

_____

_____

_____

_____

_____

_____

What's Your Status?

Continue in prayer, and watch
in the same with thanksgiving.
COLOSSIANS 4:2 KJV

Prayer can be intimidating. After all, you're speaking to the God of the universe. So, how do you begin? Is there a right way to pray? Should you speak aloud or in your head? Should you be on your knees? At church? Are any topics taboo?

If prayer is something you're uncomfortable with, think about it in terms of Facebook. You keep in touch with your friends by letting them know how you're feeling and what you're doing. That's exactly how prayer begins.

Tell God what's on your heart. You can communicate aloud, in a whisper, silently, or even by writing in a journal. God's always online. Though He already knows what's going on in your life, He loves to hear your voice and wants to connect with you on a deeper level.

The more you share with God, the more you'll learn to trust Him. There's nothing too big or too small to share. No secret words you need to say. Talk to God as you would anyone who loves you, frequently and from the heart.

God, one thing I'd like to share with You today is...

_____

_____

_____

_____

_____

_____

_____

_____

Three Little Words

The LORD delights in those who fear him, who put their hope in his unfailing love.
PSALM 147:11

They're on billboards, bumper stickers, T-shirts, even toothbrushes. Three little words: GOD LOVES YOU. This statement is tossed about so casually these days, it's almost a cliché. But don't let familiarity with the phrase diminish the power of the truth behind it.

It's not a feel-good motto. It's a steadfast promise. It's the assurance that God (the almighty Creator and Ruler of everything) loves (sacrificially, unconditionally, and eternally cares for and is devoted to) you.

It's true that God loves everyone in the world. But He doesn't love you just because you're a part of that mass of humanity. He loves you as an individual. And the good news doesn't stop there.

The Bible says God not only loves you but delights in you. When you delight in something, you celebrate it. You take joy in every detail. Picture a new mother so delighted with her child that she can't help but smile every time she catches sight of her face. You are that child. Take time to delight in your Father's love for you today.

God, knowing You delight in me makes me feel...

The Perfect Ensemble

As God's chosen people, holy and dearly loved,
clothe yourselves with compassion, kindness,
humility, gentleness and patience.
COLOSSIANS 3:12

If you're a cowgirl, you wear a hat and boots. If you're a nurse, a stethoscope and comfortable shoes are more suitable attire. If you're a judge, you'll sport a robe that differs from the one hanging by the shower. But is there an appropriate outfit for a child of God?

The outfit God asks you to clothe yourself in each day isn't one you'll find in your closet. It's one fashioned by God's Spirit. Being on God's best-dressed list means putting on things like kindness, humility, patience, and compassion. Every item on God's list benefits others, as well as yourself. It makes you more attractive because people are drawn toward those who love them well.

But God has given you free will. That means you have the option of saying yes or no to His wardrobe choice. Choices as small as really listening when someone speaks, carefully choosing your words, or being courteous to other drivers not only looks good on you, but allows others to see an invisible God in a visible way.

Dear God, please help clothe me in...

_____

_____

_____

_____

_____

_____

_____

_____

Not Always in the Spotlight

God looked over everything he had made; it was so good, so very good!
GENESIS 1:31 MSG

Who do you look up to? Chances are they're on a pedestal because they've done something you feel you can't. Maybe you can sing, but not like Celine Dion. Maybe you can write, but not like Shakespeare. Maybe you can inspire others, but not like Rev. Martin Luther King Jr.

Your inner critic is right. You'll never be anybody other than the wonderful woman God created you to be. As for Celine, Shakespeare, and King, they could never be you. No matter how hard they tried. Each person has a place in this world to fill. Though some spots draw more attention than others, the degree of notoriety you receive from others matters only to your ego. What matters in the end is what God says about you.

God looks at your heart, not your awards, accolades, or list of accomplishments. He applauds everything you do in love, regardless of whether it's acknowledged by others or accomplished in secret. When you do as God asks, you truly are a woman of worth.

Dear Lord, some things only I could do are...

_____

_____

_____

_____

_____

_____

_____

_____

_____

_____

Are You a "Yes" Woman?

God affirms us, making us a sure thing in Christ, putting his Yes within us.
2 CORINTHIANS 1:21 MSG

"Yes" seems like such a good word. A loving word. One that overflows from women who are generous in spirit and compassionate in deed.

But yes isn't always the best answer. Just because God has placed a desire in you to care for others, doesn't mean He's asked you to be everyone's answer to prayer. Your time is limited. So are your financial, physical, and emotional resources.

So, before you say yes, give yourself an opportunity to say no. Ask for time to think before answering a request. Then, talk to God. Ask for His guidance. Don't allow the emotion of the moment or pressure from others to dictate your answer. If your yes isn't wholehearted, it isn't a true answer to prayer.

Remember, "no" can also be an answer to someone's prayer. It can give others the opportunity to step up and help. It can also help the one asking to brainstorm other, and perhaps better, options.

God's the only one you should say yes to right away. Everyone else can wait until God gives you the green light.

Lord, for me the hardest thing about saying no is...

_____

_____

_____

_____

_____

_____

_____

_____

Cleaning Up Conflict

A fool shows his annoyance at once,
but a prudent man overlooks an insult.
PROVERBS 12:16

If only life were like a self-cleaning oven. Then, when anger boiled over, inattentiveness burned a relational bridge, or behavior created a royal mess, all you'd have to do is turn a dial. You could come back later and everything would be as good as new.

But no, life is more like the old-fashioned clean-it-yourself model. The longer you let things sit, the harder they are to clean up. This is especially true with relational conflict. If you don't attend to misunderstandings, hurt feelings, and offenses right away, they build up and get baked on.

Sometimes, if the controversy is exceedingly hot, it's best to let things cool down before trying to clean up. This helps both parties get their emotions in check so more angry words don't spill over. Just don't forget to come back to it.

Whether you feel you're at fault or not, you can still reach out to mend a relationship. Even if the other person refuses to reconcile, through God, you have the power to forgive. Does your relational oven need attending to today?

God, one relationship I need help cleaning up is...

The Prayer of Healthy Habits

Do you not know that your body is a temple of the Holy Spirit within you,
which you have from God, and that you are not your own?

1 CORINTHIANS 6:19 NRSV

Suppose you shatter a bottle of perfume. So what. Perfume may be valuable, but it isn't irreplaceable.

Life is both. Our bodies are incredibly fragile and complex. They can shatter, break down, or simply wear out. God hasn't given us the option of picking up a new one when things go wrong. At least not until we get to heaven. In the meantime, we have a responsibility to care for this precious gift.

We all know we should eat a balanced diet, exercise, and schedule an annual physical. However, it's easy to let these healthy habits slide when we're feeling fine. We only take action when something goes wrong.

Have you ever considered that the way you care for your body reflects how grateful you are to God for His gift? Choosing a healthy food alternative can be one way of praising God. Exercise can be a time of worship. What will you do today to show your appreciation for the body God's given you?

Because my body is Your creation, I will...

_____

_____

_____

_____

_____

_____

_____

_____

Totally Devoted to You

The LORD is faithful to all his promises and loving toward all he has made.
PSALM 145:13

It's the plot of countless chick flicks: A woman falls for the bad boy who's inconsiderate and unreliable. But she keeps coming back, entrusting her heart to the wrong guy. Then Mr. Right comes along. She's suspicious, afraid to wholly give her heart away. In time, Mr. Right's faithfulness wins her over. Roll credits.

On film and in life, both men and women are "bad boys" at times. They're selfish, insensitive, and can't be trusted to show up in a crisis. Sometimes they break their promises. Sometimes they break your heart. If people you depended on have let you down in the past, don't allow humanity's fickleness to harden your heart against the goodness of God.

God is steadfastly faithful. He's never made a promise He hasn't kept. And He promises that nothing, not even death, can separate you from Him. If you're longing for someone who's truly devoted to you, who'll never leave, whose love will never fail, there is only one Mr. Right. Entrust your heart to God. He'll never let you down.

Lord, I am totally devoted to You because...

You've Got Mail

Let the message about Christ, in all its richness, fill your lives.
Teach and counsel each other with all the wisdom he gives.
COLOSSIANS 3:16 NLT

Suppose you found your mailbox filled with letters bearing the return address of "Heaven." Each envelope addressed to you and signed "Eternally Yours, God." Chances are that after you looked around to see who might be playing tricks on you, you'd find a quiet spot and start reading, treasuring every word.

God has sent you more than just a mailbox full of letters. He's sent you a whole collection of letters, poetry, and historical records. It's called the Bible. In it, God recounts the history of your family tree, all the way back to the creation of the world. He advises you how to make wise decisions, persevere through difficult circumstances, love others well, and head home to heaven when your time on earth is through. He also includes love letters to remind you you're worth dying for.

Reading God's letters is one way of staying in touch with Him while you're here on earth. God's letters won't answer all of your questions. They can never take the place of a personal discussion. But until the day comes when that opportunity is yours, keep reading.

I'm writing back to You, God, to say...

_____

_____

_____

_____

_____

_____

_____

_____

The Sound of Silence

For God alone my soul waits in silence; from him comes my salvation.
PSALM 62:1 NRSV

How long can you sit in silence, waiting to hear God's voice? If you're like most women, you'll find yourself uncomfortable with the stillness and anxious for a little action in a matter of minutes. But the hurry, worry, and constant clamor of everyday life can drown out the whisper of God's voice. If you want to know God better, you need to become acquainted with what it means to be quiet, inside and out.

Turn off your cell phone, as well as your own list of prayer requests. Prayer is a conversation, and this is God's time to speak. His voice may come as unexpected insight into a problem or a gentle nudge to take action in a situation. Or you may simply feel the peace of His presence filling you with the quiet strength you need to face the day ahead. The more frequently you take time to sit in silence, the more comfortable it will become—and the more easily you'll recognize God's voice during those times when life refuses to quiet down.

When I sit in silence with You, Lord, I hear...

Try Compassion On for Size

Whenever we have an opportunity,
let us work for the good of all,
and especially for those of the family of faith.
GALATIANS 6:10 NRSV

Trying on shoes at the mall can be a fun way to spend the afternoon. Putting yourself in someone else's shoes is usually much less pleasant. What's it like to be an unwed mother, a cancer patient, a homeless teen, or a child on the other side of the world who goes to bed hungry every night?

In the same way an ill-fitting shoe can hurt your toes, trying on someone else's struggles can hurt your heart. That's what compassion does. It empathizes with the difficulties of others so closely that we take on their burdens as if they were our own.

Even though empathizing with the struggles of others can make us more grateful for the blessings we enjoy in our own lives, God's goal isn't for us to feel downcast about their situation. God's gift of compassion is designed to spur us into action.

What can you do to help lighten someone's load? A good way to start is with prayer. Then allow compassion, and God's Spirit, to direct your steps.

Lord, someone I have compassion for is...

_____

_____

_____

_____

_____

_____

_____

A Word to the Wise

What you say can mean life or death. Those who speak with care will be rewarded.
PROVERBS 18:21 NCV

Knives can be used to hurt or heal. They can take a life by maiming an innocent bystander or save a life by removing an invasive tumor. It all depends on how the one wielding the blade chooses to put it to use.

Words are the same way. They can be deadly weapons or healing balms. They can cut someone down to size or build someone up. How skillfully, and lovingly, do you wield the words that come out of your mouth?

For most women, talking comes easily. We speak quickly and passionately, often right over the top of one another. But the more words we speak, the better chance there is to use them thoughtlessly.

The Bible offers some great advice on how to use your words well. Be quick to listen and slow to speak. Think of each word as a gift, carefully chosen for the individual who'll receive it. Be more generous with your encouragement than with your criticism. When in doubt, hold your tongue. Wise words are a gift that fits every situation just right.

Lord, enable me to use my words to...

Ready . . . Wait . . . Go!

I wait for the LORD, my soul waits, and in his word I hope;
my soul waits for the Lord more than those who watch for the morning.
PSALM 130:5–6 NRSV

Every day you spend some of your precious time waiting. You wait at red lights, wait at the dentist's office, wait for your kids to hurry up and get ready before you hop in the car. In short, you hang around waiting to go!

Time spent waiting feels like wasted time, especially when your Day Planner has overflowed into the margins. The more hectic your day, the more just standing around can make you squirm. After all, we aren't called the human *race* for nothing!

But life is not the same kind of race that's run at the track. God's given you a "pause" button, as well as "stop" and "go." When your button gets pushed, whether by an interruption, inconvenience, or even an illness, don't lament it. Use it. It's a reminder that God's in control and you're not. Ask Him to help adjust both your pace and your perspective, so they're in step with His own.

God, a "pause" button in my life I'm frustrated with is…

_____

_____

_____

_____

_____

_____

_____

_____

Poured Out for Love

[God] gives strength to the weary and increases the power of the weak.
ISAIAH 40:29

If you're like most women, the role of caregiver plays an important part in your daily life. Perhaps you're a mom—or find yourself caring for one. Or maybe you're helping out a friend who's ill, or volunteering your time to aid those in need in your community.

As you pour yourself out for others, it's easy to find yourself running dry. One reason may be that you see the needs around you as immediate and your own as something you can attend to when you have time. The time is now.

A pitcher may be used to pour glass after glass of water for many years. However, it can only pour a limited number of servings at one time before being refilled. You're designed the same way.

God's your caregiver, the only one who never grows tired or runs dry. Call on Him to refill your energy and enthusiasm when they begin to run low. He'll teach you how to give, as well as rest and receive, so you can serve those you love with joy.

Dear God, one way You pour out Your love for me is...

_____

_____

_____

_____

_____

_____

_____

_____

_____

_____

_____

_____

Keep Holding God's Hand

The Lord is not slow in keeping his promise, as some understand slowness.
He is patient with you, not wanting anyone to perish, but everyone to come to repentance.

2 PETER 3:9

God is both patient and kind. He's not a quick-tempered parent, expecting you to do things perfectly. He's the one holding your hand as you learn to walk. Helping you move forward one step at a time. Picking you up when you fall. Cheering you on when you get discouraged. Whispering, "You can do it!" when you need to hear it most.

God knows what you're capable of, for better or worse. Though He desires great things from you, He knows the learning curve of life can be steep. He's fully aware of your fears, your failures, your weaknesses, and even your secrets. He doesn't hold them against you. He fully loves and accepts you. That's why He wants to help you get rid of anything that's preventing you from holding on tightly to Him.

God's patient love is a safety net that allows you to risk living the life He's planned for you. Just keep walking, and hold on tight.

Dear God, help me hold on to You and let go of...

_____

_____

_____

_____

_____

_____

_____

_____

_____

_____

Loving the Unlovable

Love is not rude, is not selfish, and does not get upset with others.
Love does not count up wrongs that have been done.
1 CORINTHIANS 13:5 NCV

There are some people who get on your last nerve. They're the individuals who make you thankful for caller ID. Sometimes you avoid them. When that doesn't work, you complain about them to anyone who'll listen. After all, it's hard to love someone you don't like.

God doesn't ask us to like everyone. He asks us to love them. Though love can be something we feel, it's also something we do. God asks us to use love as a verb—even with those who rub us the wrong way.

A great way to begin is with prayer. Praying for God's best in the lives of others, whether you like them or not, softens your heart toward them. This makes you more open to listening to their story, which can help you better understand why they do the things they do.

God doesn't ask you to be everyone's best friend. He simply asks that you keep their best interests at heart and love them because He does.

God, someone I need Your help loving is...

Power in the Right Hands

With God's power working in us,
God can do much, much more
than anything we can ask or imagine.

EPHESIANS 3:20 NCV

Radioactive substances are powerful. They can wipe out a city via an atomic bomb or help cure a patient of cancer. Some are also unstable, which means they have to be handled with the utmost of care. They may be volatile, but they aren't malevolent. Whether they bring destruction or healing, that kind of power demands respect.

God's more powerful than any kind of radioactive substance. He should be. He created them all. This magnitude of power is so great it's hard for us to comprehend. Just think about the powerful precision it would take to create atomic particles, the solar system, DNA, or life itself, from absolutely nothing.

While God's mighty power demands a healthy respect, you don't have to be afraid of Him. That's because He's absolutely loving, as well as all-powerful. He doesn't wield His power recklessly, but with wisdom and care. Knowing that an almighty God is for you, not against you, can give you the courage you need to handle whatever challenges today may bring your way.

Lord, I'm glad You are both almighty and loving because...

_____

_____

_____

_____

_____

_____

_____

_____

God Can Carry It All

Trust the Lord with all your heart,
and don't depend on your own understanding.
PROVERBS 3:5 NCV

Tragedy strikes. Your best friend's diagnosed with breast cancer. A coworker gets laid off work. An earthquake halfway around the world fills the news. So you pray. That's a good thing. You keep praying. That's even better. But after a while, especially if the situation doesn't seem to improve, you may begin to feel weighed down, depressed.

The more you pray for others, the more their burdens may feel as if they're your own. This can lead you to feeling personally responsible for fixing the problem.

There's only one Savior of the world and it isn't you. God loves those you're praying for more than you ever could. He also sees a much bigger picture. His answers to your prayers may not always be what you expect—or want.

Allow God to be God. When you pray, give Him more than your requests. Hand over the entire burden of what you feel responsible to help carry. It's too heavy for you. You can trust God to do the right thing, even if you don't always understand what that is.

God, would You please carry...

_____

_____

_____

_____

_____

_____

_____

_____

The Pinnacle of Perfection

As for God, his way is perfect;
the word of the LORD is flawless.
He is a shield for all who take refuge in him.

2 SAMUEL 22:31

When grocery shopping, you pass by the bruised peach or overripe banana. Before leaving the house, you make sure your hair isn't sticking up like a rooster's comb. When considering marriage, you're out to find Mr. Right, not Mr. Will-Do-in-a-Pinch.

It's human nature to favor what's unblemished over what's flawed. Given a choice, we choose the best. But often, we want even more than that. We want perfection. We desire it in what we purchase, whom we marry, and how we look. But the only place we can find perfection is in God.

Only God is flawless. He never makes a mistake. He does everything right the very first time. His love, justice, wisdom, beauty…all are without fault or flaw. This perfect God loves imperfect people, perfectly. That's because His forgiveness is as flawless as His knowledge of our lives.

Only a perfect God can be perfectly trustworthy when it comes to doing the right thing. What are you trusting Him for today?

Lord, today I am trusting You for…

_____

_____

_____

_____

_____

_____

_____

Fear Factors

This is what the LORD says to you:
"Do not be afraid or discouraged.
For the battle is not yours, but God's."
2 CHRONICLES 20:15

What are you afraid of? Every woman has her own unique list. Snakes and big hairy bugs may be on yours. But it's just as likely to include things like air travel, water, heights, enclosed spaces, or public speaking. Then there are the more personal fears. "Will my mammogram be okay?" "Will I lose my job?" "Will my husband leave me?"

Fear can stop even a bold, confident woman in her tracks. When you come face-to-face with something you fear, remember that you never face your fears alone. God is with you. Like a valiant warrior, He fights for and protects you. He wants to replace your fears with His peace.

When your heart begins to race, turn to God. Ask Him to help you sift what's rational from what's irrational. If there's a real need for caution, He can provide the wisdom you need to know what you should do. Finally, take courage. Knowing God's near can give you the strength you need to face whatever comes your way.

Lord, my greatest fear right now is...

_____

_____

_____

_____

_____

_____

_____

_____

Strengthening Your Heart

Just as you received Christ Jesus as Lord, continue to live in him, rooted and built up in him, strengthened in the faith as you were taught, and overflowing with thankfulness.

COLOSSIANS 2:6–7

If you're employed in the customer service industry, you know "the customer is always right." Or, at least you're supposed to act as though they are. Even if people are demanding or rude, your job is to put on a smile and do your best to meet their needs.

Having a servant's heart is not about customer service. It's about loving others well. That's what Jesus did. Even though He had all the power and privilege of being the God of the universe, He humbled Himself to walk on this earth. He patiently listened to those in need, healed the hurting, and sacrificed His own life for the lives of those who didn't appreciate the magnitude of His gift.

God asks you to have a heart like His, for it will take His Spirit working through you to serve others without expecting anything in return. Give your servant's heart a workout today by asking, "How can I help?"

Enable me, God, to give my servant's heart a workout by...

_____

_____

_____

_____

_____

_____

_____

_____

_____

The Freedom of Forgiveness

The Lord our God is merciful and forgiving, even though we have rebelled against him.

DANIEL 9:9

The older we get, the more pressure we feel to hide who we really are. We choose an outfit that hides those extra pounds, color our hair to cover the gray, and whiten our teeth to conceal our addiction to Starbucks. We don makeup in hopes of making up a more youthful image for ourselves. We can try to hide the truth, but we can't change it.

We can't hide the truth from God either. Good or bad, God sees it all. But the good news is that God offers you a way to erase the poor choices you've made. When you ask God to forgive you for the times you've turned your back on Him, it's as though they never happened.

God doesn't rewrite history. If your bad decisions had adverse consequences, you'll still have to work through them. But in God's eyes, it's like you've been declared "not guilty" of what you've done. He doesn't offer you a cover-up. He provides an absolute pardon. All you have to do is ask— no matter what.

God, please forgive me for...

_____

_____

_____

_____

_____

_____

_____

_____

Gratitude Always Fits Just Right

O give thanks to the LORD, for he is good; for his steadfast love endures for ever.
PSALM 107:1 NRSV

Want to know a great gift idea for God? Gratitude. You don't have to wait for a special occasion. Gratitude is a gift you can give every day of the year. The funny thing is, the more you give, the more you'll discover you have on hand.

Cultivating a grateful heart begins by slowing down long enough to notice what you have. Consider it anti-advertising. The goal of advertising is to direct people's attention toward what they're missing, to leave them feeling discontent with what they've been given.

Gratitude reminds you of what you already have, of gifts easily taken for granted. These can be as small as the beauty of an almond tree in bloom or as large as the gift of your very next breath. When you recognize every good gift ultimately comes from God, you can't help but feel grateful. This deepens the pleasure of even an ordinary day, making you not only more content, but more generous with what you've received. Gratitude is a gift that simply can't stop giving.

God, thank You so much for...

Wonderful by Design

Thank you for making me so wonderfully complex!
your workmanship is marvelous—how well I know it.
PSALM 139:14 NLT

In the mid-1800s, one nickname for women was "spare parts." Since the Bible said Eve was fashioned from Adam's rib, some people reasoned she was more of an accessory than an invaluable, indispensable creation. But the Bible tells a totally different story.

The Bible tells us God appointed women as judges and prophets. They played a vital role in the rise and fall of cities, armies, and kings. Esther saved God's people from slaughter. Deborah strategized the downfall of an evil ruler. Mary gave birth to Jesus, God's own Son.

Jesus Himself treated women with equality and respect, atypical of the custom of that day. He spoke to women one-on-one. He healed them with His touch. He invited them to sit at His feet, to listen and learn. After He rose from the dead, to whom did He appear first? Women.

Even today, some countries, cultures, and individuals regard women as second-class citizens. God never has and never will. God wove your femininity into every fiber of your design. You truly are beautifully and wonderfully made.

Thank You, God, for making me...

Giving God Your Best

But seek first the kingdom of God and His righteousness,
and all these things shall be added to you.
MATTHEW 6:33 NKJV

If you ask your family what they'd like for dinner, it's unlikely they'll shout, "Leftovers!" That's because leftovers are rarely as tasty the second time around. They take a lot less time, thought, and effort to prepare than the original meal—and it shows.

Often, that's exactly what we give to God. Leftovers. If we have a few extra minutes before we head to the office, then we'll spend some time with God. If we have a little cash left over at the end of the month, then we'll place it in the offering. If other plans fall through, then we'll share God's love by helping new neighbors unload their U-Haul.

Love can't be reheated. If it's only offered when it's convenient, it isn't really love. It's duty. It's given out of a sense of obligation instead of devotion.

Loving God with your heart, soul, mind, and strength takes more than wishful thinking. It requires your sacrifice, not your surplus; offering your best, instead of what's left. How will you choose to serve God today?

Lord, I want to give You my best by...

_____

_____

_____

_____

_____

_____

_____

_____

A Shower of Blessing

There shall be showers of blessing.
EZEKIEL 34:26 KJV

A single drop of rain glistening on your window may seem insignificant. It doesn't have the power to sustain a plant or quench a person's thirst. It simply evaporates and disappears. But consider what happens when that single drop is joined by thousands, millions, or billions of other drops. They can replenish a city's water supply, nourish a field of grain, or even carve the Grand Canyon. Single drops have incredible power when they work together.

You're only one woman out of a world of 6.9 billion people, a single drop in the sea of humanity. But God created people to live and work in community. When you work together as part of a team, the difference you make grows exponentially.

The local church is God's team. Being part of it can help deepen your relationship with God, as well as expand your circle of friends. But God's church has a bigger role to fill. Working together, you have the opportunity to become a shower of blessing, helping quench the needs of a thirsty world.

Dear God, as part of a community, I want to...

_____

_____

_____

_____

_____

_____

_____

_____

_____

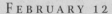

Home, Beautiful Home

*[Jesus said], "In My Father's house are many mansions; if it were
not so, I would have told you. I go to prepare a place for you."*

JOHN 14:2 NKJV

Home is a special place where you can relax and be yourself. It's often the place you share with those you love most. Home is more than just the dwelling you live in. It whispers, "This is where you belong."

When God created you, He gave you two homes. One's here on earth and the other's in heaven. It's much easier to relate to the one you can decorate and inhabit here and now. The place you live, the people you love, and the work you do help to fill your days with a sense of stability and purpose.

The thought of leaving behind what's familiar, everything we know and love, can sound scary—if it were not for the fact that Someone who loves us, and knows us, even better than our closest family has already prepared a home for us. God says our home in heaven is unimaginably beautiful, and it's one we'll never have to leave. Once we arrive, we'll realize there truly is "no place like home."

Lord, I think heaven will be like...

_____

_____

_____

_____

_____

_____

_____

_____

Rooted in Faith

I am like an olive tree growing in God's Temple. I trust God's love.
PSALM 52:8 NCV

Growth isn't always visible to the eye. It often works undercover, splitting open seeds, pushing fresh, green shoots upward toward the surface, digging sturdy roots deeper into the darkness of fertile soil.

The same is true with spiritual growth. At times you may feel you're growing by leaps and bounds. You're learning so much about who God is and seeing your life change as a result. But every growing season has its winter. There will also be times when you may feel stuck, as though no matter how much you work, pray, or read God's Word, old habits refuse to die. The warmth of God's love may feel as though it's a thing of the past. Consequently, your desire to persevere may feel like it's withering away.

When winter comes, cling to what you know about God. Trust in His unfailing love and His Spirit's power to encourage your growth. Spring will come. It's only a matter of time. Until then, don't give up drawing closer to God. Allow your roots to grow deep.

Lord, in this season of faith, help me to...

The Ultimate Valentine

In Christ Jesus you who once were far away have been brought near through the blood of Christ.
EPHESIANS 2:13

God is wooing you. Like a suitor trying to win your love, God sends valentines your way every day. When your heart responds to the splendor of a bird in flight or the unexpected gift of a rainbow, God's revealing His tender, artistic side. Like an admirer bearing a gift of homegrown roses, He's wooing you with beauty, sharing what He's created with the one He loves.

But Jesus is God's ultimate valentine. By confining His majesty to the constraints of human form, God reached out to you with a hand that could feel your pain and a heart that broke beneath the weight of the times you rejected Him. What kind of valentine will you send in return?

All God asks is your love. But as every woman who's ever been romanced knows, love's more than exchanging conversation hearts or bearing bouquets. It's opening yourself to another in an honest, intimate way. It's a commitment to share your heart, your time, your possessions, your dreams, and your life. Are you ready to say, "I do"?

Lord, be my valentine so I can share...

The Secret of Success

[Jesus said,] "Follow Me,
and I will make you fishers of men."
MATTHEW 4:19 NKJV

Jesus' disciples understood "net worth." After all, most of them were fisherman. What they brought up in their nets was a measure of how successful their day had been. But Jesus asked His disciples to put down their nets and fish for people instead. To do this type of fishing, the disciples cast out a net of love, sharing and showing others how much God cared for them.

In God's eyes, the disciples lived successful lives. They weren't rich. They weren't well educated. They didn't have fancy titles that followed their names. Most didn't even marry or raise a family. What they did was what God asked. They devoted their lives to loving others well.

God asks you to do the very same thing. You don't have to move to some remote part of the globe to share God's love. You can follow God right where you are. Ask Him to show you the secret to leading a successful life by learning to love the same way Jesus' disciples did. Then go fish.

God, I want to be successful; teach me to...

The Freedom to Follow

It was for freedom that Christ set us free.

GALATIANS 5:1 NASB

God offers you a life of ultimate freedom. Freedom from guilt, despair, judgment, condemnation...the list of things God's freed you from goes on and on. But one thing God hasn't freed you from is rules.

Wait! Isn't true freedom the option of doing anything you want? Yes and no. Some rules may limit your actions while increasing your freedom. Take traffic laws. They help make order out of potential chaos, allowing traffic to flow more safely and freely. Or how about recipes? You're free to replace sugar with ground pepper when baking brownies, but you may not be able to choke down the result.

God didn't give us commandments like, "Do not lie," "Do not commit adultery," or "Worship God above all others" because He's a control freak. He gave them because He loves us and wants the best for us. God's rules teach us how to love Him and others well. As we follow God's rules, our relationships—and therefore our lives—go more smoothly. That makes us freer to enjoy each day to the fullest.

Thank You, God, for setting me free from...

God's Answers Are Well Done

See how the farmer waits for the land to yield its valuable crop and how patient
he is for the autumn and spring rains. You too, be patient and stand firm.

JAMES 5:7–8

Even if your family were hungry, you'd refuse to serve them undercooked chicken. You wouldn't risk their health to save a little time.

God feels the same way about you. That's why He'll never serve up an answer to prayer before it's ready. You may be hungry for a change, but God won't be rushed. A significant part of your personal growth comes from learning to trust God's timing, especially when your heart is crying, "I need it now!"

Consider what it was like for Jesus' disciples when He died on the cross. They undoubtedly felt God had abandoned them. But God's plan was so much better than any answer to prayer they could've imagined. Jesus rose from the dead. He promised His followers God's Spirit would be with them until He returned again. This promise extends to you. Ask God's Spirit to help fortify your patience as you wait for His answers. Because God's timing is always right.

God, please help me watch and wait patiently for Your answer to...

Turn the Page

[God said,] "Forget the former things; do not dwell on the past.
See, I am doing a new thing! Now it springs up; do you not perceive it?"
ISAIAH 43:18–19

When reading a compelling novel, you can't wait to turn the page to find out what happens next. But when it comes to the story of their lives, some people refuse to move forward. They relive the same page over and over again in their minds. They may be stuck in heartache or regret. Or perhaps they're lost in lamenting "the good old days," when life seemed happier.

Your life story rivals any current best seller. It has it all: drama, humor, mystery, suspense, and love. But like any story, you can't understand how it fits together until you get to the end. What looks like a horrible situation somewhere in the middle may be exactly what brings the heroine (that's you!) to a place where she's able to discover her greatest joy.

If you're stuck in the past, ask God to help you learn what you can from it. Then turn the page. Leave yesterday behind. Today's ready to be written and enjoyed.

God, I'm thankful You wrote into the story of my life...

Carrying Others' Dirty Laundry

See to it that no one fails to obtain the grace of God;
that no root of bitterness springs up and causes trouble.

HEBREWS 12:15 NRSV

If someone's hurt you, intentionally or not, you try to reconcile. You explain how you feel. You accept any responsibility you have for the problem and apologize. You listen to what the other person has to say.

If that person's willing to work things out, you forgive the same way God forgave you—without conditions. If he or she isn't interested in fixing things, you still do the exact same thing. Forgive. Easy to do? No. The right thing to do? Always.

Just because that's what God asks, doesn't mean it isn't tempting to pick up a little something as you leave. It's called a grudge. But the only thing a grudge changes is you. It weighs you down and makes you bitter. That bitterness can spill over into angry, complaining words or a self-righteous attitude. Neither of these reflects the true heart of the woman God created you to be.

Carrying a grudge is like toting around someone else's dirty laundry. Ask God to help you pick up forgiveness instead.

God, once and for all, please help me forgive...

_____

_____

_____

_____

_____

_____

_____

_____

The Honest Truth

Lying lips are abomination to the LORD:
but they that deal truly are his delight.

PROVERBS 12:22 KJV

A lie is like a skirt on a bathing suit. It's an attempt to cover up something you'd rather others not see. Differentiating between a "little white lie" and a "whopper" is just another way of skirting the truth. The truth is reality. It can't be stretched. Either something's true or it's not.

It's easy to get into a habit of exaggeration, giving insincere compliments or blending truth with what we wish were true. This is often done to save face. We want people to think highly of us, to like us. Other times, we go a step further. We flat-out lie on our taxes, on an application, or even to our spouse. We don't value honesty enough to break our dishonesty habit.

Every lie, big or small, breaks God's heart. That's because honesty is a form of authenticity. God never lies about who He is or what He's done. He's true in every sense of the word. That's one reason you can trust Him. When you live honestly, authentically, that's when you're ultimately the true you.

Dear God, help me be honest when...

_____

_____

_____

_____

_____

_____

_____

_____

_____

_____

_____

_____

God's Place of Peace

You, LORD, give true peace to those who
depend on you because they trust you.
ISAIAH 26:3 NCV

Today's headlines suggest that peace is not just improbable but impossible. Wars, earthquakes, injustice, global warming, economic instability...world events proclaim that we live in a time of chaos where life is destined to go from bad to worse.

But our heavenly Father is a God of order, not chaos. Even in the direst of circumstances, He reaches out to us and offers us a place of peace. The world around us may feel as though it's falling apart, but inside God's putting us together "piece by peace."

Take your eyes off the brokenness around you. Focus on God and His promises. Allow His Spirit to bathe your heart and mind in the reality of God's big picture, His eternal purpose and plan. Trust that God has both the power and desire to bring something good out of every situation. Breathe deep, every breath a prayer.

Peace is more than a Christmas wish or the hope of potential beauty queens. It's God's gift to you today. Receive it with open arms.

God, help me find Your place of peace today concerning...

Circle of Friends

Two are better than one, because they have a good return for their work:
If one falls down, his friend can help him up.

ECCLESIASTES 4:9–10

What do you want in a friend? If you're like most women, you're probably looking for a good listener and great conversationalist with a sense of humor, someone who's loyal, honest, and kind. And that's just for starters. How do you find a friend like this? Be the friend you want to have.

People are drawn to those who genuinely care about them. That's one reason why people are drawn toward a relationship with God. His love and interest in their lives never grows cold. If you look at the qualities you desire in a friend, you'll notice these qualities reflect God's own. Your heart instinctively knows you can trust a friend like this.

It takes time to build a deep, trustworthy friendship. But that's part of the fun. The deeper your friendship grows, the more you'll bring out the "God qualities" in each other. Why not reach out today to a friend, old or new, and tell her how much she means to you?

Dear God, thank You for my friends...

Heard It Through the Grapevine

Do not spread slanderous gossip among your people.
LEVITICUS 19:16 NLT

Like grapes, women often hang out in bunches. We cluster together, waiting to hear something juicy. We chat about the latest office news, parenting tips, beauty secrets, or anything else that crosses our minds. Companionship like this can be a wonderful thing, as long as we strive to bring out the best in each other. But it's easy for the latest "news" to deteriorate into the latest "gossip."

Gossip brings out the worst, not the best, in us. It's telling a story that isn't ours to tell, often when we don't know all the facts. Once it's out of our mouths, gossip spreads like a fungus through our relational vine. Even if it's not intentionally malicious, it can wind up causing damage to reputations, relationships, and hearts. Not the least of which is our own.

Love speaks well of others. Gossip enjoys being the center of attention, with little regard for the truth. Which type of words would you like others to be speaking about you? Give away the kind of words you'd like most to receive.

Lord, instead of gossiping, help me to...

_____

_____

_____

_____

_____

_____

_____

_____

Expect the Unexpected

This is the day the LORD has made;
we will rejoice and be glad in it.
PSALM 118:24 NKJV

Today may be disguised as an ordinary day. You follow the same routine. You scrub the same dishes, clothes, and face you've scrubbed before. You perform the same tasks, pass the same people, and watch the same TV shows you always do. And when you fall asleep tonight in the same bed, you think you know what tomorrow holds. But you'd be wrong.

There are no ordinary days—or ordinary women. That's because with God, anything and everything is possible. God's power and creativity are beyond what you can imagine, beyond what you would ever dare to dream. Don't limit today by what happened yesterday. The next twenty-four hours are a limited, one-time opportunity.

So wake up every morning with your eyes wide open to the potential of the day. Old habits may be broken. Relationships may be restored. Conflict may be resolved. New friends may be made. The same God who is at work in the world is at work in you. That should be enough to get you out of bed and ready for adventure.

God, my prayer for today is...

Our Super-Sized God

How great you are, O Sovereign LORD!
There is no one like you,
and there is no God but you.

2 SAMUEL 7:22

A super moon occurs when the moon is full and at its closest point to the earth in its elliptical orbit. This makes the moon appear larger and brighter—more super! Of course, the moon remains the same size, regardless of whether it's at its perigee (closest point) or apogee (farthest point) from the earth. It's only our perspective that changes.

Like the moon, the closer we are to God, the bigger He seems. The more time we spend with Him, the more in awe we are. But as our awe increases, our understanding doesn't necessarily follow suit. Trying to comprehend an infinite God with a finite, human brain simply isn't going to happen. But that's a good thing. If we're honest with ourselves, we don't want a God who's just a tool we can use. We want, and need, a God who's bigger and wiser in charge.

Whether our relationship with God is close or distant, He remains the same—super-sized in wisdom, power, and love.

Dear God, I'm glad I'm not in control of the universe, because...

Designed to Last

Jesus said…"I am the resurrection and the life. He who believes in Me,
though he may die, he shall live. And whoever lives and believes in Me shall never die."
JOHN 11:25–26 NKJV

We consider what's disposable to be of little value. Diapers, razors, paper cups and plates…we don't get attached to them because soon they'll be headed out to the trash.

People are not disposable, though at times we treat them as though they were. Maybe it's the beggar by the bridge, the prostitute on the corner, or the hoodlum with the tattoos. Once we label people, we no longer see them as individuals. We view them more as throwaways who wouldn't be missed if they happened to disappear.

To God, we are precious regardless of the choices we've made or the situations we find ourselves in. We're so precious that God designed us to last. Like God, we are eternal. It's true that we'll all face death one day. But that isn't the end of the story. It's only the beginning.

Each person you see is a never-ending story. Ask God to help you read them with care.

Lord, I will read the stories of others carefully by…

_____

_____

_____

_____

_____

_____

_____

_____

_____

_____

You've Got the Right Stuff

*Let us draw near to God
with a sincere heart in full assurance of faith,
having our hearts sprinkled to cleanse us from a guilty conscience.*
HEBREWS 10:22

When you were born, God wove a conscience into your design. It's like He downloaded information about right and wrong straight into your heart. It let you know that hitting your siblings, saying rude words to your parents, and sneaking cookies from the cookie jar made you feel uncomfortable.

But as you matured, you discovered that sometimes the right thing wasn't easy or the wrong thing looked like more fun. Maybe you ignored your conscience. The problem is that the more often you ignore your conscience, the quieter it becomes.

Refuse to drown out God's homing device designed to lead you toward a better life. Ask God to help guide you into making wise, honest, and loving decisions. Risk evaluating how your life lines up with what's written in the Bible. Don't allow guilt or shame to masquerade as a healthy conscience. When you choose to do the right thing, God's Spirit, your conscience, and Scripture will assure you you're headed the right way.

Lord, the one "right thing" I know I need to do is...

_____

_____

_____

_____

_____

_____

_____

_____

Take a Living Water Break

[Jesus said,] "If anyone is thirsty, let him come to me and drink. Whoever believes in me,
as the Scripture has said, streams of living water will flow from within him."
JOHN 7:37–38

A bottle of water is a healthy accessory for every woman to carry. Sipping it throughout the day keeps you hydrated, fills you up, and deters you from grabbing yet another cup of coffee or can of soda.

But you have another source of refreshment readily available to you. God offers you "living water"—a well of spiritual insight, encouragement, and guidance that never runs dry.

Even if you've spent time in the morning talking to God, you're likely to face a spiritual slump later on in the day. An emotional upset, an unexpectedly tough situation, or sheer exhaustion can compound the situation. Whatever the reason, all you know is your joy level is running low.

Draw close to the source. Refocus your thoughts on God. Whisper a prayer of thanksgiving. Hum a song to worship Him. Pour out your heart in prayer. Time with God is the pause that ultimately refreshes.

Lord, during this break in my day, I want to tell You...

Find Rest in God

When you lie down, your sleep will be sweet.
PROVERBS 3:24 NIV

How do you sleep at night? With full schedules, an endless list of errands, home, family, and work obligations—you might expect to find yourself so exhausted that you flop into the bed and sleep soundly until morning. But an increasing number of women find themselves doing just the opposite. The lights are out and the house is quiet, but their minds refuse to rest, racing in circles, recalling the day's conversations, reviewing activities, problem solving. By morning they are even more exhausted.

Our bodies cannot function properly without rest. So what can you do to calm your restless mind? One solution is to find rest in God. As you lie there in the darkness, consciously hand Him each burden, each unresolved situation, each decision in the making. He doesn't mind if you unload on Him. When you've finished, ask Him to quiet your mind and body and give you a long and uninterrupted sleep. It may take a few nights before this process begins to work, but don't give up. Rest is a precious gift from God. Don't let anyone or anything take it from you.

Lord, tonight I will focus my thoughts on You, reminding myself that You are...

_____

_____

_____

_____

_____

_____

_____

_____

_____

_____

_____

Stretching Your Faith

The righteous will hold to their ways,
and those with clean hands will grow stronger.
JOB 17:9

After a Pilates class, a morning run, or a thorough scrub of the bathroom tub, your muscles may remind you that you've accomplished something significant. You've stretched yourself beyond yesterday's limits. That ache you feel is caused by tiny tears in your muscles. But these tears don't harm you. They strengthen you. As they repair themselves, they build muscle mass, making you stronger and enabling you to push yourself even further in the days to come.

Stretching your faith works the same way. Doing what God asks you to do can be uncomfortable at times. Being true to your word even when it's inconvenient, extending love to someone who treats you poorly, sharing a portion of your tight budget to help feed the hungry...doing things like these may pull you outside of your comfort zone. But they're exercising your trust in God. The more frequently you follow God's lead, the stronger your faith will grow.

It's okay to start out small. The baby step you take today will help you get in shape for the two steps you'll take tomorrow.

God, please help me stretch my faith by...

_____

_____

_____

_____

_____

_____

_____

_____

Nurture the Woman in You

She is clothed with strength and dignity; she can laugh at the days to come.
She speaks with wisdom, and faithful instruction is on her tongue.

PROVERBS 31:25–26

Whether you have children of your own or not, God wants you to become a nurturing woman. A good woman sets a godly example with her actions, as well as her words. She passes on the wisdom of her experience with humility and grace. She disciplines out of love, instead of anger. She nurtures the beauty and individuality of those in her care—and realizes she not only has a lot to teach, but a lot to learn from those who look up to her.

Even with all of these wonderful qualities, she knows she isn't perfect. She understands, however, that God's love is big enough to repair any mistakes she makes along the way, and that enables her to love with abandon, even if the ones she loves are rebellious or unkind.

There are children and young people in your life looking for someone to nurture them, accept them, and point them toward their heavenly Father. They're looking for someone just like you.

Lord, help me to nurture others by...

Promises, Promises

*I will sing praise to Your name forever,
that I may daily perform my vows.*
PSALM 61:8 NKJV

"We'll do lunch sometime." "After things settle down, I'll give you a call." "Count me in to help you move!" "I'll pray for you."

Do you ever make promises you don't keep? It's easy to do. Your intentions may be sincere, but your resolve isn't quite up to the task. You want to be there for your friends, your family, your coworkers or neighbors, but life gets in the way. Those casual promises that slipped so easily from your lips are soon forgotten. Or maybe they nag at your conscience, prompting you to avoid the person you made the promise to altogether.

God takes every promise He makes seriously. When He says, "You're forgiven," you are. When He promises, "I'll be with you," He is. When He vows, "My love will never fail," it won't. God is as good as His word. Always. That's one reason why He can be trusted.

A woman of her word can be trusted as well. Make promises thoughtfully, and carry them through faithfully. You'll honor God as well as those you love.

God, please help me become a woman of my word by...

Fall on Your Knees

Get down on your knees before the Master; it's the only way you'll get on your feet.
JAMES 4:10 MSG

You may be a CEO. You may be a genius when it comes to investing, marketing, or performing on stage. You may be a leader in your church or hold a position of power in the government. But no matter what roles you excel at in this life, you were designed for bigger things. You were designed for worship.

Worship is responding in awe to something bigger and more powerful than yourself. That's why worship comes so naturally when you focus on God. That sense of wonder that overwhelms you at the sight of God's most magnificent creations, the tears that flow unbidden when the words of a chorus touch your heart, the desire that inspires you to become a woman to whom God can say, "Well done, my beloved daughter"—these are just a few forms of worship.

Take time today to focus on who God is and what He's done for you. Respond in prayer, song, or even awestruck silence. Catch a glimpse of how big God really is. You'll never be the same.

God, I rejoice in the wonder of worshipping You by...

_____

_____

_____

_____

_____

_____

_____

_____

_____

A Vision for the Future

We can make our plans,
but the LORD determines our steps.

PROVERBS 16:9 NLT

When driving, it's wise to look farther down the road than the end of your front bumper. You need to look into the distance to see if traffic is slowing down, if your lane is going to disappear, or if your exit is coming up. You also need an occasional glance in your rearview mirror to help gain a complete picture of where you are in relation to the traffic around you.

This kind of overall vision is important in life as well as on the road. It's a matter of both planning and prayer. Though you can only live the moment you're in right now, you need to do it in light of what you've learned in the past and what direction you're headed in the future.

Since God's viewpoint is much more expansive and intuitive than your own, it makes perfect sense to ask Him to bring your vision in line with His. Don't be surprised if He stirs up some bigger, bolder dreams in your heart than you'd ever dare envision on your own.

God, please reveal more of Your vision for my life by...

_____

_____

_____

_____

_____

_____

_____

_____

_____

_____

Twin Demands

Oh, that my steps might be steady, keeping to the course you set.
PSALM 119:5 MSG

Suppose you're the mother of two children. For fun, let's make them twins—two-year-old boys. They may look alike, but that's where their similarities end. One is soft-spoken and obedient, every mother's dream. Then there's the other one: loud, whiney, and prone to throw tantrums at inopportune moments. In other words, he demands your attention.

The day ahead of you is like those twin boys. You'll encounter situations that will scream and stomp until you attend to them. Things like flat tires, car pools, or impending deadlines all fall into this category. If you let them, their urgent whine will consume all of your time.

But remember there's another child waiting on the sidelines. He may be less vocal, but that doesn't mean he's less important. Don't allow whatever shouts the loudest to distract your attention from the little things that matter most, like returning a call to a friend, spending time with God, or wholeheartedly focusing on what your children say. Ask God to help you balance your time and energy between the two.

God, things I need Your help focusing on today are...

Swimming Upstream

Peter and the other apostles replied: "We must obey God rather than men!"
ACTS 5:29

Picture yourself as a leaf, fallen on the surface of a gently flowing stream. At first, everything reminds you of your former home, an aspen branch bobbing in the breeze. You drift and twirl as the current pulls you around rocks and over slowly moving fish. It all seems so comfortable, so safe—until you hit the waterfall. You're powerless as you're pulled over the edge, led somewhere you never wanted to go.

Peer pressure can feel like that waterfall. Whether it's pressure at work to do something you feel is unethical, pressure from others to volunteer for something you really don't have time for, or pressure from friends to buy something you know you can't afford, God can supply the strength and resolve you need to do the right thing.

If you're being pushed in a direction you don't believe God wants you to go, explain that you need time to think. Refuse to make a snap decision that you may regret. Then pray for guidance and the courage to go against the flow.

God, help me do the right thing when...

What Do You Want?

Those who live according to the flesh set their minds on the things of the flesh,
but those who live according to the Spirit,
the things of the Spirit.
ROMANS 8:5 NKJV

Do you know what you want? Really? Set aside wishes for a calorie-free box of Godiva chocolates or high heels that feel like your favorite sneakers. Look closer, all the way down to the deepest longings of your heart.

God is there. Your deepest desires can only be met in Him. Your hope for a healthy investment portfolio, a steady job, or a home is really a desire for security. Your yearning for a spouse, children, and a close circle of friends is a desire for unconditional love. Your longing for success and fulfillment is really a desire for purpose and significance.

The security, significance, and love that God offers are eternal. They won't fade away in the face of an economic downfall or a poor personal choice. What women (and men) *really* want is to draw close to God. The more you recognize that God is your heart's true desire, the more fulfilled you'll be with the life you're living.

God, I will come to You with my deepest desires, including...

_____

_____

_____

_____

_____

_____

_____

_____

Seeking Peace

As far as it depends on you, live at peace with everyone.
ROMANS 12:18

Conflict can be destructive. It can wreak havoc on relationships, set emotions on edge, and open a floodgate of words you'll wish you could take back. Or not. It all depends on what you choose to do with it.

Conflict in and of itself isn't a bad thing. Considering God created every person as an individual, it's inevitable that we won't all see life from the same point of view. But when egos and agendas get involved, a simple problem of perspective can degrade into a power struggle for control.

The best resolution for conflict begins with seeking God's perspective. Ask Him to help you clearly see what's at the heart of the conflict. Many times it's not as clear-cut as it appears to be. Then ask Him how you can become a peacemaker. Listen carefully and use your words judiciously. Be willing to set your own pride aside.

View yourself as a teammate to those around you, working together toward solving a problem, instead of opponents battling over who's going to win. Ultimately, your relationship may be what's most at stake.

God, please help me resolve...

Springs of Joy

You will show me the way of life, granting me the joy of your presence
and the pleasures of living with you forever.
PSALM 16:11 NLT

If you were a nomad living in the desert, finding an underground spring would be an incomparable gift. Especially if it was one that never ran dry. God's gift of joy is like that spring. It's always there, bubbling just below the surface, offering you refreshment when you need it most.

Happiness is transient. Like a sudden rainstorm in the desert, it can surprise and delight but disappears as soon as breezes blow the clouds away. Joy lasts. It's constant, a continual undercurrent of well-being that can flood you with wonder and gratitude anytime, anywhere.

If you find yourself in an emotional desert, in need of a lift from the Lord, take a joy break. Dig down through your circumstantial sand. Ask God for a sense of His presence. Bring to mind His promises and how He's come through in the past. Count your blessings. Voice your thanks. Focus on God...His awesome creation, everlasting hope, and faithful character. Allow God's gift of joy to overflow into your life.

Lord, I long for deep reservoirs of joy in my life to overcome...

Come As You Are

Whatever you do or say,
let it be as a representative of the Lord Jesus,
giving thanks through him to God the Father.
COLOSSIANS 3:17 NLT

If you're a woman who believes in God, it's tempting to act like the perfect child. After all, you want to put God in a positive light. If others could see all of your mistakes, your questions, and your imperfections, well...they might think God isn't that powerful after all. Right?

Wrong. Every woman who's honest with herself knows she's a work in progress. There's always room for growth. Just take a look at the heroes of the Bible, men and women alike. Often, they blew it. Sometimes, they blew it big time. We read about their failures, as well as victories, because God values authenticity and honesty.

Being open to acknowledge your struggles and doubts, as well as your successes and break-throughs, is a real-life visual aid. It demonstrates to others that God's acceptance isn't dependent on how good we are. It's a reflection of how good He is.

Don't be afraid to be yourself. God's power can shine brightest through the true you.

God, please help me be more "real" about...

Lead Me, Lord

This is what the LORD says: "Stand at the crossroads and look; ask for the ancient paths, ask where the good way is, and walk in it."

JEREMIAH 6:16

Looking to an invisible God for guidance is a bit like learning to make your way through the world while wearing a blindfold. You become more attuned to the little things...the slope of the sidewalk leading down to a pedestrian crossing, the subtle difference in the sound of your footsteps as you draw closer to a wall, the smell of the bakery letting you know you're only a block from home. The more you walk the same path, the more familiar it becomes. In time, you realize you can walk confidently by faith, instead of sight.

When you're uncertain which way to turn, turn first to God. You'll discover you already have some of the information you need. Is your decision supported by what you read in the Bible? Have others who follow God counseled you to head this way? Has God's Spirit given you peace about moving forward? If so, take the first step. Keep leaning on God as you move ahead. He'll guide you where you need to go.

God, I need Your guidance with...

An Invitation to Adventure

Never be lacking in zeal, but keep your spiritual fervor, serving the Lord.
ROMANS 12:11

You've probably heard the stories...how God used Moses to part the Red Sea, how He used Joshua to direct the fall of Jericho, how He used David to fell the giant Goliath. But the truth is, God never *uses* people. He *invites people to join Him* in accomplishing the extraordinary. We always have the option of saying no. Moses, Joshua, and David, however, all wisely, eventually, responded with a rousing "Count me in!"

Today, if God asked you to join Him on a new adventure, would your first response be "Count me in," "I'm on the fence," or "Try back again tomorrow"? The truth is, God asks you that question every morning. Each new day offers a fresh opportunity to join in a novel adventure. It may be an under-cover operation of unsung kindnesses and sacrifices. Perhaps it's an all-out rescue mission where your words or actions lead someone closer to God. Or it could simply be reconnaissance, helping you gain understanding to prepare for battles yet to come. Are you ready to say yes to adventure?

Lord, I want to be "all in." Please help me...

_____

_____

_____

_____

_____

_____

_____

_____

_____

A Relational Eden

Those who are attentive to a matter will prosper,
and happy are those who trust in the Lord.
PROVERBS 16:20 NRSV

Relationships are like gardens. When well tended, watered, and pruned, they're a pleasure to visit, a place of retreat and renewal. But if left unattended for any length of time, the fruit rots, the flowers wither, and weeds take control. What was once beautiful becomes an eyesore.

Whether it's with your spouse, your children, your friends, or God, you can't expect your relationships to flourish unless you invest the time and attention it takes to keep them growing strong. The faster the pace of your life, the better chance there is that weeds may be sprouting up between you and those you love.

Let your calendar serve as a warning buzzer—when you notice the squares beginning to overflow, take a brief time-out. Ask God to bring to mind anyone you need to reconnect with—including Him. Make a date to get together, even if it's only for fifteen minutes. Then, instead of talking about how busy you are, ask questions. Listen. Deal with any weeds. Celebrate the beauty of the one you're with.

Lord, please help me connect more deeply with...

_____

_____

_____

_____

_____

_____

_____

_____

_____

_____

_____

Meekness Isn't Weakness

Your right hand has held me up, Your gentleness has made me great.
PSALM 18:35 NKJV

To say someone "hits like a girl" isn't considered a compliment. It implies that the person's actions are "meek and mild," similar to the way Jesus is described in Christmas carols. But meekness isn't synonymous with weakness—at least not in God's dictionary. It simply means gentle and humble. And believe it or not, this kind of meekness can be a source of great strength.

You can be gentle and still be assertive, humble and still set boundaries with others. Allowing others to abuse you physically, emotionally, verbally, or sexually means that you're reinforcing their ungodly behavior. You're rewarding them for treating you in a way God abhors.

If you're in a relationship that has crossed the line into abuse (or know someone else who is), don't "hit" back. Get help. Call a hotline or shelter. Talk to a pastor or counselor. In humility, you can recognize that nothing is unforgivable. But with gentle strength, you can hold your head up, walk away from the past, and head toward a future of hope and healing.

God, I believe You want me to demonstrate meekness by...

Holding On to Hope

We have [God's] hope as an anchor for the soul, firm and secure.
HEBREWS 6:19

As a little girl, you may have looked up at the night sky and fervently wished upon a star. Now that you're an adult, hope may feel like a "big girl" wish. You hope you'll get a promotion. You hope you'll find the man of your dreams. You hope the test results from the doctor will be favorable. But what, exactly, are you placing your hope in?

Placing your hope in God is not a grown-up version of wishing upon a star. It isn't expecting God to grant your every wish. It's resting in the fact that since God's character is good, trustworthy, powerful, wise, just, merciful, and generous (to mention just a few of God's amazing attributes!), you can confidently hope for God's best in every area of your life.

Regardless of the difficulties you may be facing today, don't lose heart—or hope. God is both a miracle-worker and a loving Father. Hold your head high and hope in the One who holds your past, present, and future in His almighty hands.

God, I will place my hope in You for...

Not So Precious

Test everything. Hold on to the good.
Avoid every kind of evil.
1 THESSALONIANS 5:21–22

Regardless of whether you have toddlers of your own or not, you've undoubtedly heard them scream one of their favorite words: MINE! Whether it's a beloved toy, a treasured blanket, or even a piece of discarded trash they happen to be holding on to, if someone, anyone, tries to remove it from their chubby little fingers, the tug of war begins.

Is there anything in your life that you cling to like Gollum's "Precious" in *Lord of the Rings*? God wants to help open your clenched fingers, so you can hand it to Him. Not because God's a killjoy, wanting to deprive you of what you enjoy just to prove how much you love Him, but because God wants to set you free.

Whatever you cling to has a grip on you. Is it your finances? Overeating? Shopping? The car you can't afford? A youthful appearance? A relationship you know is drawing you farther away from God? Ask God to help you release anything masquerading as precious that's robbing you of what's truly valuable in this life.

God, please show me what to release and help me to cling to...

_____

_____

_____

_____

_____

_____

_____

_____

The Time Is Ripe

[Jesus] said to them, "Come with me by yourselves to a quiet place and get some rest."
MARK 6:31

In the century before Jesus was born, the Latin poet Horace wrote two little words that remain a popular catchphrase even today: *Carpe Diem*. In light of the brevity of life and our desire to use well the time God's given us, seizing the day seems like wise advice. It encourages us to burst onto the dawn of each new day fully caffeinated, motivated, and ready to go-go-go!

But the original translation of Horace's advice really means "pluck the fruit when ripe." In other words, do the right thing at the right time. Sometimes, the right thing to do is nothing at all. Believe it or not, that advice comes straight from the Bible.

After completing creation, God took a day off. He sat back and celebrated everything He'd accomplished in the last six days. He encourages you to follow His example. Life isn't all about doing. It's also about "being," simply enjoying God's good gifts and the results of your hard work. Taking a time-out isn't wasted time. It's time that's ripe for rest and renewal.

God, teach me how to "be" by letting go of...

Relational Solitaire

God sets the solitary in families.
PSALM 68:6 NKJV

You don't have to be alone to feel lonely. It can happen when you're in a crowd, late at night after the rest of the family has gone to sleep, or even when you're out with a group of friends. It's that feeling of isolation, of not belonging, of being totally on your own.

You were not created to live a solitary life. God made people dependent on each other and on Him. He wove that longing for companionship deep into your heart and soul. Loneliness is a warning signal that something's interfering with that connection. The best place to reconnect is at the source.

Ask God to help you understand what's really going on. Is there an emotional disconnect? A relational rift you need to address? Is it time you risked reaching out, expanding your circle of friends? Are you expecting others to fill the place only God can fill in your heart? Recognize loneliness as a relational wake-up call—and rest in the fact that it's a call God wants to help you answer. Opening up to others may well open you up to a fuller life.

God, when I feel alone, please...

_____

_____

_____

_____

_____

_____

_____

_____

Give All You've Got

Whatever you do, work at it with all your heart, as working for the Lord, not for men.
COLOSSIANS 3:23

Striving for excellence is different from promoting perfectionism. After all, only God is perfect. For Him, excellence is synonymous with perfection. For the rest of us, excellence means doing our very best, even if our best means making a few mistakes along the way.

Excellence begins with an attitude that says, "I'll do this job as if I were doing it for God Himself." Imagine how that would change even the minor jobs before you today. If you were preparing breakfast for Jesus, making His bed, attending to a project He put in your in-box, wouldn't each task be done to the very best of your ability?

In actuality, everything you do is a thank-you gift to the One who created you. You alone determine the quality of the gift you give. Again, God isn't asking for perfection. He's simply asking you to put your heart into everything you do. When you do, you receive more than you give. Enthusiasm, joy, accomplishment, fulfillment...the gifts keep accumulating when you live life with excellence and heart.

Lord, the job I need help doing with my whole heart is...

Change Is on Its Way

The LORD will be your confidence, and will keep your foot from being caught.
PROVERBS 3:26 NKJV

If only every change in your life was as easy as changing your clothes. But putting on things like a brand-new age, address, occupation, or marital status can leave you feeling anxious, even if you consider the change a positive one. There's comfort in what's familiar, in maintaining the status quo. But change is inevitable. So it's good to learn how to embrace it with open arms.

God can teach you how to do just that, since He's the author of change. Life was God's idea. An integral part of life is growth, and at its heart, growth is change. When you're facing a change, think of it as an opportunity for growth. Even if it's a change you dread, ask God to help you face it with courage, confidence, and optimism.

God has something for you to learn, some new direction for you to grow every time change enters your life. The sooner you embrace the change you face, the sooner it will change yet again—from new to familiar, from complication to transformation.

God, a change I'm anxious about is...

The Little Things

In my distress I called to the LORD, and he answered me.
From the depths of the grave I called for help, and you listened to my cry.
JONAH 2:2

In hospital rooms, on battlefields, when faced with tragedy, trauma, or some kind of dire dilemma, people cry out to God. Even those who don't believe God's there instinctively turn to prayer in times of need. But when times are good, the exact opposite often occurs. We depend less on God and more on our own abilities to handle everyday concerns.

God isn't a backup plan when life goes awry. He's a parent who loves you. Like a mother who wants to hear all about her child's day, God cares about the tiniest details of your life. But He'll never meddle. He waits for you to come to Him.

You're an intelligent, capable woman. Turning to God isn't a sign of weakness; it's a sign of wisdom. God's in control. Not you. The more frequently you turn to Him, the more you realize you need Him—and the more your love for Him continues to grow.

Father, I invite You into every part of my day, including...

_____

_____

_____

_____

_____

_____

_____

_____

_____

_____

100 Percent Genuine

When you give to the needy,
do not let your left hand know what your right hand is doing,
so that your giving may be in secret. Then your Father,
who sees what is done in secret, will reward you.

MATTHEW 6:3–4

Good deeds are a bit like jewelry. Some of them are expensive. They can cost you time, energy, resources, comfort, and convenience. But when your heart is genuinely in love with God, and He urges you to fill the need, the only answer that feels right is yes.

Sometimes, though, acts of service are motivated by guilt, the need to be needed, or the need to look good in front of others. These deeds resemble costume jewelry. They may sparkle like the real thing, but their worth is significantly less.

Everything you do for others is valuable. But when your actions are motivated by a genuine concern, that's when your love resembles God's own. Don't beat yourself up if you feel your motives aren't absolutely selfless. Every woman is a work in progress. But if you're tempted to perform instead of serve, try helping others in secret. You can trust God sees every beautiful thing you do.

God, please help me genuinely serve others by...

When Teardrops Fall

He will wipe every tear from their eyes.
There will be no more death or mourning or crying or pain,
for the old order of things has passed away.
REVELATION 21:4

They show up when you're joyful. They flow when you hear bad news. They appear when you're angry, when your hormones are on the rampage, when you pray, or sometimes, for what seems like absolutely no reason at all. Tears can be a nuisance. But no matter how hard you try, it's tough to keep them inside when they're crying to get out.

It can feel uncomfortable to cry, especially in front of others, because it's such an intimate act. It reveals there's something going on inside that runs deeper than words can express. The Bible says that God keeps every one of your tears in a bottle. He knows when and why each one falls. He doesn't consider crying weak or unnecessary. After all, Jesus wept when His friend Lazarus died, even though He was about to raise Him from the dead.

God promises that one day, tears will be a thing of the past. Until then, picture Him drying your tears. What breaks your heart breaks His.

God, when I'm brokenhearted, help me remember...

_____

_____

_____

_____

_____

_____

_____

_____

_____

_____

Trust and Obey

If anyone obeys his word, God's love is truly made complete in him.
This is how we know we are in him.

1 JOHN 2:5

You've seen them at the grocery store...kids gone wild. They put things in the cart when Mom isn't watching. They scream when Mom won't purchase something they want. They lie on the floor like a limp noodle when Mom tries to lead them in a direction they'd rather not go. All you can do is try and ignore them—as long as you're not the one they call mom.

Obedience is an attractive trait for children, including children of God. But just like little kids, we want what we want. At times, what God asks is contrary to what we have in mind. But as the incomparably wise parent, our Father really does know best.

When God asks you to do something, there's a good reason behind it. Even so, He'll patiently allow you to go your own way, play with things you shouldn't, and even act as though He's not there. But you'll never fully mature until you learn the beauty and benefit of doing things His way.

Father, the hardest thing I find about obedience is...

_____

_____

_____

_____

_____

_____

_____

_____

_____

Staying Grounded

[The man said to Jesus,] "I do believe; help me overcome my unbelief!"
MARK 9:24

Once upon a time, people believed the world was flat, the sun revolved around the earth, and mermaids were demonic creatures who seduced sailors in order to steal their souls. Over the years, myths have been debunked, and science has set our solar system straight. But that doesn't mean we hold the answers to every mystery of life.

When it comes to God, faith and doubt often go hand in hand. That's because it's hard to gather concrete evidence about someone we can't see, hear, or touch. Of course, we don't have to totally understand how gravity works to believe it's real. And the same is true with God.

Don't allow doubts or unanswered questions to construct a myth about who God is and what He's like. Rest in God's millennia-long track record of loving faithfulness by reading accounts of people just like you as recorded in the Bible. Keep a journal of how you've seen God at work in your life. Then reread your own faith journey whenever doubts arise. God, like gravity, will keep you grounded.

God, please put my doubts to rest about...

_____

_____

_____

_____

_____

_____

_____

_____

I Surrender

Submit yourselves, then, to God.
JAMES 4:7

The words "surrender" and "submit" have negative connotations, especially for women. It's reminiscent of raising a white flag, throwing in the towel, or accepting defeat. It implies you're giving up your rights or something dear to you. But instead of picturing yourself losing something, consider these two words an invitation to become part of something greater than yourself.

If you're on the freeway merging into traffic and a mammoth semi is in the lane you want to enter, you surrender your position—or get squished demanding your desired piece of asphalt. In the same way, when you're merging into a relationship with the almighty God, you surrender your own plans in light of His. You submit yourself to Him. That doesn't mean you leave everything you've dreamed of by the side of the road. It's more like your agendas come together as one. However, any time your plans run in direct opposition to God's, it only makes sense that you're the one who must yield.

You won't lose yourself by surrendering to God. Instead, you'll discover what it's like to be fully, intimately, unconditionally found.

God, help me fully surrender...

_____

_____

_____

_____

_____

_____

_____

_____

_____

Making Sense of Cents

Why do you spend money for what is not bread,
and your wages for what does not satisfy?
ISAIAH 55:2 NKJV

Money masquerades as a universal remote control. It promises that if you point enough of it at any problem, you can fix it. Insecure about your appearance? Change your looks with a new pair of boots or a tummy tuck. Unhappy with your job? Keep playing the lottery, and one day you can retire on your own private island. Distraught over relational conflict? Cheer yourself up with a trip to Vegas.

Money makes a lot of promises it can't deliver. Like a bandage, it can cover up a problem, but it can't fix whatever's broken inside of you. Only God can do that. Invite God to help you see money for what it is: a tool whose value is determined by the way in which you use it. Using this tool wisely includes getting out of debt, putting a portion into savings, refusing to use it as an emotional crutch, and generously sharing what you have with others. With God's help, you'll discover how rich you really are, regardless of how much money you have.

Lord, You've shown me that I'm rich in...

Beyond Compare

Each one should use whatever gift he has received to serve others,
faithfully administering God's grace in its various forms.
1 PETER 4:10

Being a comparison shopper in the produce aisle is a smart move. You choose one banana over another because it's riper or bruise-free. You pick one bag of spinach over another because it's on sale. You want to get the most for your money.

Similarly, women often compare themselves with other women to assess their own value. But comparing yourself to others will always be apples to oranges. You're unique and, therefore, incomparable. Weighing assets like appearance, IQ, abilities, achievements, or spiritual growth against others will only bear bitter fruit. Pride, jealousy, discouragement...that's the kind of harvest you can expect when you use anyone other than yourself as your measuring stick.

The only person you can fairly compare yourself with is who you were yesterday. Each day offers a new opportunity for growth. Are you learning from your mistakes? Loving God and others more deeply and freely? If so, celebrate it. If not, ask God to help you change. Then, stop scrutinizing and get on with living a fruitful life.

God, help me stop comparing and see myself as...

March 30

Great Expectations

*[Jesus said,] "Blessed are those who mourn,
for they will be comforted."*

MATTHEW 5:4

You know exactly how everything's going to turn out. You've pictured it in your mind a thousand times. Then the unexpected happens. Reality paints a totally different picture than the one you'd hoped and prayed for, leaving you bewildered and discouraged. How do you keep moving forward when you're headed in a direction you never imagined you'd go?

Jesus' followers knew this kind of disappointment. For centuries the Jews anticipated a Messiah, someone akin to a king, who would bring the Jewish people back to the height of political power. Then came Jesus. Not only was He a different kind of Savior than they were expecting, He was arrested and crucified. Talk about discouraging news! But God's plan was better than anything the Jews ever imagined. Jesus arose from the dead, bringing the power of God's Spirit and the promise of forgiveness to everyone, not just the Jews.

When disappointment leaves you discouraged, remember God has something better in mind. Trade your heartache for anticipation as you wait for the beauty of God's plan to unfold.

Lord, please give me a new vision to replace my discouragement over...

Under the Influence

Blessed is the man who walks not in the counsel of the ungodly,
nor stands in the path of sinners.
PSALM 1:1 NKJV

We're all under the influence of someone. As kids, it's usually our parents. As teens, it's often our peers and teachers, as well as the fashion trends of celebrities we idolize. As adults, things get a bit more complicated. Our lives intersect with those of so many others, both personally and virtually, that we need to be intentional in choosing whom we'll allow to be role models in our lives.

The more time we spend with people, the more easily they influence us. We pick up their speech patterns, adopt their fashion trends, try on their habits for size, and begin to evaluate our beliefs in light of theirs. God doesn't ask you to be an island, shunning those who differ from the kind of woman He desires you to be. However, the Bible notes that when you hang out with wise women, their wisdom will rub off on you.

Be aware of the influence others have in your life. Hang out with those who give you a hand up, instead of pulling you down.

God, I'm concerned about how I'm being influenced by...

The Attitude of Aging

Even when I am old and gray, do not forsake me, O God,
till I declare your power to the next generation, your might to all who are to come.
PSALM 71:18

What comes to mind when you think about getting older? Wrinkles, menopause, and the benefits of an eighteen-hour bra? Or wisdom, experience, and freedom from the pressure to be fashion forward? The kind of woman you'll grow up and grow old to be depends a lot on the attitude you bring to each season of life.

Society may not fully value those who're considered over the hill as much as those still climbing it, but we can. We know God does. In the Bible, we read how He invited Moses, Abraham, and Sarah to do amazing things when they were well past their prime. Who knows what God has in store for you?

God says He numbers our days. We don't know why some die young and others live to celebrate the century mark. What we do know is that getting older is a privilege. Each new day and every season is a gift. Accept them with open arms.

God, one attitude about aging I need Your help changing is...

Being Wise in God's Eyes

The LORD gives wisdom and from his mouth come knowledge and understanding.
He holds victory in store for the upright.

PROVERBS 2:6–7

Being called a wise guy isn't a compliment. Being regarded as a wise woman, that's something else altogether. While it's true that some people seem more intuitively sensible and levelheaded than others, wisdom isn't an ability you're born with. It's insight accumulated through experience over time. When you use that insight to make good choices, share astute advice, and speak with discernment, that's when wisdom shows itself for what it is: the key to living a godly life.

No matter how wise a woman you grow to be, God is wiser still. And He's promised to share that wisdom with you if you'll only ask. Prayer primes the pump of God's wisdom so it can flow more freely into your life. Understanding the importance of relying on God when you're faced with a difficult decision or struggling for the right words to say is simply more evidence of how wise you really are.

Do the right thing, the wise thing, by crying out to God. A wise woman knows she can't make it on her own.

God, I need Your wisdom for...

The Gift of Praise

Praise God in his sanctuary; praise him in his mighty heavens.
Praise him for his acts of power; praise him for his surpassing greatness.

PSALM 150:1–2

We all enjoy praise. Being told, "You look amazing in that dress!" or "Just watching you inspires me to be a better mom," can really make our day. That's because praise is more than a compliment. It's an affirmation. It confirms the truth about who we really are. Sometimes, we need to hear that truth because we still have doubts about our own worth.

If we're worthy of praise, how much more deserving is God? But it isn't because God's ego needs stroking or His low self-esteem can use a boost that we're encouraged to praise Him. It's because praising God reminds us of how incredibly remarkable He really is. It shines a spotlight on what's truly deserving of glory.

Why not take a moment to praise God right now? Applaud His goodness by describing how His love has changed your life. Tell the truth about Him—to Him. You'll find that praise is a gift to give as well as receive.

God, You're so worthy of praise, I want You to know…

_____

_____

_____

_____

_____

_____

_____

_____

_____

Renovation and Renewal

According to God's mercy he saved us,
by the washing of regeneration,
and renewing of the Holy Ghost.

TITUS 3:5 KJV

If you're going to remodel an outdated bathroom, what's the first thing you do? You get rid of the old stuff. You strip away the tropical fish wallpaper. You donate the cotton candy-colored commode to your local Goodwill. You prepare the tile for regrouting. You can't install what's new until you discard everything else that stands in its way.

The same is true as God is remodeling you. You aren't outdated. You're growing. Your character's becoming more like God's each day. That means some things simply have to go. Bad habits, selfish motives, past regrets...they all need to be stripped away. This sounds like a tough job, but it isn't a project God expects you to take care of on your own.

God's Spirit is ready to get to work in your life. He has the power to tear down walls you've built or replace faulty perceptions about Him. But just as a contractor requires a building permit, He awaits your permission to get started. Is there anything holding you back from a complete renovation of your life?

God, I want to work with You to rebuild...

_____

_____

_____

_____

_____

_____

_____

_____

Balancing Act

Let us therefore come boldly to the throne of grace,
that we may obtain mercy and find grace to help in time of need.
HEBREWS 4:16 NKJV

Have you ever watched jugglers place an overabundance of plates on wooden dowels, balancing them on their feet, nose, chin, forehead...you name it? Then they set them all spinning. If you're like many women, you can't help but feel you're witnessing a metaphor for your life.

Trying to balance all the plates of responsibility you carry and prevent them from crashing to the ground isn't as entertaining in real life as it is beneath the Big Top. But it can be done. Begin by inviting God to help you evaluate your priorities. Putting God first in your life doesn't mean He's the biggest, heaviest plate you have to bear. Instead, He's there to help you keep those that are worthwhile in the air.

First thing every morning, lay each of your plates before Him. Ask for wisdom in knowing which ones to pick up, which ones you can put off carrying until later, and which ones to toss. Only God can help you accurately weigh what's worthy of your time and heart.

God, right now my load of plates feels...

One Step at a Time

I am the LORD your God who takes hold
of your right hand and says to you,
Do not fear; I will help you.

ISAIAH 41:13

As a kid, you learned how to run. You put one foot in front of the other. Pretty simple, right? But what if you wanted to run a marathon? Running that kind of race takes more than just picking up your feet while wearing expensive sneakers. It takes training and perseverance.

Not all marathons are athletic events. Some are financial. Others are relational. They can also be emotional, physical, or spiritual. Sometimes they're races you choose to run, like losing ten pounds, earning your master's degree, or raising a child. Others you may be thrown into without warning, like being diagnosed with breast cancer or losing your job. For the latter, there's no time to train. You may feel as though you didn't even have the chance to grab your shoes.

God's presence provides the power you need to persevere. He isn't an "easy button" that whisks you to the finish line. He's a coach, running beside you, offering you perspective, strength, and encouragement every step of the way.

God, please help me keep moving forward with...

_____

_____

_____

_____

_____

_____

_____

_____

_____

_____

Identity Theft

The Spirit himself joins with our spirits to say we are God's children.
ROMANS 8:16 NCV

Many women have become victims of identity theft. Perhaps you're one of them. You didn't hold tightly to your identity and somewhere along the way, it was lost. Perhaps in a tempting moment, you surrendered your identity for something that looked more fun, more interesting. You forgot you were a child of God.

You neglected to call your Father. You didn't read the love letters He'd written. You figured you'd strike out on your own. After all, picking up another identity was easy enough. All you had to do was blend in with the crowd. Maybe you did a few things you were ashamed of. At times, you considered calling home but figured it was too late. You'd made your choice. You were no longer the woman you'd been before.

The truth is, your identity can never be lost or stolen. The Bible says God's Spirit holds it safe throughout eternity. Once God's called you His child, you can never be anything else. Your identity and destiny are secure. Even if you turn your back on God, He'll never turn His back on you. The reach of His enduring love will always lead you home.

God, being Your daughter means...

_____

_____

_____

_____

_____

_____

_____

_____

God's There When You Grieve

[God says,] "As a mother comforts her child, so I will comfort you."
ISAIAH 66:13 NRSV

God grieves. He understands the anguish of being separated from someone you love. That's why Jesus sacrificed His life, so that death wouldn't be a final good-bye. Jesus' death paid the price for our rebellion and opened the gates of heaven. Now we have the assurance of being with God throughout eternity.

But what about our grief, the profound emptiness we feel when someone we love crosses from this life into the next? Yes, God's assurance of heaven remains steadfast for those who love Him. But what about us, the ones left behind?

Everyone grieves as uniquely as they live. People can give you advice on what helped them in their time of need. They can comfort you with kindness and prayer or reach out to help in practical ways. But only God can heal the sorrow you feel. His gifts of peace, comfort, and compassion may feel elusive at times. But remember, feelings don't paint an accurate picture of the truth. Keep reaching out to Him, even when tears are all you have to offer.

God, help me see You in the midst of grief like...

_____

_____

_____

_____

_____

_____

_____

_____

_____

_____

Pollution-Free Living

Obscene stories, foolish talk, and coarse jokes—these are not for you.
EPHESIANS 5:4 NLT

When a metropolitan area issues a high pollution alert, it isn't pretty. Once blue skies are now blanketed with a sickly yellow haze. Visibility is impaired. Your eyes burn, and if you're prone to a respiratory disease, your lungs can as well. Compare that picture with one of crystal-clear skies, viewed from a pristine alpine valley in the shadow of an isolated mountain peak. No one has to guess which is more appealing.

Pollution isn't attractive in nature—or in your character. That's why God appeals to you to be pure. Pure is defined as a single substance that isn't mixed with or contaminated by anything else. God is 100 percent pure, wholly Himself, nothing else added. You were created in this pure, unpolluted image.

If you question what purity looks like in real life, your heart has a clue. Ask yourself: If Jesus walked in right now, would He enjoy the movie I'm watching? Compliment the outfit I'm wearing? Celebrate the relational choices I'm making? When it comes to your character, keep it pure!

God, help me stay pure, especially when...

Finding Solace in Solitude

[Jesus] went out to the mountain to pray, and continued all night in prayer to God.
LUKE 6:12 NKJV

You weren't created to live a solitary life. God designed you to love and be loved. But sometimes finding a quiet place where you can be by yourself is exactly what you need. Jesus needed it. He often headed off to a solitary place. Sometimes it was a mountaintop. Other times it was a garden. That doesn't mean Jesus was alone. Jesus sought a secluded spot so He could spend some one-on-one time with His heavenly Father.

Jesus sought solitude when He heard John the Baptist had been killed. He took time out when crowds of needy people kept Him so busy that He couldn't find time to eat. And right before He was arrested, Jesus was having a heart-to-heart discussion with His Father in an olive grove.

Anytime you're overwhelmed, follow Jesus' example. Take a walk or head to a park bench. If you have small children, head into the closet or the bathroom and close the door for a minute or two. God's there in the silence, waiting to quiet your heart.

God, a solitary spot where I'd like to meet with You is...

Free Your Muse

A desire accomplished is sweet to the soul.
PROVERBS 13:19 NKJV

When was the last time you invited your inner muse to come out and play? If you don't consider yourself artistic, it may have been awhile. But you were created in the image of the Creator. That means creativity is part of God's plan for your life.

Don't panic. You don't have to open your own gallery, write the Great American Novel, or start hawking your wares at craft shows. It simply means you have what it takes to create. Better yet, freeing your creativity can help you share God's love in inventive ways.

The possibilities are as endless as your imagination. Create a fanciful meal for someone in need. Teach your children about God through storytelling and role-play. Help a friend decorate her home. Greet a new neighbor with a garden-picked bouquet. Write out your own psalm of thanks to God. Be a singing telegram for someone who's housebound. Don't feel pressured to deliver an artistic tour de force. Simply do your best with what you've been given. A work of heart is always a masterpiece.

God, I would like to use my creativity to...

Picture Perfect

How good and pleasant it is when
brothers live together in unity!
PSALM 133:1

A puzzle is a great example of unity. Each distinctive piece interlocks with those around it. Together, they form a picture that can only be seen when every piece is in its proper place.

God calls His children to be "one" in Him. But unity doesn't equal uniformity. At times, this causes division. One woman raises her hands while singing in church. Another doesn't feel comfortable being that demonstrative. She may feel the first woman is distracting or even believe she's doing something God wouldn't approve of. Soon, the two have their eyes on each other—judging each other—instead of having their eyes on God.

God's children worship, pray, celebrate communion, and interpret the Bible in different ways. After all, God designed us to be individuals. It's healthy to discuss our differences. But after all is said and done, we need to pull together as one.

Together, God's children create a picture of what God's like. We're on display for the world to see. The more closely we're unified in love, the more accurate that picture will be.

God, help me paint a clearer picture of Your love by...

_____

_____

_____

_____

_____

_____

_____

_____

Eternal Energy Source

This is what the LORD Almighty...says:... "I will refresh the weary and satisfy the faint."
JEREMIAH 31:25

When you need a burst of energy, where do you turn? Perhaps you grab a venti macchiato, head to the gym, or turn on your favorite music at full blast. You have another option. God is the ultimate power source. That means where energy is concerned, He has an unlimited supply.

When you're running on empty, run to God instead of Starbucks. He won't leave you feeling wired. He'll help clear your mind and strengthen your resolve. By plugging into prayer, reading a single Psalm, repeating a favorite verse of Scripture in your mind, or turning on a CD that provides a soundtrack of praise, God can help get you up and out of the rut you may have slid into. If you're seriously lagging, consider taking a quick nap in His arms. Close your eyes and ask Him to refresh you, body and soul.

You can plug into God anywhere by drinking deeply of His presence. Connecting with Him is a caffeine-free way to add a bit of bounce to your step.

God, I could use an energy boost from You today to...

_____

_____

_____

_____

_____

_____

_____

_____

_____

You're Cordially Invited...

The world cannot accept [the Spirit of truth],
because it neither sees him nor knows him.
But you know him for he lives with you and will be in you.

JOHN 14:17

Your heart beats about seventy times every minute. Every hour, your lungs take in over seven hundred breaths. You blink your eyes more than twenty thousand times each day. But God's gift of life is more than heartbeats and respiration. It's things like joy, love, growth, and purpose.

When God set your heart beating in your mother's womb, He did more than turn a switch to the ON position. He extended an invitation to join Him in celebrating an unparalleled adventure. But to join the celebration, you need to do more than receive an invitation. You also need to accept it.

It may take awhile to understand God's invitation, to believe He's at work behind the scenes. It may take even longer to accept it, to reach out in humility and say, "I believe." But once you do, that's when your life truly begins.

One day, your heart will stop beating. But this new life will continue. Your adventure with God is one that never ends.

Lord, accepting Your invitation means that I...

_____

_____

_____

_____

_____

_____

_____

_____

_____

_____

Law and Order

Everyone must submit to governing authorities.
ROMANS 13:1 NLT

Benjamin Franklin said, "Nothing is certain except death and taxes." You already know what God says about death: because of Jesus' sacrifice, the door of eternal life has been swung wide open, so there's nothing to fear. But does God have anything to say about taxes?

Yes, He did. When religious leaders asked Jesus whether they should pay their taxes, Jesus pointed out Caesar's picture on their money. He then told them to give Caesar what was his. Though we have leaders like Ben Franklin instead of Caesar on our currency, the principle behind Jesus' words still holds true.

Following the laws of the land is one more way of honoring God. Driving the speed limit may be a struggle when you feel everyone else is ignoring it. But it's still the right thing to do. The same goes for accurately reporting your taxes, showing respect for those in governmental authority, and exercising your right to vote. Unless the government's laws are in direct opposition to His own, God asks us to honor those laws as a way to honor Him.

God, the law I struggle most to follow is...

_____

_____

_____

_____

_____

_____

_____

_____

_____

Attitude Check

Whoever says, "I abide in him,"
ought to walk just as he walked.
1 JOHN 2:6 NRSV

Suppose you're the mom of a hormonal teenage girl. Even if you aren't, you can imagine what it's like. After all, you once walked in those conflicted shoes. Picture yourself asking your daughter to clean her room before she heads out with friends. What's her first response? Probably a big, fat, juicy serving of attitude.

Your daughter may begrudgingly do what you ask, accompanied by mumbling, grumbling, and heavy sighs. Procrastination may play a part in the process as well. As for the quality of her work, she'll probably do the minimum required to meet your request. Chances are it will be far below what you'd consider her best effort.

When God asks you to do something difficult, inconvenient, or out of your comfort zone, what's your first response? Do you ignore it, procrastinate before diving in, or simply grit your teeth and obey? As every parent knows, attitude plays a part in obedience. When you wholeheartedly do what God asks, you're doing more than simply obeying. You're lavishing Him with love.

God, in checking my current attitude about serving You, I feel...

_____

_____

_____

_____

_____

_____

_____

_____

Down and Out

[Jesus said,] "Do not let your hearts be troubled. Trust in God; trust also in me."
JOHN 14:1

A traffic sign reading DIP provides advance warning of a depression in the road. Unfortunately, life doesn't come with bright yellow signs. Sometimes, things like depression catch you by surprise.

Everyone faces sadness on the road of life. It's natural to feel sad when facing a significant loss or traumatic event. But sometimes those feelings won't go away or they show up when life seems to be moving along just fine. If this happens, openly sharing your feelings with God is important, so is doing all you can to make positive, healthy choices and changes in your life.

But suppose these feelings still won't let up. If sleep begins to elude you, you find it hard to concentrate, you begin to gain or lose weight, you feel hopeless, worthless, or suicidal, call on God—but call on others as well. Depression is more than just melancholy. It doesn't show a lack of faith to ask for outside help when you need it. A doctor or counselor may be the answer God's providing to your prayers.

God, today I'm feeling...

_____

_____

_____

_____

_____

_____

_____

_____

_____

_____

A God Worth Celebrating

O clap your hands, all ye people;
shout unto God with the voice of triumph.

PSALM 47:1 KJV

When we focus on character traits like God's righteousness, justice, and sovereignty, it's easy to lose sight of the fact that He's also a God of celebration. Throughout the Old Testament, God invites His children to celebrate various feasts and festivals. In the New Testament, our reunion with God in heaven is described as a joyous wedding banquet.

Celebration binds relationship and remembrance together with joy. The closer you draw to God, the more joyful celebrations like Christmas, Easter, and birthdays become. But don't stop there. Why not initiate some spiritual festivals of your own? When you receive an answer to prayer, a desire of your heart becomes reality, or you simply find yourself overflowing with thanks for who God is and what He's done, do more than pray. Party!

The party theme is up to you. Special food, gifts, music, prayer, praise...let your imagination run wild. Why not gather family and friends to join in the celebration? With a God as awesome as ours, any time is the right time for declaring a personal day of Thanksgiving.

God, something I'd like to celebrate with thanksgiving is...

When "I'm Sorry" Isn't Enough

Repent and be baptized,
every one of you, in the name of Jesus Christ
for the forgiveness of your sins.
ACTS 2:38

Every mother of more than one child has said, "Tell your sister (or brother) you're sorry." While you can encourage your child to say she's sorry, you can't change her heart. If her apology doesn't reflect true remorse, she's more than likely to do what she did all over again.

When we confess to God what we've done wrong, His forgiveness is absolute. It's as though what we did never happened. That's a wonderful thing! But if we aren't truly contrite, we use the magnitude of God's grace as an escape hatch. That means there's a good chance we'll go out and do the same thing all over again—then come back and say we're sorry once more.

But if we recognize how what we've done hurts the Father we love and we're genuinely penitent, we'll do more than apologize. We'll change our ways. The Bible calls this repentance. It means to "turn around." We'll turn from the wrong direction we're headed and go back toward the One who calls us His beloved daughter.

Father, I'm truly sorry for...

_____

_____

_____

_____

_____

_____

_____

_____

God's Gift of Enough

I have learned in whatever state I am, to be content.
PHILIPPIANS 4:11 NKJV

The Rolling Stones sing with great abandon about how they "can't get no satisfaction." But the closer you draw to God, the more you realize you're more than satisfied. You're wholeheartedly content.

Contentment is a gift that can make other gifts unnecessary. It works like a time-released capsule, gradually over time. Little by little, you realize you want less and have more than you ever noticed before. Your desire for a bigger, better home is replaced by gratitude for wherever you live. Trips to the mall center more on spending time with friends than coming home with bags. Even the way you see yourself changes. Your appearance, your weight, your abilities, your age...you're more comfortable with who you are, as well as with what you have.

As God helps you see more clearly what really matters in this world, contentment spreads its sense of peaceful appreciation deeper into your soul. That hunger to strive for more is replaced by a hunger to know more of God. That's what lies at the heart of living a full life.

God, I see Your gift of contentment working in...

Welcome Home

Do not neglect to show hospitality to strangers,
for by this some have entertained angels without knowing it.
HEBREWS 13:2 NASB

Hospitality isn't about making your home a showcase, being able to whip up a killer soufflé, or organizing an evening of entertainment that rivals a night at the Met. It's about making others feel at home.

Opening your home begins with opening your heart. If you welcome others with the same love and acceptance God extends to you, they can't help but feel at home. This may be easy with close friends and family. But God asks you to extend hospitality to those who wouldn't make your usual guest list—including people you haven't met before. This doesn't mean you should start bringing home random strangers. But when you hear of someone in need, talk to God about how you can help. Perhaps the home they need is yours.

If you don't have the means to invite others into your home, you can still make them feel like part of the family. Prepare a meal for a new mom or someone who's grieving or ill. True hospitality extends far beyond your front door.

God, I want to share my home more freely. Help me...

_____

_____

_____

_____

_____

_____

_____

_____

Hiding in Plain Sight

Nothing in all creation is hidden from God's sight.
Everything is uncovered and laid bare before the eyes of him to whom we must give account.

HEBREWS 4:13

Your life is an open book to God. He's aware of everything you do and every word you say. That isn't a threat. It's a reassurance. God won't up and leave, get distracted, or be pushed out of your life. Knowing this might lead you to believe all your secrets are safe with Him—except that not all secrets are worthy of being kept.

Is there anything you're hiding from your spouse, kids, family, or friends? A secret you'd be ashamed for anyone at church to find out? If so, chances are it's something God wishes to bring out into the light. If it's a habit that needs to be broken, being accountable to someone who knows the truth can strengthen your resolve. If it's a past transgression God's already forgiven, sharing your experience might keep someone else from making the same mistake.

You don't have to be an open book to the world. But God can show you what secrets need to be shared.

God, reveal any secrets I need to bring into the light and help me to...

Who Are You Looking For?

He that cometh to God must believe that he is,
and that he is a rewarder of them
that diligently seek him.
HEBREWS 11:6 KJV

Are you looking for God, but feel as though He can't be found? Perhaps the God you're looking for differs from who God really is.

Consider who God is not. He's not a cosmic, short-order cook, ready to serve up whatever you order in answer to your prayers. He's not a stone-faced judge, weighing your efforts on a moral scale to determine if your "good" is "good enough." He's not an impersonal power who set the world in motion then sat back to watch the show. He's not a purveyor of good karma, doling out good lives to good people and hard lives to the rest.

God is the God of the Bible. The more you read about Him, the more accurate your picture will be. If you want to understand what He's like, look at Jesus. Read the books of Matthew, Mark, Luke, and John. Note His love and humility. That's the God who's reaching out to you. If you seek Him, you will find what you're looking for.

Father, I want to know You for who You really are. Open my eyes to...

Just a Thought

You are my lamp, O Lord;
the Lord turns my darkness into light.
2 SAMUEL 22:29

Did you ever regret watching a movie? Maybe it gave you nightmares. Perhaps the sex scenes made you blush. Possibly you found yourself laughing at jokes you knew God would sadly shake His head over. Regardless of what inspired your regret, what makes matters worse is that those words and images have been downloaded into your memory. Not even a *Bambi* marathon can erase them from your mind.

Your mind is a complex creation. God entrusts you with the freedom to choose how you're going to use it. Like a computer, your mind follows the GIGO principle: Garbage In, Garbage Out. By making a conscious choice to set your mind on what's truly worthy of your time, you can change that to: Good In, Good Out. That's one reason why reading the Bible is so important. It fills your mind with good things. If you find yourself down in the dumps, focusing on "garbage" such as disturbing images, critical words, unhappy memories, or self-deprecating thoughts, change the channel. Repeat the good words God has shared with you.

God, a channel I need Your help to change is...

_____

_____

_____

_____

_____

_____

_____

_____

On the Wings of Love

*The prayer of the upright
is [God's] delight.*
PROVERBS 15:8 KJV

From Senegal to Siberia, Timbuktu to Toledo, there are individuals who could use a friend like you. They need someone to feed them, to educate them, to heal them, to stand up for them, to tell them the story of God's love.

You're only one woman with limited time, energy, and resources. Yet you serve an unlimited God. When God says, "love your neighbor," He invites you to think farther than just down the street. With God's help, your love can travel around the globe, across borders and boundaries, breaking through language barriers, cycles of poverty, and even prison bars.

Begin praying your way through the morning paper or the evening news. As your heart is stirred to aid various countries or causes, seek out relief or missions organizations that serve in these areas. If you attend church, become aware of local and international outreach opportunities. Then, ask God how you can help. Writing letters, packing supplies, fundraising, financial support, perhaps even a trip abroad...who knows where God will lead your gift of love.

God, a global concern I'd like to pray for right now is...

_____

_____

_____

_____

_____

_____

_____

_____

APRIL 26

A New Kind of Princess

Be imitators of God as dear children. And walk in love, as Christ also has loved us.
EPHESIANS 5:1–2 NKJV

Princesses are "in." Little girls celebrate their birthdays wearing the frocks of fairy-tale royalty. Big girls wear T-shirts with PRINCESS emblazoned in rhinestones across the front. Royal lineage or ruling a principality isn't required. However, an attitude of entitlement often seems to be. But demanding to be pampered is never attractive, even if you're sporting a crown.

The truth is, you really are a bona fide princess. You're the daughter of the King. But you're a new kind of princess, a more beautiful one. Like Jesus, love will lead you to serve others, instead of expecting others to serve you. The Bible says you'll receive a genuine crown in heaven, but even then you won't place it proudly on your own head. Awe and humility will lead you to lay it at the King's feet.

Being a child of the King carries with it incredible privileges, such as grace, unconditional love, and eternal life. When you bear these royal privileges with the attitude of a loving servant, that's when the true princess in you shines brightest.

God, seeing myself as Your princess makes me...

Just Say "Know"

Incline your ear and hear the words of the wise, and apply your heart to my knowledge.
PROVERBS 22:17 NKJV

In the classic TV show *Dragnet*, Sgt. Joe Friday is best remembered for his line, "The facts, ma'am, just the facts." In the information age in which we live, we have access to facts regarding just about anything. All we have to do is log on to the Internet.

Being knowledgeable is more than just knowing the facts. It's understanding why they matter and how they fit into the context of how we live and what we believe. So, why would Jesus tell us to have the faith of a child? Children aren't known for their expansive knowledge. True, kids don't know it all. But neither do adults. What makes children's faith so exemplary is they're aware they don't know it all. They trust those around them to teach them. They lean on others for help. They're always ready to learn, so their knowledge is growing every day.

Come to God like a child, inquisitive, trusting, and ready to learn. He'll help you apply what you know in ways that will help you grow. And that's a fact.

God, help me become more knowledgeable about spiritual things like...

Warding Off Worry

*[Jesus said:] "Give your entire attention to what God is doing right now,
and don't get worked up about what may or may not happen tomorrow."*
MATTHEW 6:34 MSG

Picture your mind as a pot of cool, still water sitting on the stove. Then picture worry powering the heating element beneath it. A little fretting here and there sets the water simmering, disturbing the once smooth surface as bubbles begin to roil. Now, turn up the heat a bit more. Mild concern becomes anxiety. Before long, this boils over into full-fledged panic. Where's God when you need to turn down the heat?

As always, God is there. He's already given you all you need to keep worry in the OFF position. When you find yourself concerned about something, refuse to let things heat up. Point your concern upward instead of inward. Dwelling on the "what ifs" of life has the power to do nothing but give off steam. Releasing every care into God's hands is like letting a bubble take flight. Before you know it, it's no longer in sight.

Refuse to let worries disturb your peace of mind. Let God take the heat.

God, one worry I'd like to release to You is...

_____

_____

_____

_____

_____

_____

_____

_____

_____

Standing Up for What's Right

Learn to do right! Seek justice, encourage the oppressed.
Defend the cause of the fatherless, plead the case of the widow.
ISAIAH 1:17

It's been said that nice girls don't fight. But there are things worth fighting for. Not with your fists, but with prayer, wise words, and loving actions. These battles are never compelled by anger, but inspired by concern and compassion. They aren't fought against others, but for them...for the poor, for the innocent, for widows and orphans. They may be personal battles, like fighting to save your marriage or something more public like trying to abolish child trafficking.

If your heart is stirred to consistently pray over an issue, the best thing to do is wait for God's call to battle. Listen carefully after you pray. Does God bring any Bible verses to mind that support you taking a stand? Do wise words weigh on your heart, crying out to be spoken at the right time to the right person with the right, loving attitude? Is there a practical, biblical course of action you believe God is leading you to take? If so, step up and fight for what's right.

God, I believe You are asking me to fight for...

The Ultimate Makeover

Let us leave the elementary teachings about Christ and go on to maturity.
HEBREWS 6:1

Funny thing about clothes...one day you buy them and they're the height of fashion. A decade or so later, those items you once thought looked perfect are now perfectly awful. They're too tight, too short, too loud, too everything! You wouldn't dream of wearing them out in public. The only logical thing to do is to get rid of them.

As you spend time with God, you'll notice that some things that used to fit your lifestyle don't seem to fit anymore. Maybe certain movies, music, or books you used to enjoy now make you uncomfortable. Perhaps what you used to consider a great weekend now feels like a waste of time and money. You realize some things feel wrong that never did in the past.

Just as a child outgrows her clothes, a child of God will outgrow immature habits and pursuits. Like shoulder pads and parachute pants, these need to be bid *adieu*! When God gives you a makeover, you can trust it will bring out the very best in you—and will always fit just right.

God, some changes I see You making in me are...

And the Answer Is...

*[Jesus said,] "Whoever practices and teaches these commands
will be called great in the kingdom of heaven."*
MATTHEW 5:19

Do you know which of these sayings are found in the Bible: "Cleanliness is next to godliness." "God helps those who help themselves." "Money is the root of all evil." "God won't give you more than you can handle"? Guess what? Not one of them is there.

Lots of words and actions often attributed to God are nowhere to be found in Scripture. That's one reason why it's important to read the Bible for yourself. Then you'll be able to distinguish God's words from spiritual-sounding proverbs.

If you do read the Bible, you'll discover that two of the aforementioned sayings *almost* sound like Scripture. The Bible says that various evils stem from the *love* of money and that we'll never face a *temptation* stronger than our ability to resist it. There's quite a difference between what's written and what's often quoted. To live a life of faith, you need to be sure your faith is placed in what's true.

You can't believe everything you hear. But when it comes to the Bible, you can believe everything you read.

God, I want to know the true You, so please help me...

Order in the Court

[Jesus said,] "Judge not, and ye shall not be judged: condemn not, and ye shall not be condemned."
LUKE 6:37 KJV

Not all judges sit in courtrooms and wear official robes. Some sit in car pool lanes, on mall benches, or front porches. Some even sit in churches. They may wear the latest fashions or something they picked up at Goodwill. But each one of these self-appointed judges has something in common. They harbor a critical heart.

Judging your own actions is one thing. God wants to help you learn to discern right from wrong, to help you make choices that will benefit you, not harm you. But when you take what you've learned and use it as a weapon on those around you, love drops out of the picture.

God's the only one qualified to judge those around us. He's the ultimate authority on right and wrong. We judge by what we see. God, on the other hand, sees the whole story, including what goes on behind the scenes. Best of all, God's judgment comes from a place of love and mercy, instead of criticism. Anytime you're tempted to pass judgment, pass that job onto Him.

God, You're the only judge. Please help me...

A Prayerful Lullaby

I will lie down and sleep in peace, for you alone, O LORD, make me dwell in safety.
PSALM 4:8

God never sleeps. At times, it may feel as though you're following in His footsteps. As you're tossing and turning in bed like seasoned vegetables in a wok, all you can think of is the time you're wasting. You're frustrated because you're not doing anything productive. You're worried because in the morning your sleep-deprived brain won't be able to efficiently accomplish the tasks on your to-do list. And you're tired, physically and mentally.

Sleep seems so simple. Babies do it anytime, anywhere. They just close their eyes and turn off their brains. But when your brain gets stuck in the ON position, what can you do? Talk to God. He's up, just like you are. If you're worried, in pain, or can't seem to slow your racing thoughts, breathe deeply. Change your focus. Concentrate on the fact that God's right there with you. Curl up in His arms and tell Him what's on your heart. You won't hurt God's feelings if you fall asleep in the middle of prayerful conversation. God never sleeps, so you can.

God, help me to sleep peacefully by first telling You...

Free to Dance

It is God who is at work in you, enabling you both to will and to work for his good pleasure.

PHILIPPIANS 2:13 NRSV

You're a composite of different women. You're the little girl who dances when no one is looking. You're the teenager, unsure of how she fits into the world. You're the young woman looking toward the future with anticipation and trepidation. You may also be a mother, musician, widow, mechanic, adventurer, or poet. Every experience and moment of your life adds a bit of color or shadow to who you are.

Those around you don't see the whole picture. They see you as you are right now. They may see a driven thirtysomething career woman, a sleep-deprived new mom, or a frail great-grandmother in assisted living. They're unaware of the little girl that continues to dance on the inside. But God knows she's there. He's been dancing right along with you through every season of your life, even when you were unaware He was there.

True wholeness comes from embracing your history in light of His story. By staying in step with Him, you can freely reveal all of who you are.

God, I can trust I'm whole and complete in You, because...

One Thing Leads to Another

This is what the LORD Almighty says: "Give careful thought to your ways."
HAGGAI 1:5

Mouse Trap was a popular kids' game in the sixties. Kids would construct a trap out of plastic wheels, tubes, funnels, and slides. When complete, they'd release a metal ball that would roll, tumble, and twirl from piece to piece until finally lowering a cage that would catch a plastic mouse.

Everything you do is like one plastic piece of a Mouse Trap game. It interacts with something or someone else. Choosing paper or plastic at the grocery store affects the environment. Choosing a kind word over a harsh one affects your relationships. Choosing to follow God or your own fickle feelings affects the heart of the woman you're becoming day-by-day.

Living intentionally means living thoughtfully and prayerfully. It means considering more than what feels good, looks good, or seems harmless right now. It means taking the future into consideration— so you don't wind up being the one caught in a trap. Decisions have consequences, short-term and long-term, positive or negative. Ask God for the wisdom you need each day to put the right piece into place.

God, help me evaluate the long-term impact of...

Shake What You've Got

Let your conversation be always full of grace, seasoned with salt,
so that you may know how to answer everyone.

COLOSSIANS 4:6

Pretzels, hot dogs, nachos, peanuts, popcorn...they're the all-American snack food of movie theaters and baseball diamonds. Healthy? Not especially. Tasty? You bet. But remove just one ingredient from these tasty treats and their overall appeal is reduced to that of a sheet of notebook paper. Lose the salt, and they lose their flavor.

Very few people would choose bland and blah over savory and salty, unless out of concern for their health. Salt not only enhances food, it's used to preserve it. That's why it's significant that God uses "salt" to describe you.

When you choose to follow God, you make others thirsty for more of Him. The loving way you live, the encouraging words you say, the evidence of God's hand at work in your life invites others to taste and see that God is good. When you share what you understand about God, you offer others a chance to preserve their lives with God's help. In a world hungry for God's goodness, you offer a taste of the real thing.

God, help me to be salt in the life of...

_____

_____

_____

_____

_____

_____

_____

_____

_____

Just Do It

*[Jesus said,] "I must work the works of Him who sent Me while it is day;
the night is coming when no one can work."*
JOHN 9:4 NKJV

Review your mental to-do list. Consider the things on that list you never seem to cross off. Or perhaps they never actually make it on the list. They're the things you keep putting off, the jobs that seem too difficult, the appointments you wish you didn't have to make, the problems you hope will simply fade away.

Procrastination only accomplishes one thing. It weighs you down. Whether it's getting the oil changed in your car, scheduling your mammogram, resolving a conflict with a friend, or losing the ten pounds you've picked up over the last few years, choosing to put them off never makes accomplishing them any easier. It can even make things worse. The engine in your car seizes up. A small lump grows larger. A misunderstanding becomes a relational rift. Ten pounds become twenty.

Don't delay another day. List everything you've been putting off. Ask God to strengthen your resolve to complete one thing on your Wish-I-Didn't-Have-To-Do list every day. You'll feel lighter, no matter what you weigh.

God, today help me tackle...

_____

_____

_____

_____

_____

_____

_____

_____

All Together Now

If God has given you leadership ability, take the responsibility seriously.
ROMANS 12:8 NLT

When it comes to leadership, we're all just part of the band. Some of us may play lead guitar, while others play more of a supportive role as bass. Some were designed for percussion, keeping a consistent beat in the background. Then there are the flutes, tambourines, cowbells, and euphoniums. Depending on the musical selection, there's room for every musical instrument ever created to participate.

Some instruments are destined for the spotlight more than others. But every so often, there comes a call for a drum solo or more cowbell. Are you ready when the call comes to step up and take the lead?

A good leader understands the significance of her own part. She plays it confidently, while carefully harmonizing with those around her. She follows the music, knowing when to crescendo, repeat, and rest. Whether your opportunity to lead comes at home, at work, at church, or in your community, step up with confidence. Allow God to lead the leader in you. Let His voice be the music that moves you as you humbly move others.

God, help me develop the leadership role of...

_____

_____

_____

_____

_____

_____

_____

_____

_____

R-E-S-P-E-C-T *Is a* C-h-o-i-c-e

[Jesus said,] "In everything, do to others what you would have them do to you."
MATTHEW 7:12

When Aretha Franklin asks for just a little R-E-S-P-E-C-T, it seems like a reasonable request. She sounds like a woman worth admiring, someone who's strong, confident, and supremely talented. But what do you do when God asks you to respect those you don't feel are worthy of honor?

The Bible tells us to honor various groups of people including our parents, the elderly, the government, and those in authority. It also instructs wives to respect their husbands and husbands to honor their wives. Scripture doesn't say this kind of respect is dependent on whether others have earned it or deserve it. It simply says we're to freely offer it.

When others treat you poorly or act in ways that are less than admirable, this type of offering may feel like an out-and-out sacrifice. God doesn't demand you offer your admiration, just your consideration. Showing a little R-E-S-P-E-C-T simply means treating others with thoughtfulness and dignity. When you honor others with kind words and actions, you honor God at the same time.

God, please help me better understand how I can respect...

In Step with Purpose

When you walk, your steps will not be hampered; when you run, you will not stumble.
PROVERBS 4:12

Some women search for God's purpose for their lives the same way they look for a great pair of shoes. They're searching for something that's comfortable, that fits their own personal style and their budget. They try on one shoe after another. One's too constricting. Another, too costly. The next, so last year's style. So they keep searching, hoping one day they'll find the pair that fits just right. Then finally they'll know God's plan for their lives.

God's purpose for you is more like a closet full of shoes than one ultimate pair of peep-toes. God clearly states that His will is for you to love Him and others. How you live that out day-to-day will change throughout your lifetime. You may wear the shoes of a mother, a missionary, a friend— or all three. Sometimes, your feet may ache, not because God's shoes are ill fitted but simply because the road is long. If every step you take is directed by love, you can be fully confident you're on the right path.

God, I believe living out Your purpose in my life today means...

Fragile Beauty

The joy of the LORD is your strength.
NEHEMIAH 8:10

Porcelain is known for its strength and translucence. Of course, strength is a relative term. While porcelain is strong for fired clay, it easily chips, cracks, and breaks. It will never win a battle against a slate floor. But this weakness doesn't make porcelain less attractive or desirable. In fact, its delicacy adds to its beauty.

Fine porcelain is so translucent that the shadow of the hand of the one holding it can be seen right through it. The same can be said of you. It's true that God's a source of strength. But you're still fragile. Even your areas of greatest strength hold weaknesses and vulnerabilities. But God can use all of who you are, even your weaknesses, to do amazing things.

When you feel small or incapable of handling a task you know you have to face, pray for God's power to work mightily in your life. But remember to look for the shadow of His hand, gently holding you close. When you're weak, God's strength has a chance to shine through you in unexpectedly beautiful ways.

God, the weakness it's hardest to trust You with is...

Something for Nothing Isn't Free

*It was not with perishable things such as silver or gold that you were redeemed...
but with the precious blood of Christ.*
1 PETER 1:18–19

It pays to clip coupons. Saving a dime, a dollar, or cutting the price of an item in half is nice. But what's really worth celebrating is when a coupon entitles you to something for nothing. Whether it's a tube of toothpaste, a ride on a carousel, or a lunch buffet, getting it for free makes it seem extra special.

The next time you redeem a free coupon, remember that's what God did for you. Through Christ's sacrifice on the cross, you've been redeemed. The term "redeemed" sounds like a highfalutin churchy word. But when you think of it in the same light as coupon redemption, it's easier to understand its significance.

God's gift of forgiveness, grace, and eternal life is free. But that doesn't mean it didn't cost anything. It cost Jesus His life. The gift was free to you because someone else paid the price, just like those promoting their product or service through coupons pay for what you receive free. Let every coupon you redeem remind you of the true cost behind "free."

Jesus, thank You for the free gift of...

_____

_____

_____

_____

_____

_____

_____

_____

The Battle of the Sexes

God created human beings in his own image.
In the image of God he created them; male and female he created them.
GENESIS 1:27 NLT

Are you a warrior in the battle of the sexes? When you find yourself in the company of men, either at work or socially, do you feel you have something to prove? Do you deliberately dress in a way guaranteed to catch their eye? Are derogatory jokes about the opposite sex a recurring theme when you celebrate a girls' night out?

God designed men and women to be allies, not adversaries. But with encouragement from the media, fluctuating hormones, and an age-old debate over whether men or women truly are the superior sex, it's easy to find yourself involved in a battle you never intended to fight.

Whether you're single or married, it's time to lay down your weapons. Men and women were created to complement not compete with each other. Sure, we have our differences. But our similarities are so much greater. There's room to celebrate both.

Ask God to help you see every individual, whether male or female, through His eyes. We're all His children, uniquely designed and infinitely loved.

God, teach me to love and honor men, especially when...

_____

_____

_____

_____

_____

_____

_____

_____

_____

A Legacy of Love

The world and its desires pass away,
but the man who does the will of God lives forever.
1 JOHN 2:17

You're walking through this life on the sands of time. Each step you take leaves a footprint, marking a path for those who come after you. One day those footprints will stop in their tracks, and you'll begin walking on a heavenly shore. At that moment, you'll leave behind property, possessions, and perhaps a few items on your bucket list. But those footprints will remain, a legacy of how you've lived your life. Will they leave a path worth following?

You can work hard to make a name for yourself, to accumulate things of value so you can leave a substantial inheritance behind. But in the long run, the legacy of your love has the power to outlast and outshine them all. Keep in mind that what you choose to do today is what forms those indelible footsteps. Your words, your generosity, your attentiveness, your compassion, your faith...if those you love followed your lead, would you rejoice at where your footsteps led them?

Plan for the future. Live a life of love today.

God, the kind of legacy I want to leave is...

_____

_____

_____

_____

_____

_____

_____

_____

Time for a Change

Because he himself suffered when he was tempted,
Christ is able to help those who are being tempted.

HEBREWS 2:18

We all have control issues—self-control issues. What's yours? Do you cave at the sight of red velvet cake? Do you continue swiping your credit card, even after your budget yells, "Whoa!" Do you wish you could rewind the words that just came out of your mouth? Do you promise yourself, "Just one more time," but there's always a time after that and a time after that...?

Willpower can only take you so far. That's because instant gratification holds more appeal than the promise of long-term results. When trying to break a destructive habit, having someone you trust hold you accountable to your goal can be a tremendous help. Hands down, the best accountability partner is God.

The Bible says true self-control is evidence that God's Spirit is in control. The more you rely on God, the stronger your desire becomes to be the woman He created you to be, one who's free from any habit that threatens to enslave you. Why put off any longer giving up what you've wanted to let go of for so long?

God, let me partner with You to break my habit of...

Hero Worship

I will sing aloud of Your mercy in the morning;
for You have been my defense and refuge in the day of my trouble.
PSALM 59:16 NKJV

You know you want him...a Clark Kent to your Lois Lane, a Spiderman to your Mary Jane, a Robin Hood to your Maid Marian. You long for a hero who'll proclaim your beauty, fight for your honor, and never fail to come to the rescue when you're in danger. The champions you're drawn to in books and movies are actually poor reflections of a perfect God. Your heart responds to their strength, devotion, and bravery because they remind you of another story—a greater story—one written by almighty God.

When you're longing for rescue from fear, loneliness, discouragement, or pain, you have a champion in your corner. He's always near, ready to fight for you. Like the superheroes found in comic books, His true identity is often hidden. His rescue may arrive under the guise of a human hand, an inexplicable burst of joy, or the faint whisper of an almost-forgotten promise. Wait for Him. Watch for Him. He's a hero who will never fail.

God, thinking of You as my hero makes me...

_____

_____

_____

_____

_____

_____

_____

_____

_____

Please, God, Can I Have...

Let your conduct be without covetousness; be content with such things as you have.
For He Himself has said, "I will never leave you nor forsake you."
HEBREWS 13:5 NKJV

When fictional Oliver Twist utters, "Please, sir, I want some more," he has good reason. He's hungry, as are the rest of the workhouse children. Unlike Oliver, we don't always ask for more because we need it. Sometimes we just want it. More money. More shoes. More techno-gadgets. More of what we see advertised on TV or parked in our neighbor's garage.

God speaks strongly about our lust for more, using a term we don't hear much in today's society: the word "covet." It means to desire something strongly, often something that belongs to someone else. When our desire for more is stirred by what we see around us, we're doing just that. Coveting. Even if we don't follow through and purchase more of what we want, our desire to possess it is just as destructive. Constantly wanting more tells God His provision isn't sufficient; His blessings aren't enough.

When the urge for more tugs at your heart, count your blessings—literally. Gratitude transforms you into a spiritual Oliver Twist, always hungry for more of God.

God, help me overcome my coveting for...

_____

_____

_____

_____

_____

_____

_____

_____

Note Worthy

He put a new song in my mouth, a song of praise to our God.
Many people will see this and worship him. Then they will trust the LORD.
PSALM 40:3 NCV

What's the soundtrack of your life? What radio station do you play in the car? What's downloaded to your iPod? What songs do you hum in the shower? If you long to grow deeper in your faith or are struggling with a sense of melancholy in your life, perhaps it's time you changed the station.

What we listen to plays in our minds long after the song is through. That's why listening to music that honors God is doubly beneficial. Not only do we have the opportunity to worship God and connect with Him outside church walls, but our hearts, minds, and spirits also get a needed boost of joy and truth throughout the day.

Today's Christian music is much broader than old-time gospel. It spans the genres of country, rap, folk, soul, R & B, pop, rock, and alternative...to name a few. Pick up a compilation of various artists. Then, open wide and sing along.

God, the part music plays in my life is...

_____

_____

_____

_____

_____

_____

_____

_____

_____

_____

Go Ahead... Kid Yourself

Celebrate with joy before the Lord your God.
LEVITICUS 23:40 NLT

Paint a mental picture of a godly woman. What does she look like? How does she act? What does she say? Does she take time to play? Whoa...what does play have to do with the serious business of faith?

Jesus tells us to be like children. Children know how to play. They dance, draw, sing, explore, tell stories, climb trees, and imagine all kinds of things they'll later label "impossible." The childlike spirit God bestowed on you before birth is alive and well. But if you haven't let her out to play in a while, she may feel a bit out of practice.

God reveals His playful side throughout creation. Otters, orangutans, the duck-billed platypus, and the aurora borealis...wonder and whimsy abound in this world and beyond. Jesus invited little children into His arms. Play isn't foreign to our almighty God. It shouldn't be foreign to you, God's daughter, either.

Need help relearning how to play? Hang out with kids. Don't have any of your own? Borrow some from a friend. (She'll thank you!) Godly women make time to exercise their juvenile joy.

God, thinking of myself as being playful makes me...

_____

_____

_____

_____

_____

_____

_____

_____

As Good As His Word

The LORD is good to all; he has compassion on all he has made.

PSALM 145:9

God is good. What you read in the Bible and glean from your own personal experience attests to this truth. When words like abundance, health, and prosperity describe your life, it's easy to offer thanks to God and praise the faithfulness of His character. But good times are not the only times you'll experience in this life. Jesus Himself reminded His disciples and those who came after them of this very fact.

However, God's character remains steadfast. He's still good, even when your situation is not. When you're struggling—when grief, loss, pain, or discouragement are the words that best describe your life—feel free to share your heartache with God. But refuse to focus solely on your feelings or the difficult situation you find yourself in. Focus on who God is, the beauty of His unchanging character, and the depth of His love for you. Being fully loved by someone who's wholly good means you can trust that whatever He's doing will turn out for the best. The day's coming when that goodness will be evident to all.

God, You've shown Your goodness to me by...

_____

_____

_____

_____

_____

_____

_____

_____

Your Favorite Toys

Good will come to him who is generous and lends freely, who conducts his affairs with justice.
PSALM 112:5

When kids are together in a room full of toys, what's the toughest lesson they have to learn? Sharing. If it happens to be *your* house and *your* toys, the lesson's even harder. Sharing means putting something you're attached to into the hands of kids who may not treat it right. They may lose it, break it, or even take it with them when they leave. The more attached you are to the toy, the harder it is to let it go.

Grown women often resemble those kids and their toys. We're hesitant to lend what we treasure, even more so to outright give it away. But everything we have has been given to us. Every possession is a gift from God. Appreciating these gifts is important. But holding too tightly to them squelches a spirit of generosity.

Practice the art of letting go. Lend freely. Give when God prompts you to give. The more loosely you hold on to things, the more room you'll have in your heart to hold tightly to what's truly worth treasuring.

God, help loosen my grip on...

_____

_____

_____

_____

_____

_____

_____

_____

Avoiding Prickly Situations

*The proof that we love God comes when we keep his commandments
and they are not at all troublesome.*

1 JOHN 5:3 MSG

Some people view God as a cosmic killjoy. They believe being asked to refrain from things like gossip, getting drunk, or having sex outside of marriage are archaic rules set in place by an out-of-touch God. Nothing could be further from the truth. Anything God asks of us, He does because it's best for us.

Life can be like a cactus. When you look at it, the big quills are easy to see. Refraining from things like murder, robbery, and abuse are obvious ills to avoid. But cacti often have two kinds of quills, the ones you can see and the ones you can't. It's the tiny quills, almost invisible to the eye, that work their way into your skin. They're difficult to remove and guaranteed to make you miserable.

God loves you. He doesn't want you to suffer needlessly. He sees the tiny quills that hide in some things that don't look all that bad. Following His lead is the best way to get to where you truly want to go.

God, please help me trust Your wisdom and words concerning...

_____

_____

_____

_____

_____

_____

_____

_____

_____

_____

Absolutely Fabulous

When pride comes, then comes disgrace; but wisdom is with the humble.
PROVERBS 11:2 NRSV

You are one hot mama. God says so. You're uniquely gifted, utterly irreplaceable, and eternally beautiful. You're worth dying for. So how can someone who's so absolutely fabulous be absolutely humble? By learning to see yourself through God's eyes.

God plays a part in everything you accomplish in this life. Every natural ability and opportunity you have is a gift. Even the skills you work hard to learn are only achievable because God has given you the abilities you need to learn them. You have much to offer and much to learn—and God plays a part in both.

When you're able to hold on to the best in you without closing your eyes to the worst in you, that is when you're most teachable. Invite God to help you grow in maturity, ability, and humility. It will mean facing some difficult truths about yourself, as well as celebrating some wonderful ones. But that's how you become a woman who's truly worth looking up to, someone who's secure in who God's created her to be, confident and humble at the same time.

Lord, grant me the humility I need in order to face...

Hooked on Comfort

When my soul fainted within me,
I remembered the LORD.
JONAH 2:7 NKJV

Are you in the zone? The comfort zone, that is. It can be a place of peace and contentment, a God-given season where your heart has a chance to heal and your emotions call a time-out to rest. But a comfort zone can become a hiding place. The longer you hide, the more likely it is that your desire for comfort will turn into complacency.

Neverland was Peter Pan's comfort zone. Leaving it meant growing up—and growth always involves risk. Is there any area of your life you've declared a Neverland? Maybe you've felt a tug at your heart to get acquainted with your neighbors, volunteer in your community, or change a long-standing lifestyle choice or bad habit. Perhaps discomfort has led you to keep a particular area off-limits in your relationship with God or someone you care about.

Whatever your personal Neverland, make the choice to step up and step out. Consider the amazing things you'd have missed if you remained a child your entire life. Risk growing up. God's there to catch you if you fall.

God, help me see where I've grown complacently comfortable and...

_____

_____

_____

_____

_____

_____

_____

_____

Consolation Is Golden

Encourage the timid, help the weak, be patient with everyone.
1 THESSALONIANS 5:14

You know people who are hurting. They've received devastating news. They're facing seemingly impossible odds. They've been abandoned, betrayed, deceived, or abused. There's nothing you can do to fix things. Words feel inadequate. To tell the truth, you feel inadequate in light of what's happened. You assure yourself there's someone better equipped than you who can help. So you turn away and go on with your life.

Consoling others through what feels inconsolable is hard. It opens you up to feel a small part of their pain. It can make you feel awkward and stir up questions you can't answer. But it's one of the greatest gifts you can give.

If you struggle with knowing what to do, try the Golden Rule. Doing unto others what you would have them do unto you is a biblical principle—as well as great advice. If this happened to you, what would you need? What would bring you comfort? What would you need to hear? God can turn the little things you do into something more significant than you'll ever know.

God, if I were going to console others like I would like to be consoled, I would...

An Up-Side to Housework

Everything is for your sake, so that grace, as it extends to more and more people,
may increase thanksgiving, to the glory of God.
2 CORINTHIANS 4:15 NRSV

Cleaning the house doesn't rank too highly on most women's list of favorite things to do. However, it's usually on their to-do list, over and over again for years on end. So what can you do to turn cleaning time into meaningful time? Celebrate Thanksgiving, any time of the year.

As you clean out the dishwasher, thank God for the meals you've eaten and those who sit around your table. Sorting laundry? Praise God for running water and having a choice of what you're wearing today. While folding clothes, pray for others. If washing windows is on the agenda, thank God for how He's helped you see more clearly what truly matters in life. Yes, even scrubbing toilets is cause for thanks when you sing the praises of indoor plumbing.

Taking care of the home God has provided for you is one way of thanking Him for His gifts. Spending time talking to Him, as every parent knows, is an even more welcome form of thanks.

God, help me turn house cleaning into time with You by...

_____

_____

_____

_____

_____

_____

_____

_____

_____

Shopping for Inspiration

Everything that was written in the past was written to teach us,
so that through endurance and the encouragement of the Scriptures we might have hope.

ROMANS 15:4

Malls provide a great way to shop. You can find everything from swimsuits to pretzels to haircuts, all under the same roof. At the West Edmonton Mall in Canada, you can even find a skating rink, amusement park, and indoor wave pool, along with more than eight hundred stores and restaurants. That many choices can leave you feeling a bit overwhelmed.

Some people view the Bible like the Edmonton Mall, as daunting in size and scope. So, they scan it to choose only what they want. They try on a few verses for size. They discard what they don't like and keep whatever fits their personal point of view.

But the Bible isn't a one-stop shop for inspiration and advice. It's more like one perfect outfit made up of different parts. You may not fully appreciate, understand, or feel comfortable with it all, but it's all the Word of God. Every page counts. The longer you wear it, the better you'll find it fits.

God, these are some of the ways Your words fit into my life...

Time to Be Kind

Try to do good to each other and to all people.

1 THESSALONIANS 5:15 NLT

In the dictionary, the word "kind" is described as an attribute of someone who gives pleasure or relief. What a beautiful picture of how God treats us. Would God, and those who know you best, use the same word to describe you?

You can give pleasure or relief without knowing someone well. You can offer a cold bottle of water to the teen selling magazines door-to-door in the summer heat. You can compliment a stranger on how beautiful she looks. But the better you know people, the better able you'll be to extend acts of kindness that do more than brighten someone's day. They have the power to encourage a weary heart.

Why not schedule a surprise massage for a new mom and babysit her newborn? Reach out to a friend on the anniversary of a loved one's death? Use your experience to help a new grad assemble her first resume?

Creativity and kindness are great partners. Ask God to help you better see others' needs. Then seek innovative ways to provide pleasure or relief.

God, I want to be kind. Teach me to...

_____

_____

_____

_____

_____

_____

_____

_____

God's Ultimate Plan

[God said,] "As I have designed, so shall it be;
and as I have planned, so shall it come to pass."

ISAIAH 14:24 NRSV

The phrase "God has a plan" is a bit of an understatement. After all, God's plans are so much grander than anything we'll ever pull together. Our plans include things like calling a plumber to fix the toilet, organizing a birthday party for our two-year-olds, or scheduling a camping trip to a national park. God's plans include creating that national park—as well as the universe it's located in.

So when you hear *God has a plan for your life*, think big. The possibilities are as endless as the number of days eternity holds. As you live out your days here on earth, the minor details are the ones you'll see at close range. But not all of these will go smoothly. You'll deal with the plumber who doesn't show up, the birthday cake that didn't rise, or the wet wood that wouldn't burn.

When things don't turn out the way you've planned, remember God doesn't have that same problem. Nothing can prevent His good plan from being fulfilled in your life.

God, I believe one part of Your plan for me is...

Heads Up

The very hairs of your head are all numbered.
LUKE 12:7 NKJV

Consider the attention you give your hair. You wash it, cut it, highlight it, condition it, color it, tease it, spray it, mousse it, and straighten or curl it. The time and money you spend on what grows out of your head reflects how much you care about it.

God cares too, but He doesn't care if your gray is showing or if you're wearing the latest style. He cares about what goes on inside your head more than what's on it. He cares about the true you, the woman beneath the "do." He's cognizant of every detail about you, which includes numbering every hair on your head.

God's aware of every breath you take, every beat of your heart, each ache and pain. He knows whether you've having a good hair day or a bad one. He's more intimately involved in your life than anyone else ever could be.

So as you get ready each morning—think of Him. You can be certain He's thinking of you.

God, knowing You're so intimately involved in my life makes me feel...

_____

_____

_____

_____

_____

_____

_____

_____

_____

Full Speed Ahead

[One who] is slow to anger is better than the mighty.
PROVERBS 16:32 KJV

Rhinos are accidents waiting to happen. They can only see as far as the length of a tennis court in front of their lumpy, horned noses. But they run at thirty mph. They're also extremely ill-tempered. Between their near-sightedness, their speed, and their disposition, it's little wonder a herd is called a "crash."

Rhinos react without forethought, charging anything in their path. The faster you move through life, the easier it is to wind up in a rhino-like situation. When your schedule is overbooked to the breaking point, it's tough to focus on anything other than what's directly in front of you. Like a rhino, you end up crashing into whatever or whoever gets in your way.

When your schedule threatens to get wild, stop in your tracks. Ask God to help you refocus. Temporarily drop any commitments that aren't absolutely necessary. Renew your commitment to make time for what matters, like your family, your health, and your relationship with God. Then, go ahead and get moving.

God, some of the changes I need to make in my schedule are...

Faith's Beautiful Bouquet

Blessed are those who trust in the Lord....
They are like trees planted along a riverbank with roots that reach deep into the water.
JEREMIAH 17:7–8 NLT

If you're planting a flowerbed, you choose between annuals and perennials. Annuals need to be replanted, year after year. Perennials bloom, die back, go dormant, and then bloom again, season after season.

Which type of blossom does your relationship with God most resemble? If you're an annual, you bloom as long as you're enjoying a growing season—when life is going well, you see your prayers being answered, and your emotions attest to the fact that God loves you. But if these things change, so does your faith. It begins to wither and die.

If you're a perennial, you may not always be in bloom. You go through seasons of struggle. Perhaps even doubt. You may not feel God's presence, but you continue to hold on to the truth that He's near, that His love for you will never fail. Perennials are deeply rooted in God through prayer and reading God's Word.

Plant yourself in the soil of faith, not feelings. That's where true life eternally continues to bloom.

God, I feel my faith is like a...

_____

_____

_____

_____

_____

_____

_____

_____

Interior Decorating

God's temple is holy, and you are that temple.

1 CORINTHIANS 3:17 NRSV

Many women have a gift for home decorating. They can transform an ordinary guest room into a spread from *Better Homes and Gardens* in an afternoon. Whether you have that gift or not, there's something you decorate every day. Your body. You dress it, primp it, and preen it. You may paint your nails or even change your hair color to match your mood.

God refers to your body as His temple. That means He views it as a home where He resides. If you were decorating God's home, what would it look like? What materials would you use?

Knowing what you do about God, you're already aware that the exterior of this temple isn't as important as the interior. But you have to make certain the structure is sound before you start nailing things into the walls. That means caring for your health. Next, you'd add beautiful things to make God feel at home. Adorning your character with traits such as love, forgiveness, and generosity would be the perfect decor. Is it time for a little interior redecorating in your life?

God, as Your temple, I want to be...

That's Not Fair!

The LORD longs to be gracious to you; he rises to show you compassion.
For the LORD is a God of justice.

ISAIAH 30:18

As kids, we moan that life is unfair. Brother gets a room to himself. The girl next door gets the bike *we* wanted for Christmas. Dad gets a bigger piece of cake.

Then we grow up. And we do the very same thing. Our neighbors' prayer is answered while our request seems to fall through the cracks. We claim that life *and* God are unfair. And we're right.

Honestly, we only want things to be fair when it's to our advantage. What if we divided the world's resources, which means taking away your home, car, and savings? How would fair sound then? Or how about if everyone got cancer? Would that be equally fair?

Like any loving parent, God bestows gifts, discipline, and answers to prayer in ways that best fit each individual. In His ultimate act of unfairness, God showers us with His love. We get what we don't deserve—forgiveness and unconditional love. Thank God for the unfairness He's shown to you.

God, You've been unfair to me in wonderful ways, such as...

_____

_____

_____

_____

_____

_____

_____

_____

_____

Love Story

God is love, and those who abide in love abide in God, and God abides in them.
1 JOHN 4:16 NRSV

How do you define love? Your definition may come from fairy tales and involve chivalry, magical kisses, happily ever afters, and a great pair of shoes. Or perhaps it's tempered by those who said they loved you and then betrayed your trust. You may love chocolate, your children, and your job. "Love" is one little word with a lot of definitions.

One of these definitions is "God." The Bible says God does more than love us. He *is* love. So how do you take all of those images of love and wrap them around our infinite God? Very carefully. This kind of love isn't a feeling that ebbs and flows. It is love in its purest, truest, most selfless sense.

Since God is love, He's absolutely relational. Everything He does is an expression of His devotion. The Bible says this devotion extends to the whole world. God's love is as infinite as His existence, which means there's more than enough to go around. Allow God to rewrite your definition of love in light of who He is.

God, if You are love, then true love is...

_____

_____

_____

_____

_____

_____

_____

_____

_____

Up and At 'Em!

Cause me to hear Your lovingkindness in the morning, for in You do I trust.
PSALM 143:8 NKJV

Do you ever have a morning when you just don't feel like getting out of bed? Maybe you're exhausted. Maybe you're coming down with a cold. Maybe you're dreading something on today's to-do list, like having a root canal or speaking before an audience.

Whatever the reason, the next time a morning like this rolls around, roll back into bed—momentarily. (Set the snooze alarm for five minutes if there's a chance you'll head back to dreamland!) Instead of reaching for a cup of coffee, take a deep drink of God's presence, wisdom, and joy. Tell Him what you're facing, especially anything you dread. Ask Him to help you picture the day ahead with Him by your side. His gift of today may hold challenges, but it also holds once-in-a-lifetime opportunities. Every day does.

After five minutes, picture God pulling you up out of bed and onto your feet. Then, get up and face your day with confidence. Continue to picture God by your side throughout the day. It isn't a dream. He's always there.

God, the time I need You most by my side is...

_____

_____

_____

_____

_____

_____

_____

_____

Ridding Yourself of Rubbish

As far as the east is from the west, so far has [God] removed our transgressions from us.
PSALM 103:12 NKJV

Garbage men, sanitation engineers, trash collectors...whatever you choose to call them, the people who remove our rubbish are unsung heroes. They handle what others shun, the smelly, discarded, unusable waste of life. Only a crazy woman would run after the truck and grab her bag back out because she simply can't refuse to part with it.

Yet spiritually, we do this all the time. We cling to what's hurt us. We tote around wrongs God's already forgiven. We hold on to regrets. Then, we open our trash bags and paw through them. We may even put our favorite discards on display. Eventually, our garbage bags of guilt, shame, and pain are worn to shreds. Wherever we go, we leave behind a trail of trash. No wonder those around us start steering clear of our company.

God offers Himself for the ignoble task of removing your rubbish, once and for all. There's no recycling plan or dump you can visit. Once you give it to Him, it's gone for good. Trash day is here.

God, trash I need You to take out today is...

Our Daily Bread

O give thanks to the LORD, for he is good; for his steadfast love endures for ever.
PSALM 106:1 NRSV

Tradition can be a wonderful thing. Egg hunts on Easter morning. Opening gifts with those you love on Christmas. Watching fireworks light the sky on Independence Day. They're all great ways to celebrate something worth remembering. But when we do things over and over again, it's easy to forget why we're doing them and simply go through the motions.

This is often true of saying grace. Some people reserve praying before meals for holidays. Others only do it around the family table. Some bow their heads while others join hands. Some repeat the same words before every meal.

There's no commandment that tells us to pray before we eat. But we are told to be thankful in all things. The food we receive every day is certainly cause for thanks. We couldn't live without it. That's why this prayer is called "grace." Only by God's grace do we have enough to eat. Whether what's set before you is a feast or a simple bowl of soup, it's all a gift. And every gift deserves a thank you.

God, when I say a quick prayer for my food, what I really mean is...

Prayer for the Prodigal

Jesus said, "In the same way, I tell you, there is rejoicing
in the presence of the angels of God over one sinner who repents."
LUKE 15:10

What do you do with a wayward child? If you love her, you refuse to turn your back on her. You're patient with her but continue to set boundaries. You allow her to experience the consequences of her own actions, so she'll understand the benefit of changing her ways. You celebrate her victories and hold her close when she fails. You tell her you love her, even if she claims to hate you. You never give up.

Are you that wayward daughter? Even if you view yourself as a good girl, you can still nurture rebellion in your life. God will never give up on you, even if you've given up on yourself. That doesn't mean He won't challenge you to change. God's love is strong enough to comfort and confront.

If the wayward child is yours, take heart. God's at work. Lean on Him for the wisdom to comfort or confront. There's always hope. It's not what you're hoping for, but who your hope is in, that makes the difference.

God, my definition of hope is...

_____

_____

_____

_____

_____

_____

_____

_____

_____

Who Will You Be?

Good people can look forward to a bright future.
PROVERBS 13:9 NCV

When you were a little girl, what did you want to be when you grew up? A dancer? A teacher? A race car driver? A wife and mom? An explorer? A pilot? A poet? However you pictured your future back then, how does that picture line up with who you are today?

Chances are, reality wrote at least a few unexpected storylines into your childhood dreams. But it's time to dream a new dream. This time, instead of pondering what you want to do, ask yourself, "Who do I want to become?"

Picture yourself five years from now. Ten. Twenty. What kind of woman do you hope to be at the end of your life? Regardless of your age at this moment, your future holds as much potential as it did when you were a child. A woman of God is always growing, always becoming more of who she was created to be. This can mean acquiring new skills, as well as new character traits. What will your future hold? Patience? A pilot's license? Only God knows for sure.

God, as a woman who is trying to please You, I see myself...

Your Presence Is Requested

Jesus said to his disciples, "If anyone would come after me,
he must deny himself and take up his cross and follow me."
MATTHEW 16:24

Amid the bills, catalogues, and sales flyers that fill your mailbox on any given day, there's one envelope that is always a joy to receive. That's because it holds the precious words "please come." An invitation means there's cause for celebration. It may be for something as grand as a wedding or as simple as friends coming together to share a meal. An invitation lets you know this is more than a random gathering. It's an occasion. What's more, your presence matters.

An invitation is a sign of relationship. It's an open hand, extending a welcome, announcing that you belong. In the Bible, we read that Jesus extended a simple, verbal invitation to His future disciples: "Come." His disciples accepted the invitation by following Him. Once they did, their lives were never the same.

Jesus continues to say, "Come," today. While most invitations are offered to a select group of family or friends, Jesus' invitation is open to everyone. To RSVP, all you need to do is follow Him. Don't hesitate. Celebration awaits!

Jesus, Your invitation makes me feel...

_____

_____

_____

_____

_____

_____

_____

_____

Some Assembly Required

My people will live in peaceful dwelling places, in secure homes, in undisturbed places of rest.

ISAIAH 32:18

The concept of family is God's idea. He created men and women to be drawn together in love and to complement each other in design. Then, God allowed the physical expression of this love to create new life. Inside the mother's womb, a child's frame is first fit together. But there's more to a child than his frame and more to a family than its godly design.

God isn't the sole architect who determines how a family is built. It's more like He hands us the pieces we need, and our job is to put them together the right way. Love, patience, self-sacrifice, forgiveness, respect, tenderness...these are all available for us to use. But sometimes, they got tossed off to the side, like leftover parts from a build-it-yourself kit.

Whether the family you grew up in was solidly constructed or wobbled with the slightest breeze, you have a chance to build something that lasts. Build into your family only what strengthens it. Remodel old habits if necessary. What's well built today, future generations can build on tomorrow.

God, I pray for every member of my family, including...

_____

_____

_____

_____

_____

_____

_____

_____

_____

Betrayal's Bitter Fruit

Bless those who curse you, and pray for those who spitefully use you.
LUKE 6:28 NKJV

Jesus knows the pain of betrayal. One of His twelve closest friends sold Him into the enemy's hands with a kiss. After His arrest, His other friends fled. Shortly afterward, one of them denied even knowing Him—not once, but three times.

Perhaps you've tasted the bitter fruit of betrayal firsthand. A spouse is unfaithful. A coworker takes credit for something you've done. A friend's spiteful words, whispered behind your back, become known. Being hurt by strangers or those who dislike you is bad enough. But having those you love turn their back on you can feel like a wound that will never heal.

Jesus understands what you're feeling. That's why He asks you to do what He did while suffering on the cross—forgive those who betrayed Him. He doesn't ask you to excuse what happened or pretend it doesn't matter. He wants you to let go of the pain and the blame. That's how healing begins. Let Him deal with those who betrayed you. Refuse to let their actions poison your own.

Jesus, the pain and blame I need help letting go of is...

_____

_____

_____

_____

_____

_____

_____

_____

_____

From the Heart

A generous man will prosper;
he who refreshes others will himself be refreshed.
PROVERBS 11:25

God's a great gift giver. One reason is He knows each recipient so intimately. But God isn't the only one who gives. Whether it's for a special occasion or as a token of affection for someone you care about, the gifts you give reflect how well you know those receiving them. Before you pick up another innocuous bouquet of flowers, think carefully about the person you're paying tribute to.

People feel honored in different ways. Some people respond best to words. For them, a card may be the most important part of a gift. Tell them how you feel, verbally or in writing. Others long for the gift of your company more than one that you wrap in a box. For them, spend the day together doing something you enjoy. Others could use a break from caring for an elderly parent or need a listening ear. Give them the gift of your time and energy. Still others treasure a heartfelt hug or prayer.

Next time you're ready to give a gift, open your heart before your wallet.

Lord, I desire to give the gift of...

Blending In or Being Real?

Do not conform to the evil desires you had when you lived in ignorance.
1 PETER 1:14

Are you a chameleon? You don't have to sleep upside down, change color, or be part of the lizard family to qualify. If you clean up your language when you run into someone who shares your faith, act helpless around the opposite sex (when in real life, you're not), or pretend to enjoy things you really don't, just to fit in with a certain crowd, you have definite reptilian characteristics.

A real chameleon blends in with its surroundings as a form of protection. Changing your words, actions, or appearance depending on the audience you're with may stem from the very same need. If those you're with would reject the true you, they're not really your friends. However, your deeper fear may be that the true you isn't enough, that you really aren't worth loving.

If there's an area in your life you know God wants you to change, address it. Don't dress it up to fit in. Allow those you care about to have the opportunity of loving the true you, the woman God knows and loves.

God, help me be more authentic in the areas of...

_____

_____

_____

_____

_____

_____

_____

_____

What's Your Opinion?

I will praise the LORD, who counsels me;
even at night my heart instructs me.

PSALM 16:7

In the *Peanuts* comic strip, the character of Lucy offered advice to her peers for only five cents. Today, you can get it for free. Television talk shows, radio call-in lines, newspaper advice columns, or countless Internet sites will answer your questions on any and every topic. Add the advice of family, friends, neighbors, pastors, and coworkers, and how do you decide who to listen to?

The Bible tells us it's smart to seek the counsel of others. But unless those counselors are both godly and wise, the advice you receive may not lead you in the direction you truly want to go.

Seek advice from people you respect, those whose lives exhibit traits in line with God's own character. Talk to more than one person. Weigh their words against what God has to say in the Bible. Then, ask God to help you sift through what you've heard and take appropriate action. The next time you're asked for advice on the subject, you'll have both experience and wisdom to share.

God, some of the people I might be able to seek advice from are...

_____

_____

_____

_____

_____

_____

_____

_____

_____

A Glorious Purpose

Give to the LORD the glory due His name;
bring an offering, and come before Him.
Oh, worship the LORD in the beauty of holiness!

1 CHRONICLES 16:29 NKJV

It's been said the ultimate purpose of every man and woman is to give glory to God. But what does that mean? "Glory" isn't a word we use every day, but it's used more than four hundred times in the Bible. So what is it, and how do we give it?

Glory is defined as the honor, praise, and distinction given to those who achieve an impressive accomplishment. It also describes something marked by incredible beauty. Both of these definitions describe God. What He's done is without precedent. As for His beauty, the word "glory" is too limited to describe His actual splendor.

So to give God glory means to see Him for who He is and respond in the only way possible when we do—with thanks and praise. We don't have to wait until we get to glory (a nickname for heaven) to give glory to God. The better we know Him, the clearer we see Him, and the more glory we want to bestow in return.

God, You are worthy of glory because...

_____

_____

_____

_____

_____

_____

_____

_____

The Ultimate Mystery

[God] made known to us the mystery of his will according to his good pleasure.
EPHESIANS 1:9

Not all mysteries are detective stories. The Bible is filled with mysteries. The creation of the world, Jesus' birth, His resurrection from the dead, the gift of the Holy Spirit, the intimacy of the marriage relationship, what eternity is really like...the list of mysteries God's been gracious enough to share with us is long.

Since by definition a mystery is anything that leaves us feeling baffled or is difficult—even impossible—to understand or explain, the Bible is a great mystery. How could something that attempts to tell the story of what is seen in light of all that is unseen be anything less? So don't feel foolish or intimidated if you don't understand everything you read. Mysteries, by nature, boggle the mind.

Take action on what you can understand and keep reading and pondering the rest. Over time, some mysteries will become clearer. Others will remain profoundly puzzling until they're fully revealed in heaven.

So, the next time someone asks you if you've read any good mysteries lately, you can say, "As a matter of fact, I have...."

God, one mystery that really baffles me is...

_____

_____

_____

_____

_____

_____

_____

Victory's in Sight

With God we will gain the victory.
PSALM 60:12

You're a victorious woman. God reminds you of this truth through Scripture, as well as through His Spirit as you pray. His whisper confirms it in your heart. But victory isn't all fireworks, parades, and cheers from an appreciative crowd. It's about overcoming. Unfortunately, that means it requires some obstacle to overcome.

It may be hard to see your life as victorious in the face of failure, disappointment, or continued conflict, but every war that's ever been fought was won through a series of battles. Not every individual battle will be victorious. What matters is how it turns out in the end.

Is a major conflict raging in your life? A rebellious child, chronic illness, the loss of a job, a betrayal by someone you love...whatever your struggle, both you and God are on the battlefield. Even if victory doesn't seem close at hand, God is. Your fight is also His. Be strategic and courageous in pursuing the right course. Don't let discouragement tempt you to give up. Today's skirmish may be the decisive battle that wins the war.

God, to me real victory looks like...

_____

_____

_____

_____

_____

_____

_____

_____

_____

One Life to Live

The LORD will work out his plans for my life.
PSALM 138:8 NLT

Body snatchers are the stuff of horror films. But you don't have to snatch someone else's body to try and snatch control of their life. God gave you one life to live. Are you content with His gift, or are you trying to live vicariously through someone else?

There are several favored victims for this crime. By far the most popular for women is their kids. If you have kids, it's important to be involved in their lives. But when your self-esteem gets wrapped up in theirs, their successes and failures begin to feel like your own. Children are not your second chance for a perfect childhood. They have their own God-given life story. You're there to help guide them, not rewrite the storyline to fit your own hopes and dreams. That storyline is something they'll write alone with the help of their heavenly Father.

Don't miss out on the life God has given you to live. It is a gift, graciously given by your Creator. Embrace it; revel in it.

God, I may be crossing the line between love and control when...

_____

_____

_____

_____

_____

_____

_____

_____

_____

The Strength to Endure

May you be made strong with all the strength that comes from his glorious power,
and may you be prepared to endure everything with patience.
COLOSSIANS 1:11–12 NRSV

Endurance is the ability to continue exerting yourself over a long period of time. In other words, it's the opposite of being a couch potato. Slowly building your physical endurance takes time and effort. But whether you're preparing for a marathon or simply want a healthier heart, it's essential.

Life itself can be an exercise in endurance. It will test your physical, mental, emotional, and relational limits. But unlike a marathon, there's no official starting line. Once you're in the race, it's too late to prepare. That means the time to begin building endurance is now.

Learn to trust Him. Choose to listen to Him. And call out to Him long before you reach the limits of your own endurance. Exercising your faith in God each and every day will help get you in great spiritual shape. Then you'll have the strength and resolve you need to keep moving forward regardless of how long the race you face may be.

God, I want to get in better spiritual shape. Help me...

Mental Overload

Preserve sound judgment and discernment, do not let them out of your sight.
PROVERBS 3:21

There are two sides to every brain. Literally. The left side excels in logic, encouraging sequential and rational thinking. It understands things by dividing them up into parts. The right side is more intuitive and creative. It tends to be more of a big-picture thinker.

For women, the connective tissue between these two sides of the brain is thicker. This is why women tend to use both sides of their brains at once to solve a problem, while men use one side at a time. This is one reason why making a firm decision can elude us at times. We've simply got too much going on in our heads.

When you're at an impasse over a choice you need to make, ask God to help rein in your thoughts. Spend a few moments focusing on Him instead of the problem. Allow His Spirit to clear the static of nonessentials out of the way, so He can guide you toward a wise answer. Then, refuse to keep second-guessing your decision. Act on it.

God, help me clearly understand what I should do about...

Always Abundant

"Test me in this," says the Lord Almighty,
"and see if I will not throw open the floodgates
of heaven and pour out so much blessing
that you will not have room enough for it."

MALACHI 3:10

Infomercial advertisers know the secret words that speak directly to many women's hearts: limited time only. The fear that if we don't act now, we could lose the opportunity to own a fantastic kitchen gadget, innovative exercise aid, or miraculous beauty cream can be overwhelming.

But a life of abundance doesn't come from acquiring just the right products. It also isn't threatened by recession or financial loss. It's a gift from God that is held, not in our hands, but in our hearts.

Three telltale signs of an abundant life are gratitude, contentment, and generosity. If these are evident in your life, you've hit the abundance mother lode. Regardless of your circumstances, your life will continue to overflow with more than enough. However, if this promise rings as true to you as an infomercial endorsement, it's time you and God had a heart-to-heart. The more you desire Him, the less stuff you'll desire to fill your life. Ask Him to introduce you to true riches.

God, I think true abundance is...

_____

_____

_____

_____

_____

_____

_____

_____

The End's a New Beginning

I saw a new heaven and a new earth.
REVELATION 21:1

Beginning a book by reading the final chapter takes away the suspense. Once you know the heroine is rescued, the hero survives, and their love for each other blossoms into happily-ever-after, what's the point of reading the rest of the story?

Yet that's exactly what God invites you to do. He's given you the final chapter of this life in the book of Revelation. This final book in the Bible assures you that Jesus will return, you will be rescued, and your love for each other will grow throughout eternity. Knowing the end of this story isn't a "spoiler." It's a comfort.

The Bible doesn't spell out what's going to happen today. Today everything may go exactly the way you've pictured in your mind. Or an unexpected storyline might take you in a direction you never dreamed you'd go. Regardless of what today holds, you know how the story ends. That means you can trade fear and worry for confidence and peace. Best of all, after the final chapter, an even more wonderful Part II begins.

God, for me, knowing what's coming means I...

_____

_____

_____

_____

_____

_____

_____

_____

_____

On the Job

Surely the LORD your God has blessed you in all your undertakings.
DEUTERONOMY 2:7 NRSV

The phrase "labor force" doesn't paint a particularly pleasant picture for women. Anything involving labor sounds painful and exhausting. But if you receive a paycheck, this force includes you. If you're a stay-at-home mom, you may not officially be part of the force, but that doesn't mean you don't labor right along with the rest of them.

God didn't design work as drudgery or a pastime to keep us occupied until we're home in heaven. God intended work as a gift with a purpose. In the Bible we read about those who built God's temple. Some were assigned jobs as singers, others as artisans. There were carpenters, goldsmiths, musicians, and priests. Everyone's job was important. They were also in line with their individual skills and talents.

Not every job you do will utilize all of your skills. But every job will offer you the opportunity to work hard at doing something well. When you do this, you'll have something in common with those who built the temple. What you do will honor God.

God, I believe what I do matters in these ways...

_____

_____

_____

_____

_____

_____

_____

_____

Marked by Love

[God] set his seal of ownership on us, and put his Spirit in our hearts as a deposit, guaranteeing what is to come.

2 CORINTHIANS 1:22

Chances are it's happened to you. You buy something. But the moment you try to leave the store an alarm sounds. As everyone turns to look at you, you want to cry out, "Not a shoplifter!" Instead, you dutifully head back to the register so the clerk can remove the security tag attached to your purchase.

God has a security tag on you. It doesn't make an obnoxious noise if you pass a certain point or spray dye on your clothes if you try to remove it. It's more like a royal seal. God's own Spirit has marked you as His child. Your life was purchased, so to speak, by Jesus' death on the cross. He paid for the wrongs you've done, and now you're secure in His love.

Nothing can separate you from His presence, His forgiveness, or His grace. You can't be hidden from His sight or cut off from His power. You are safe and secure in His care from now until you're home with Him in heaven.

God, to me, being secure in You means...

_____

_____

_____

_____

_____

_____

_____

_____

_____

Mercy Me

Who is a God like you,
who pardons sin and forgives the transgression of the remnant of his inheritance?
You do not stay angry forever but delight to show mercy.

MICAH 7:18

Throwing yourself on the mercy of the court may sound romantic in a fictional courtroom drama. But what it actually means is that a client hopes that by telling the judge the story behind what happened, the judge will exercise compassion and excuse laws that have been broken due to extenuating circumstances. The client is guilty. That part is clear. It's the sentence that's up in the air.

God extends His mercy to you whether there are extenuating circumstances or not. You're guilty, but declared not guilty. Any sentence you would have received, Jesus has taken on Himself. The final judgment is freedom.

Suppose someone then commits an offense against you. If God's compassion has made a true difference in your heart, mercy will influence how you respond. You'll offer what you've received... kindness, forgiveness, and freedom. The truth is, God's the only true judge. Extend mercy to others and let God handle the rest.

God, some of the ways I can extend mercy are...

_____

_____

_____

_____

_____

_____

_____

_____

Unpredictable Love

*He who covers over an offense
promotes love.*
PROVERBS 17:9

The people we love are not machines, but sometimes we act as though we wish they were. We want them to be predictable. We want to say, "Do this," and have them do it the way we want it done. We want them to continue serving us with a smile even when we're less than congenial. Oh yes. And if they could read our minds, that would be a plus.

But relationships are not mechanical. They're dynamic, unpredictable, and emotional. They can leave us in stitches, as well as in tears. We can't just drop them off for a tune-up when things go wrong. We have to get our own hands dirty and play a part in fixing the problem.

God could have made us machines that never did anything wrong. With His limitless power, He could have made us love Him. But love that isn't given freely isn't love at all. So, here we are. Human. Let God show you how to love the fallible, unlovable people in your life the way He loves you.

God, some of the people I need help loving are...

_____

_____

_____

_____

_____

_____

_____

_____

_____

Caring for God's Gifts

God is not the author of confusion but of peace.
1 CORINTHIANS 14:33 NKJV

On which side of the organizational scale do you fall? Do you alphabetize your spices and color code your closet? Or are you more of a "let the chips fall where they may" kind of gal? Meaning, if chips fall between the couch cushions, that's where they'll stay—at least until the relatives are in town.

If you're in need of an organizational consultant, God can help. He certainly has the track record to display He has the skills. Our solar system, our bodies, the seasons...each one's a masterpiece of organization and planning. Begin by asking Him what's necessary and what's not. If you're overly obsessive about tidiness, He may challenge you to deal with control issues in your life. If you fall into the messy camp, make a list of big and little projects. Choose one little project to finish each day and one big one each week. If you need outside help, find a way to get some. Taking good care of everything God's given you is one way of showing your thanks.

God, please help me take better care of...

Taming Your Temper

In your anger do not sin; when you are on your beds, search your hearts and be silent.

PSALM 4:4

Someone hurts your feelings. Your child has done what you've asked her not to do four times already today. Your husband forgets the onion dip you asked for at the store. You're rear-ended in rush hour traffic. No matter how even-tempered a woman you are, there are plenty of things, big and small, that can push you to the breaking point. If anger is inevitable, is it wrong?

After all, even Jesus got angry. When He saw people selling goods in the temple and cheating others out of their money, He even turned over a few tables to display His displeasure. Jesus was upset because people were not loving God and others well.

However, even if your anger stems from something that would displease God, you're still responsible for every word and action. Where you let your anger lead you is where things can go wrong. Let it lead you to God. When you start to fume, talk to Him. Make sure that when you open your mouth, the words you say are true, loving, and necessary.

God, some of the areas of life that make me really angry are...

_____

_____

_____

_____

_____

_____

_____

_____

_____

Designer Genes

The LORD who made you and helps you says: Do not be afraid...my chosen one.
ISAIAH 44:2 NLT

You can learn a lot from a label. You can find out if your new dress is washable, where it was made, its fiber content, and who designed it. But supposed someone sewed the wrong label into the garment. You might care for it improperly. You might iron a rayon blouse or toss a wool skirt in the dryer.

God put a label on you before you were even born. It read: precious, one-of-a-kind, handle with care. But as you got older, you may have switched out this label with one of your own. Perhaps it read: stupid, loser, ignore me. Or maybe: unlovable, unattractive, abuse me. Labels like these are rarely written alone. Others in your life, often those closest to you, help you write them. But that doesn't make them true.

Like a fake Coach bag sold on a street corner, you're pretending to be something you're not. But unlike that imitation, you're the real thing. You can trust that what God says about you is true. Any other labels should be removed.

God, I believe the label You've written for me reads...

Confidence in Him

I trust in God, so why should I be afraid?
PSALM 56:11 NLT

Who of us hasn't, at one time or another, lacked confidence? We sometimes perceive others as being smarter, more sophisticated, or more knowledgeable than we are, and deep down inside, we wonder if we can measure up.

On our spiritual journey, the same thing can happen. Some of our fellow travelers have been lifelong Christians, talk easily about God, and know the Bible inside and out. We wonder if we could ever become so spiritually self-assured!

The Lord invites you to look at things from His perspective. When He sees you, He sees you alone. Whether your prayers come from church tradition or spring from your own heart, He treasures the sound of your voice. God's love for you is the same whether you're able to ace a graduate exam in theology or you're only beginning to explore your relationship with Him. His love is incomparable, and He compares you with no one else in the world.

When you lack confidence in yourself, He reminds you to take your confidence from Him and in His high regard for you.

Dear God, help me find my confidence in You when...

_____

_____

_____

_____

_____

_____

_____

_____

Time for R & R

By the seventh day God had finished the work he had been doing;
so on the seventh day he rested from all his work.

GENESIS 2:2

Long summer days are made for relaxation. You might go on a morning stroll, spend an afternoon at the pool, or sit on the patio and watch the sun set. But if you're like most women, you won't be doing any of those things today. Why? Because you're too busy!

At the beginning of time, God set aside for Himself a day of rest, and He commanded His people to do the same. This shows the importance God puts on keeping work and relaxation in balance. Perhaps now more than ever—with our 24/7 activities and ever-increasing connectivity— His example speaks to our needs.

Time out for recreation releases tension and anxiety, and time spent following your own thoughts frees your imagination and creativity. Time set aside for prayer and worship nurtures your soul, and time reserved for loved ones builds relationships.

God intends for you to have meaningful work, and He will show you how to balance the gift of work with His blessing of relaxation.

Lord, I find it difficult to relax when...

For All Eternity

If the earthly tent we live in is destroyed, we have a building from God,
an eternal house in heaven, not built by human hands.

2 CORINTHIANS 5:1

If you like puzzles, try this one on for size: God is eternal. That means He has no beginning and He has no end. Can you wrap your mind around the concept? No one can!

Easier to grasp is this amazing truth: we possess an eternal soul. We don't know all the specifics, but we're able to conceive of existence beyond the life we know right now. We can picture being with God in His kingdom, a place called heaven, where the constraints of time no longer exist. We can imagine eternity.

It's no puzzle at all why God wants you to think about eternity. It's His way of showing you the difference between what is transitory and what is permanent, and what will pass away and what will live forever. Eternity points you toward firm and time-honored principles. Here and now, you start choosing for yourself eternal values.

Your awareness of eternity opens to you a future of hope and fulfillment. And this is the never-ending future your eternal God has in mind for you.

Thank You, Lord, for the promise of...

Something to Celebrate

The heavens declare the glory of God;
and the firmament shows His handiwork.
PSALM 19:1 NKJV

Some cities in the United States go all out for the Fourth. Crowds gather on beaches, fields, lakeshores, and riverbanks, to thrill to an awesome array of spectacular fireworks of all shapes, sizes, and colors.

Every night, however, the skies provide something even more breathtaking than holiday pyrotechnics. Stars glisten from horizon to horizon, and planets charted by the ancients continue their course across the deep expanse. The moon—from subtle shadow to glorious fullness—reigns over a kingdom of infinite splendor. All this is God's creation, and it all reflects His infinite majesty.

As God's creation, you, too, are made to reflect His infinite majesty. Your desire to know Him better leads you to take on His characteristics and that, in turn, allows your words and actions to illuminate His compassion, purity, wisdom, and tenderness in a world dark with pain. You sense His Spirit as He dispels lingering shadows of doubt with the brightness of His light in you.

The skies are alive with splendor, and so are you. It's something to celebrate every day of your life.

God, I would like to reflect You by...

A Good Question

Everyone who asks receives; he who seeks finds;
and to him who knocks, the door will be opened.

MATTHEW 7:8

Have you ever been afraid to ask a question? Perhaps you felt everyone else knew the answer, and you didn't want to sound ignorant. Chances are, however, others had the same question but were afraid to ask for the same reason. That's why, before inviting audience participation, many moderators say, "There are no stupid questions!"

God assures you of the same thing. Spiritually, there are no stupid questions. Indeed, your questions show you're thinking through what you hear from Him and about Him. Your questions reveal a desire to learn more and know more of what He has to say. All your questions are good ones to ask.

Whether your questions spring from doubt or confusion, or you're simply wondering, ask. Ask Him how to handle a sticky situation in a Christ-like manner, or how to see a current event from a godly perspective.

Find God's answer in the Bible, or talk to a mature Christian minister or friend. Ask, because a question is the beginning of wisdom.

Lord, I have a question for You...

Hand and Heart

O LORD my God,
I called to you for help and you healed me.
PSALM 30:2

The Bible recounts many instances of Jesus using His divine power to heal physical ailments. He restored sight to blind eyes, strength to weakened limbs, and health to bodies wasted by disease. His purpose was not to magnify Himself but to demonstrate something deeper—God's power to bring spiritual healing to all who come to Him.

When you approach God, you are assured He stands willing and able to help you. You can look to Him for spiritual enlightenment and increased faith. You can depend on Him to renew and restore a spirit worn down by life's trials. Jesus lived on earth so you could glimpse His healing powers and His ability to make you whole.

Did you know He gives you the power to heal? When you comfort a mourner or encourage a struggler, you are providing God's healing action to others. When you speak for the voiceless, give support to the weak, and protect the vulnerable, you are doing what Jesus did to bring hope to a hurting world. You are God's hands and heart.

Dear God, help me to bring healing to...

_____

_____

_____

_____

_____

_____

_____

_____

_____

_____

_____

The Beauty of It

I the LORD do not change.
MALACHI 3:6

Most of us freely admit it—we're not always consistent in word and action, or in mood and emotion. When accused, we'll laugh and claim the right to change our mind!

God makes no such claim because He's a God of perfect consistency. He never varies in temperament or attitude. Promises He made to people long ago apply to you today, and what He said in the past was true then and is true now and will be true in the future.

How comforting to know that the compassion God feels for you right now is the compassion He will feel for you tomorrow too. The arms He holds out to you at this moment are the same arms that will open to you whenever you reach out for His tender embrace. His ear, bent to hear you today, always will be there for you.

Your God is not subject to variation. Despite the changes that ever have or ever will take place in your life, His love for you will never change. That's the beauty of it.

Lord, enable me to show consistency in my love for...

When God Speaks

...After the fire, a still small voice.
1 KINGS 19:12 NKJV

Have you ever had trouble hearing God's voice? It's not surprising if your answer is yes. The clatter of the world around you, as well as the clamor of your own thoughts, can muffle the clear, unmistakable sound of God speaking to you.

Once, the biblical prophet Elijah was deeply discouraged. Only after Elijah stilled the tumult of his emotions, however, could he hear God speak. In the silence of his soul, God's voice came as gently as a whisper, as tenderly as a kiss. In the stillness of his spirit, God's renewing, encouraging, and life-giving words restored him.

Today, God speaks to you softly, with gentleness and compassion. In the stillness of your spirit, He whispers words of assurance. In the quietness of your soul, He murmurs expressions of love and affection.

You won't have trouble hearing His voice when your mind—and ears—are turned to Him. And with inner distractions gone, you have the bonus of also hearing the voices of those around you.

Dear God, open my ears to hear Your voice as I...

All in His Family

Come, let us return to the Lord.

HOSEA 6:1 NLT

In most families, there's a relative who is rarely mentioned. Generally, this person has done something that has brought shame or embarrassment to the family.

Did you know that God's biblical family is full of embarrassments? Throughout Scripture there are accounts of liars and adulterers; tricksters and thieves; braggarts and even murderers. Yet God did not stop calling these men and women His own, and He never stopped loving them. In each case, He yearned for His loved one to return to Him.

Our heavenly Father feels the same way about the members of His family today. No matter what we have done, He longs for us to return to Him. He calls our name, loudly and clearly. He will tell anyone that we belong to Him, and even the weakest among us remains His pride and joy.

If anything holds you back from calling yourself His beloved daughter, run to Him now with it and talk to Him. You won't embarrass Him! Let your mind and heart be filled with the assurance of your place in His family today.

Dear God, the embarrassing thing I would like to overcome is...

Just in Time

God, who has called you into fellowship with his Son Jesus Christ our Lord, is faithful.
1 CORINTHIANS 1:9

You may be familiar with the just-in-time business model. Under a just-in-time plan, managers strive to produce merchandise at the same rate their customers order it. They want to avoid the expense of holding excess product, yet remain able to meet demand. Ideally, the process provides businesses and customers with what they need when they need it.

In many ways, God sends His blessings into our lives in a just-in-time process. He is the provider of everything we need or will ever need, though He does not give it to us all at once. We would be overwhelmed if He did! Yet He will never withhold from us what we need, nor is He ever slow in providing it.

God's just-in-time plan for you is twofold. First, it leads you to ask Him for your daily needs. Second, it prompts you to trust Him to meet your future needs. Yes, He knows what they are (even better than you do!), but He desires to hear your requests.

God will be there just in time for you—every time.

Today, Lord, I come before You to request...

Space for Him

*When you pray, go into your room
and shut the door and pray to your Father.*
MATTHEW 6:6 ESV

Perhaps you have a corner or room in your home that you regard as yours alone. It might be where you sew, scrapbook, read, or exercise. You have decorated and equipped this space so when you enter it, you can get right to work.

A space set aside for prayer and meditation might be something you will want to consider. A designated space helps you turn your mind from the larger world and into the spiritual realm. In this space, you might see a comfortable chair, rug, inspirational painting, Bible, prayer book—whatever assists you during your time alone with God.

As in a well-organized workroom, you would avoid clutter that can distract you from keeping your attention on God. This might include your radio or TV, your cell phone, or your to-do list. You not only have the right but the responsibility to set boundaries on outside intrusions.

Your God-space—whether a chair or a chapel—is where you enter to learn more about the space God has for you in His heart.

Dear God, let me look to You this day for...

Luster of Love

As a face is reflected in water, so the heart reflects the real person.
PROVERBS 27:19 NLT

If you wear silver jewelry, you probably have noticed that it tends to tarnish. When that happens, a little rubbing with a treated cloth returns the item to its original luster.

When God created you, He intended for you to reflect His glorious image. Talk about luster! But chances are you feel intimidated by God's high expectations. That's why He rushes to assure you that He has taken on the responsibility of restoring your original shine.

As you continue to read about Him, pray to Him, and think about Him during your day, He is doing the work of making you more reflective of His glory. Through the gift of His Spirit in you, God turns your heart toward His will and sets your eyes on His ways. More and more, the shine of joy and contentment brightens your life, and the sheen of gentleness and peace touches those around you.

As you can see your face reflected in a perfectly polished piece of silver, others see God's face reflected in the luster of your God-given love.

Lord, let me shine with Your love when I...

Smile of God

Greet each other with Christian love.
1 PETER 5:14 NLT

You have a lot to smile about! You have been touched by the beauty of God's love, and you're becoming aware of His daily care for you and His purpose for your life. Are you ready to lift the spirits of others with God's smile?

Bringing God to the people you meet every day doesn't necessarily demand a confession about the way He has worked in your life, a discussion about theology, or a sermon about His plan for the world. Instead, God is shared most convincingly when one person humbly reaches out to another with compassion, patience, understanding, and genuine caring. It can begin with something as simple as a smile.

A warm smile on your part can ease a heart heavy with workaday worries. A friendly greeting from your lips can touch a spirit weary with sorrows beyond your knowing. Maybe you will glimpse the glimmer of a response in return. Or maybe not. But you will know this for sure: you have touched another soul with the beautiful, unmistakable smile of God.

Dear God, today I pray to touch the heart of...

A New Wardrobe

Clothe yourselves with humility toward one another.
1 PETER 5:5

Ahhh, summertime! Winter coats, hats, gloves, and mittens have been pushed far to the back of the closet, and fresh summer dresses and cool cotton shirts hang front and center. It's time for shorts and tops, flip-flops and sandals. It's the season for lightness and joy.

As you continue to walk with God, you may be noticing a certain lightness of spirit and newfound joy flowing from deep within yourself. Past fears of His judgment have been cast aside like an old winter coat, now that you know Him as a God of unending mercy and compassion. The emptiness of sorrow and the weight of regret have no more room in your life, because today you are basking freely in the warmth and sunshine of His love.

So slip on the chemise of His goodness. Let the billowing folds of His faithfulness swirl around your ankles as you walk, and let the mantle of His holiness float around your shoulders. Pin on, next to your heart, the fresh, bright, beautiful blossom of His love for you.

Today, dear God, help me clothe myself in...

_____

_____

_____

_____

_____

_____

_____

_____

_____

_____

House in Order

I stand at the door and knock.
If anyone hears my voice and opens the door, I will come in.
REVELATION 3:20

When company's coming, we're eager to get our house straightened up! In fact, some of us go to great lengths to make sure there's not a speck of dust to be seen or a pillow out of place.

Sometimes we carry the same thinking into our spiritual lives. Before we invite God in, we want to get past a current crisis, wait for a change in our circumstances, mend an important relationship, or feel we have more time for Him in our day. We want things just right before He enters in.

God, however, is the kind of guest you want to have over at any time, especially when your spiritual house is out of order. God can help you straighten out the mess, because that's something He knows you can't do all by yourself. He knocks at the door, not of people who have nothing to talk to Him about, but of people who do. People like you.

Today, throw open the door for Him—He's an expert at putting houses in perfect order!

Dear God, the mess I need help with is...

_____

_____

_____

_____

_____

_____

_____

_____

_____

Design of Wholeness

We are the clay, you are the potter;
we are all the work of your hand.

ISAIAH 64:8

You may enjoy needlework, but if you don't do it yourself, you may still appreciate the stunning creations of those who do. Indeed, women throughout the ages have excelled in the art of bringing simple strands of thread together to a complete and pleasing whole.

A rainbow's range of colors goes into most needlework projects, but until the design is finished, the creator doesn't know for sure what it will look like. She begins with the hope it will come out as planned, and she proceeds on faith.

Consider the many and various threads of your life—self, spirit, family, friends, work, service. Each day, your words and actions weave them together, but you don't know what your completed picture will look like. God assures you, however, of this: it will be beautiful, because His Spirit blesses every strand of your life with His goodness and truth.

As you extend your hands to others in love, friendship, and service, the threads of His love create a stunning design. Chances are, those around you are already admiring it!

Lord, I'm beginning to see a design take shape in...

Before the Rainbow

I have set my rainbow in the clouds.
GENESIS 9:13

A surprise summer storm can shut down a picnic, at least for some of us. While adults scoop up the food and run for cover, kids keep on playing—now with the added attraction of splashable puddles!

Troubles rain into our day when we least expect them, and our first reaction might be to complain because now our plans have been ruined. Or we could look at it this way: though things have changed, we'll find the good and delight in it.

Your perspective changes when you walk with God. No longer alone in facing adversity, you now have a source of strength and protection. Rather than crying out in alarm, you pose a simple question from your childlike heart: Where's the good in this situation? Where are the puddles to splash in?

From time to time, dark clouds will rain on your spiritual progress, but don't let them shadow the joy that belongs to you. Instead, treat surprise storms as just another way to discover His will for you. And remember: after the rain comes the rainbow.

God, help me see the good in the situation of...

An Abundance of Flowers

Other seed fell on good soil.
It came up and yielded a crop, a hundred times more than was sown.

LUKE 8:8

During the summer, flowers gush over the fences of lovingly tended gardens, shout along the roadways, dance across fields, and luxuriate in vacant lots. Wherever there's a bit of dirt and a dab of water, a flower will lift its head to the sky and sing.

Your spirit is like rich soil, and God's presence like the life-giving sunshine of summer. As in tended gardens, the seed of God's love grows in plots prepared for Him. These are the areas of your life where you have asked for God to enter, where you readily invite Him in. Here, the flowers of God's love bloom in wild profusion.

Then there are spots where you never expected Him to come. Perhaps these are areas in your life where you have given up, or that you have reluctantly left behind as days and events moved you forward. But look! A far-away memory warms your heart. A long-forgotten talent reemerges. A tender blossom brightens a corner of your life.

When God plants, He plants abundantly. Plan for flowers—everywhere!

Dear God, I was surprised to see You in...

Shine Like a Diamond

The one who is the true light, who gives light to everyone, was coming into the world
JOHN 1:9 NLT

Perhaps you or one of your girlfriends has had a chance to show off a bright, sparkling diamond ring. The gem catches the light, each facet alive with the brilliance of little suns.

Unlike a precious gem, God's brilliance comes from Himself—He is the light of lights. But it's helpful to picture each of God's glorious characteristics as one of the innumerable facets of His glory.

The sparkling splendor of God's mercy floods your heart when you approach Him in need of His renewal and restoration. The glowing warmth of His compassion embraces your soul when you come to Him in sorrow. The fiery passion of His love rekindles your devotion to Him when you consider all He has done and continues to do for you. And this is only the beginning!

Look closely at God. Examine who He is by watching Him shine in the various aspects of your life. See how your hands and heart, your thoughts, words, and actions are gleaming like facets of His astounding glory.

Dear God, one of the facets of Your glory I find brilliant is...

_____

_____

_____

_____

_____

_____

_____

_____

_____

_____

History of His Presence

I will cause your name to be remembered in all generations.
PSALM 45:17 ESV

We can't help but smile as we recall good times spent with family and friends. Our fond memories remind us that their love and laughter, understanding and care, and warmth and encouragement have always been there for us.

In the Bible, God's people frequently recounted how He had been with them through all the events of their history. He walked ahead of them, opened the way for them, and guided them back when they veered from His path. He made His presence known through the warnings of His prophets and the witness of women and men of faith whose words were repeated from generation to generation so all would remember.

You, too, are a part of the history of God's people. Through you and through the people around you, God continues to work out His plans and purposes. Through events and celebrations, the words of Scripture, and the insights of spiritual thinkers, God makes His presence and His history known.

Lord, thank You for the time when You...

_____

_____

_____

_____

_____

_____

_____

_____

_____

_____

The Size Is Right

How much more will your heavenly Father
give the Holy Spirit to those who ask Him!
LUKE 11:13 NKJV

You probably know the frustration: everything about the dress is right, except the size. You check each garment crammed on the rack, but your size is missing. On the website's menu, your size flashes "unavailable." Your only option is to make a second choice.

When you ask for spiritual blessings, such as increased faith, more patience, or deeper joy in Him, God has these blessings in abundance and will not fail to give them to you. When you pray for spiritual gifts of grace, faithfulness, peace, love, and holiness, your prayers are granted. God will never tell you to opt for something else!

Unlike with prayers for physical blessings, you do not need to ask if a spiritual blessing is God's will for you. Prayers for spiritual blessings reflect God's will, and He desires to lavish them upon your heart. You can get up off your knees and consider it done.

At any time, spiritual blessings are yours for the asking. Rest assured that God has a wardrobe of them in just your size.

Dear God, today please dress my spirit in...

_____

_____

_____

_____

_____

_____

_____

Some Spiritual Housework

Peace I leave with you;
my peace I give you.
JOHN 14:27

Decluttering a room can morph into a major undertaking. What do you do with knickknacks—store, sell, or toss? Where do you put keys, mail, and magazines so they're easily accessible? Yet once the tasks are done, the room radiates a new mood—peace!

In the room of your heart, spiritual decluttering helps set the tone for stillness, serenity, and peace. Mind-clutter includes distractions such as anxiety, worry, and nagging thoughts, but it goes even deeper, reaching into your feelings and emotions.

When your feelings are in conflict, your spiritual space buzzes as you weigh pros and cons and analyze various scenarios. Perhaps you can think of a time when your feelings simply would not rest. Similarly, when your emotions pull you from one mood to the other, your spiritual harmony is thrown out of kilter by your inner commotion, and you cannot rest.

God can declutter spiritual rooms. He can separate what you need to keep from what you need to let go. Let Him show you how to bring peace to your heart.

Dear God, help me declutter my heart's room by...

_____

_____

_____

_____

_____

_____

_____

_____

Fragrance of Prayer

Let my prayer be counted as incense before you.
PSALM 141:2 NRSV

Many women enjoy wearing a delicate cologne or perfume. They choose it with care, and the scent becomes that woman's unique fragrance. Perhaps you know someone whose person and perfume are beautifully matched!

As a woman of God, your prayers are like your unique fragrance. The words you use and the feelings you bring before your heavenly Father are yours alone, and no one speaks them quite the way you do.

Your prayer may take the form of a few words asking God for healing on behalf of a friend, its distinctive scent lingering to comfort the saddened heart and mind. Your prayer might appear as your hands taking on a task for someone overburdened, its singular fragrance evident in her gratitude to you.

Your personal, heartfelt prayers of all kinds rise to God, surrounding His throne with the perfume of His love given freely to you, now returned to Him fully blossomed, fragrant, and exquisitely pleasing to Him.

The perfume of prayer is your beautiful, God-given signature. Wear it and let its fragrance linger on everything you touch.

Dear God, I come to You in prayer with...

True Love's Ways

God is love.
1 JOHN 4:8 NRSV

You can easily spot a happily married couple! Their joy is unmistakable in the way they smile at each other, the tone of voice they use to talk to each other, and the respect they show each other. The love they share together draws others to them, eager to discover for themselves the secret of their beautiful relationship.

In God, you possess an even greater love. His love is noble and generous, patient and kind, without limits and conditions. Its presence permeates your heart with gentleness and peace, confidence and grace. With His love as your daily companion, you think, speak, and act with a joy that attracts others to you.

Though human love may fade over the years, God's love—like God Himself—remains constant and strong. Though your love for Him may falter at times, God's love for you stays steadfast and true. Other loves in your life may take you to the heights, but God's love surpasses them all.

People notice people in love. Don't be surprised if someone asks you the secret of your love, because true love is unmistakable.

Dear God, I love you so much because...

_____

_____

_____

_____

_____

_____

_____

_____

A Glass of Water

*The water I give him will become in him
a spring of water welling up to eternal life.*

JOHN 4:14

In the middle of a hot summer day, nothing tastes better than a glass of cold water. Not only does pure water slake our thirst, but it refreshes our tired spirit as well.

During His earthly ministry, Jesus met a woman who had come to draw water from a well. The woman was surprised when Jesus told her about the water He possessed—Living Water, He called it. With this water, He said, she would never thirst again!

She may have imagined not having to carry jars of water from the well anymore, but it was a higher freedom Jesus promised her. With her faith placed in Him, she would never again experience the thirst of not knowing God. With her hope in His saving words to her, she would always be refreshed by the wellspring of eternal life within her.

Do you thirst for His refreshment? Then picture God handing you a tall glass of His Living Water. Bring it to your lips and take a long, slow swallow. Let the cool fountains of His goodness satisfy you now and forever.

My spirit is thirsty, Lord, for...

_____

_____

_____

_____

_____

_____

_____

_____

Life Is Good

[God] chose us in [Christ] before the creation of the world
to be holy and blameless in his sight.

EPHESIANS 1:4

Many of us dream big about doing good for others. But these dreams melt away like mist under the stark sunshine of specifics. Do we have the resources to end world hunger, rescue a continent's orphans, or underwrite a local hospital? Few of us do.

There's a dream even bigger than doing good, however, and that's the dream of being good. This is God's dream for you, and He has the power to make it real. Through the presence of His Holy Spirit in your heart, He enables you to receive His good gifts of mercy and compassion, generosity and self-forgetfulness, forgiveness and love. He works in you a supernatural, life-affirming awareness that you—yes, you!—are good.

God has put His goodness in you, and it shows in your kindly thoughts, your readiness to help, and your encouraging words. Your goodness dwells not in big dreams, but lives in little ways among the people you live with, work with, and see every day.

When you are good, doing good just comes naturally.

Thank You, Lord, for Your good in me that shows when...

_____

_____

_____

_____

_____

_____

_____

_____

Better Than Perfect

There is no fear in love; but perfect love casts out fear.
1 JOHN 4:18 NKJV

The spotlight's on you as you finish your performance. Though almost blinded by the floodlights, you make out the judges' scores—a perfect ten all the way!

In life, we're not overseen by a panel of judges scrutinizing our moves (whew!), yet we're often scoring ourselves. From minor infractions to major blunders, we subtract point after point until by day's end, we're often at zero.

The burden of perfectionism is one God stands ready to lift from your shoulders. In its place, He provides you with another way. It is a way that requires no judges (not even you) and no scorecards. It is a way that guarantees you a perfect ten every time, even if you miss the mark, fumble the move, or land flat on your fanny. It is a way to do things perfectly, because they're done from a heart perfected in love.

Your God-gifted heart of perfect love will take joy in helping, encouraging, and cheering on the efforts of others, because that's what God is doing for you right now.

God, help me not to judge myself when...

_____

_____

_____

_____

_____

_____

_____

_____

A Different View

Blessed are your eyes for they see, and your ears for they hear.
MATTHEW 13:16 NKJV

Your circumstances may not have changed over the course of your life. But even if they haven't, it's a good chance you find yourself viewing things differently than you did in the past. It's bound to happen when you look at the world through spiritual eyes.

Your life continues to have good things in it, but now you recognize them as blessings from God. You enjoy them more, because you know whom to thank. Worry about keeping them forever? No, because your eyes are not on the gifts, but on the Giver.

In the same way, your life continues to have things in it you wish you could change. But now they serve not to bring you down, but to lift you up to God as you lean on Him for courage and strength. Despair about the future? No, because your focus is not on your power, but on His.

What a difference in how things look when they're seen from a believing heart! And this is the kind of difference people need to hear about. It's a different view you can help them see.

Lord, one thing I see differently now is...

Signs of Love

*God so loved the world,
that he gave his only Son.*
JOHN 3:16 ESV

When someone says he loves you, you expect to see signs of love. Perhaps you look for flowers, chocolates, or a ring as a symbol of his devotion.

God is no exception. He says He loves you, but He doesn't ask you to put your faith in His words alone. To prove His love, He created a beautiful world for you to live in. He opened the stars of the sky to you and the expanse of the heavens for your appreciation; He formed seas and prairies, mountains and deserts for your exploration and delight.

Even more, He sent His Son Jesus to show His extraordinary love for you and to assure you of His continuing care. Through Jesus, God demonstrated His authority over temptation and sickness, nature and death. All this He did at considerable cost to Himself. All this He did to extend His hand of reconciliation, friendship, and love to you.

You can count on Him. You have the signs of His presence, and so do those you have touched with your God-kissed kindness, gentleness, and love.

Lord, Your love is evident to me when...

_____

_____

_____

_____

_____

_____

_____

_____

In All Fairness

He gives his sunlight
to both the evil and the good,
and he sends rain on the just and the unjust alike.
MATTHEW 5:45 NLT

Sometimes we wonder why a certain person has it so good. Doesn't God realize this woman scoffs at His people? So why is she being rewarded while the more worthy among us are left out?

By human standards, God isn't fair. As the warming rays of the sun make no distinction between the gardens of rich and poor, God showers His blessings on everyone, believers and unbelievers alike.

God's "unfairness" stems from His overwhelming love for all people, whether or not they are willing to show Him love in return. Though He may never hear one word of gratitude from their lips, He continues to provide for their needs.

In doing this, God has set an example for you. He desires you to extend your kindness to those who are sure to thank you, and to those who will never acknowledge your goodness. He invites you to help those who can repay, and those who will never return the favor. It's not a question of fairness. It's simply the beauty of showing love to all.

Lord, today I will make it a point to bless...

_____

_____

_____

_____

_____

_____

_____

_____

Time for Tootsies

How beautiful on the mountains are the feet of the messenger who brings good news.
ISAIAH 52:7 NLT

Most of us don't regard our feet as our most beautiful feature. Though the sandal lovers among us may enjoy the luxury of a summer pedicure, we're still unlikely to hold our feet up for friends and strangers alike to admire.

Pampered or ignored, clad in socks, sandals, or slippers, your feet are beautiful in God's eyes. They're the feet that bring you to the side of a friend who longs for a few words of comfort and caring. They're the feet that hit the ground running when help is needed, and take you where you need to be. Beautiful feet are the ones you possess as a woman God has placed in His world, among His people, and showered with unique talents and gifts to share.

With God, your beautiful feet are traveling along a path of lasting joy and peace. What's more, you're taking others with you through your presence and example! Isn't that good reason to treat your tootsies to a little special attention today?

Dear God, thank You for my feet. They help me...

_____

_____

_____

_____

_____

_____

_____

_____

_____

You Are Here

Show me the right path, O LORD; point out the road for me to follow.
PSALM 25:4 NLT

On road trips, most of us have gotten lost at one time or another. We realized we were headed south instead of north, or street names bore no relation to what we saw on the map.

If at times you have found yourself going in the wrong direction on your spiritual road, you're not alone. Sometimes the way isn't clear, and sometimes you're given erroneous advice. But when the signs you're seeing make you uneasy, it's time to ask directions.

God knows the map. He has traveled every highway, boulevard, and back road, and there's no place you can be that He can't locate you. Stop and talk to Him, and He will offer you safety, shelter, and refreshment. Ask Him, and He will take you back to the path of purity and holiness—the path He set out for you long ago.

Lost on a road trip? You might want to reprogram your GPS or find a friendly service station. Spiritually adrift? Then listen to Him say, "You are here with Me."

Lord, I'm unsure which direction to go when...

_____

_____

_____

_____

_____

_____

_____

_____

_____

_____

_____

_____

Privilege of Prayer

The prayer of a righteous man is powerful and effective.
JAMES 5:16

For no particular reason, a person's name pops into your mind. You wake up in the small hours of the morning burdened by the plight of people in a faraway land. To many women and men of God, these seemingly random thoughts prompt a call to prayer.

God desires to hear you asking Him to bless your friends, loved ones, and causes you care about. Sometimes, however, He may invite you to pray for someone you haven't seen for a while, someone you barely know, or even a stranger you met only in passing. Through the stirrings of His Spirit, God brings to mind a situation pleading for your heartfelt prayer.

God builds in you a source of power—power to make a difference. Just as His words called the world and everything in it into being, so your God-inspired words continue His creative work among people. Your prayers, spoken according to His will, put you in partnership with Him as He comforts and cares for, leads and guides, lifts and saves fearful and endangered hearts.

Dear God, I pray for...

_____

_____

_____

_____

_____

_____

_____

_____

_____

Heard in a Heartbeat

The LORD hears when I call to him.
PSALM 4:3 NRSV

An indifferent "uh-huh" says it all—our words have fallen on deaf ears. The person isn't listening to what we have to say.

Though you may have been frustrated by someone's failure to listen to you, your heavenly Father's ears are always open. He possesses perfect hearing, and indifference to the voice of His beloved daughter—you—goes against His love for you. When you talk, He is listening. He responds to the words you say and also the ones you don't say. He picks up on your meaning, even before your thoughts have fully formed in your mind.

This is the kind of listening His Spirit enables you to do. Because you care about your loved ones, you hear not just their words, but the emotions expressed. Because you're willing to take the time, you hear the hurt behind the mask of casual conversation. You know what it means to listen, because you know that God continues to listen to you.

It's not hearing the words that matters, because listening—perfect listening—happens in the heart.

Hear me, dear God, and help me to listen, especially when...

A Model Look

[Your beauty] should be that of your inner self, the unfading beauty of a gentle and quiet spirit, which is of great worth in God's sight.

1 PETER 3:3–4

Runway models practice their blank, unseeing stare. That's because they've been hired to draw attention to the designer's clothes, not to show off themselves. When they prance, strut, and twirl on stage, it's the drape of the fabric and the cut of the garment that's on display, not the person.

You may never have modeled clothes, but you are a model. As your creator, God designed you to show off His goodness and to highlight, in your words and actions, His kindness and gentleness. Ever increasingly, your life becomes less about you and more about Him.

No, He doesn't ask you to erase your God-given personality or hide your thoughts and feelings under a mask of spiritual makeup! But when you allow Him to swathe your thoughts, words, and actions in His love, your unique personality will highlight His beauty.

When you walk into a room, expect to be seen, because your Designer's touch is evident to all.

Dear God, help me model Your goodness to...

Top Spiritual Condition

Stand fast in the Lord, beloved.
PHILIPPIANS 4:1 NKJV

There are all kinds of ways to get your daily exercise. You can jog or dance, swim or stretch, bicycle, walk, or bend like a jackknife. More important than what you do is that you keep doing it.

Spiritual exercise works the same way. There's no one-size-fits-all method to get your daily spiritual exercise, yet exercise is vital to keeping spiritually fit. You may choose to spend time reading the Bible or an inspirational book. If your reading brings you spiritual sustenance, then you will want to come back for more. You might prefer a small group Bible study where you can share your insights with others. If you come away revitalized, you will look forward to your next get-together. You might feel closest to God when you meditate on His characteristics or on how He has worked in your life. If this exercise floods your heart with joy today, you will have no trouble repeating it tomorrow.

As with physical exercise, you may choose more than one form of spiritual exercise. There are many ways to keep you in top spiritual condition!

My favorite spiritual exercise right now is...

Keep On Practicing

Let's not get tired of doing what is good.
GALATIANS 6:9 NLT

"Practice makes perfect." We've heard it said, usually by mothers or teachers urging our little-girl selves to try again at the piano or free throw line. As adults, we may have used the same words ourselves to encourage kids to not give up.

If you're ever discouraged in your spiritual journey, you might hear "practice makes perfect" whispered in the recesses of your heart. That's God's Spirit reminding you not to let a bad day or an off moment turn you away from practicing spiritual values and principles. Do not give up simply because you lost your temper, said words you wish you could take back, or neglected to do what you knew was right. When that happens, practice going to God in prayer and asking His forgiveness. It will be yours.

Then, get right back to practicing the beautiful strains of His love in your life. Your growing proficiency becomes unmistakable, and before you know it, your practice yields life-changing results.

Remember, practice comes before perfect—and perfect will come when you're standing with Him in heaven.

Dear Lord, I want to be more practiced at...

Let Him Help

You are not in the flesh, but in the Spirit.
ROMANS 8:9 NASB

It looks easy! The do-it-yourselfer dives into the project, realizing only after long hours of back-breaking work that it's not easy at all. If your enthusiasm has ever outdistanced your skill, you know the feeling!

Living a spiritual life might look easy too. That is, until you get serious about actually living it.

No matter how well you know what God's will is for you, carrying it out day by day can be another matter. It takes God-given self-control to hold your tongue when you want to let loose with a few choice words. It takes Spirit-strengthened conviction to speak up in defense of godly choices. It takes being holy, and that's something you can't do for yourself. No one can.

Except God. Through the power of His Spirit at work in your mind and heart, He stays with you step-by-step as you grow and mature in holiness. With Him at your side, what you want to do will be accomplished, and what you never knew you could do, will be done. Just don't try to do it yourself!

Dear God, I need Your help with...

An Aura of Humility

Before honor is humility.
PROVERBS 15:33 NKJV

Do you know someone you consider humble? What are her attributes? How does she show evidence of genuine humility? Chances are, you can't put your finger on what she does; it's more a feeling you get when you're around her. She exudes an aura of humility.

The woman of true humility is far from hesitant, insecure, or self-effacing. She speaks her mind, not to show off but to point out truth and stand up for justice. She'll step up in front of others, not to lord it over them but to lead them in the right direction. She'll put herself forward, not to swipe the spotlight but to shine it on everyone who helps, supports, and encourages her along the way.

And yes, she accepts earned praise and hard-won accolades because it's dishonest not to. Yet she does so with head and heart bowed in grace and gratitude.

God invites you to embrace His gift of humility, because it's yours. Its aura comes from within, and that's where He's working in you right now. In all humility, offer Him thanks and praise.

Lord God, I have trouble clothing myself in humility when...

_____

_____

_____

_____

_____

_____

_____

_____

_____

_____

The Next Level

*He will provide and increase your resources
and then produce a great harvest of generosity in you.*
2 CORINTHIANS 9:10 NLT

The rumble of the big yellow bus down your street marks the beginning of a new school year. The familiar sight prompts memories of reconnecting with friends, exploring new books, and getting a fresh start in the next grade.

While no semesters mark your spiritual progress, there are times along the way when you want to reach further into your studies about God. As in the academic world, the spiritual world offers many opportunities to expand and grow in faith.

The next level for you could be a Bible commentary to deepen your understanding of Scripture. It might include a Bible class to learn practical ways to apply God's teachings. Or the company of a friend with whom you can share together what you experience as faithful women of God.

When others see you taking your spiritual education seriously, it works like the rumble of that big yellow bus—it prompts them to think about their own spiritual schooling. You just might find yourself a mentor to someone who's just beginning the school of the Holy Spirit!

Lord, I'd like to take the next step and...

_____

_____

_____

_____

_____

_____

_____

_____

_____

_____

Something Worth Keeping

Imitate those who through faith and patience inherit what has been promised.
HEBREWS 6:12

There are things worth holding on to. Grandmother's vanity mirror, mother's pendant necklace, a great-aunt's handmade shawl—though of little use today, we treasure them because we treasure the person who gave them to us.

God has handed down to you a wealth of things worth holding on to—things as relevant to you today as they were to His people of long ago. His commandments haven't changed over the years in their usefulness to show His way of holiness and truth. God's warnings remain valid, as the world has not lost its power to tempt and sway.

Also worth keeping are God's words of forgiveness and comfort, which still soothe a wounded heart and renew a broken spirit. You don't have to be an especially sentimental woman to find worth in the love He hands down from generation to generation—the love He showers on you today in so many ways.

Cling to your inheritance. Its value never changes, except to become more beautiful as you learn about the God who hands it to you.

The thing I value most from you, dear God, is...

_____

_____

_____

_____

_____

_____

_____

_____

Greatness by Serving

You were washed, you were sanctified,
you were justified in the name of the Lord Jesus Christ
and by the Spirit of our God.

1 CORINTHIANS 6:11

One evening before dinner, Jesus wrapped a towel around Himself and performed the duty of a lowly household servant. He washed the feet of all those in the room. In doing so, Jesus—the greatest among them—demonstrated how to gain greatness of eternal worth.

When you begin to study what makes a person great in God's eyes, you'll quickly discover that God values very different traits than the world does. The Holy Spirit will open your eyes to the true greatness of servanthood.

God-given servanthood stems from your Spirit-fed willingness to give of yourself to others. It blossoms in your readiness to do whatever needs to be done, from the lowliest task to the greatest responsibility. It flowers in your equal regard for the needs of the poorest and the richest, from the voice of the lowest ranking to that of the highest.

It's from the position of His servant that you are great in God's eyes.

Lord, open my eyes to servanthood and...

The Dirty Details

He who guards his mouth and his tongue keeps himself from calamity.

PROVERBS 21:23

You've just heard a delicious piece of gossip.

Your next steps are what count with God. First, you might say that you'll remember the person in your prayers. Now the conversation has shifted from the shadows of secrecy to the light of genuine caring.

Second, consider whether or not the information you've heard is true, and if it is true, whether or not you need to repeat it. The Holy Spirit provides good counsel for questions like this because the reputation of another child of God is at stake.

Third, implement your God-given judgment by doing the kindest thing you can. Sometimes kindness lies in speaking of the matter in the best terms possible in keeping with the truth; at other times, in remaining silent. What you say or don't say lightens the burden of gossip for another person and heightens the respect others hold for us.

The next time you hear all the dirty details, respond with God's Spirit of kindness, truth, and love. After all, this is how He responds to you every day.

Dear God, guard my tongue and help me to...

_____

_____

_____

_____

_____

_____

_____

_____

It Takes Two

"Come now, and let us reason together,"
says the Lord.
ISAIAH 1:18 NKJV

Have you ever asked someone to sit down with you for a private heart-to-heart? Perhaps something that person said hurt or angered you, and you want to understand. Maybe that person's recent behavior worried you, and you want to share your concerns. You're left with no hope of resolution, however, if he or she is unwilling to talk to you.

Similarly, your continuing relationship with God depends on a two-way conversation. Whenever you're burdened with doubts, especially about His love for you and His presence in your life, He urges you to sit down for a heart-to-heart with Him. He's there to listen when worries threaten to seize your thoughts and rob you of the peace you have found in Him. God wants to have an honest conversation with you when your heart is heavy with anxiety, frustration, or disappointment.

When there's a misunderstanding between you and someone else, God desires resolution. Invite the person for a heart-to-heart. When there's a misunderstanding between you and God, go ahead and sit down, because He's already there, waiting for you.

Dear God, I want to talk with You about...

_____

_____

_____

_____

_____

_____

_____

_____

No Experience Possible

Samuel answered, "Speak, for your servant hears."
1 SAMUEL 3:10 NKJV

If you have ever applied for a job, the interviewer probably asked about your work history. She wanted to know what experience you could bring to the company and how much further training you might need to fill the vacant position.

When you approach God, however, one thing's for sure: He won't spend time asking about your qualifications. Why? Because spiritual qualities come from His Spirit, and you practice them as you are enabled by Him to grow in spiritual experience and maturity. With God, no experience is necessary because there's no earthly experience possible to prepare you for the spiritual position He has in mind for you.

There's one thing, though, that God would ask of you, and that's to undergo spiritual training. Just as on-the-job training prepares you for the tasks of the position, so in-the-Spirit training gets you ready for your responsibilities in God's family. These are to model His qualities, to reflect His beauty, and to radiate His peace.

For His beloved daughter, it's not only a job for a lifetime, but the job of a lifetime!

Dear God, direct my spiritual training so I can…

_____

_____

_____

_____

_____

_____

_____

_____

The Why of Things

All Scripture is inspired by God
and is useful to teach us what is true
and to make us realize what is wrong in our lives.
2 TIMOTHY 3:16 NLT

Why? If you have ever been around a two-year-old, you're very familiar with the question. Tots are curious, and it seems that one answer only leads to another question beginning with the word "why"!

As you get deeper into the Bible, you might find yourself asking God why when you run across a verse that doesn't make sense to you, or a passage that leaves you scratching your head. Yes, the Bible is God's answer book, but no, the Bible doesn't answer every question you might ask.

When it comes to life's most important questions, however, the Bible has definitive answers. Question His love for you, and God answers with crystal-clear promises of His presence. Question His attitude toward you, and God answers with an unqualified picture of it in the saving work of His Son Jesus. Question His plans for you, and God answers with the glories of heaven.

Go ahead and ask why—ask like a two-year-old. Just realize that you already have the answers to all the most important questions.

God, I'm curious about...

_____

_____

_____

_____

_____

_____

_____

_____

Model of Holiness

Just as [God] who called you is holy, so be holy in all you do.
1 PETER 1:15

She's your role model. She's a teacher, a public figure, a friend's mother, or maybe your own mother. In her, you see the woman you would like to be. Very often, her influence has changed the course of your life, and because of her guidance, encouragement, and belief in your abilities, you are who you are today.

God, in His holiness, desires to be your spiritual role model. He comes into your life as a ray of pure light, without a speck of imperfection or a shadow of hidden faults. Once you look on Him with Spirit-gifted vision, the course of your life changes. Because you have seen holiness, you desire to be holy.

It is impossible to match God in His holiness. That is what prevents Him from giving you a task you could never accomplish. His Spirit fills you and gives you the spiritual gifts you need. His love fills you and embraces you in His grace. His power fills you and makes you into the holy woman He has created you to be.

Live today in holiness.

Grant me holiness, dear God, especially when...

_____

_____

_____

_____

_____

_____

_____

_____

Put to Good Use

If we live by the Spirit, let us also walk by the Spirit.
GALATIANS 5:25 ESV

It's no secret: God has plans to put you to good use!

When a neighbor thanks you for the kindness and thoughtfulness you have shown, know that God is using you to touch another with His compassion. When a loved one notices your courage and optimism, realize that God is using you to demonstrate His ability to restore and renew. When a friend asks you about the aura of joy around you, understand that God is using you to speak of His unfailing love.

When people who know you describe you to others as a woman they can trust and depend on, God is using you to remind them that His standards and values apply to life today.

It might be the cross on your necklace or the smile on your face that gets someone's attention. It could be the loveliness of your words or the grace of your being that sparks a conversation about the gifts of His Spirit.

Yes, people can see that He's putting you to good use—praise God!

Dear God, thank You for using me to...

_____

_____

_____

_____

_____

_____

_____

_____

_____

_____

A Place for You

God saw everything that he had made,
and indeed it was very good.
GENESIS 1:31 NKJV

Imagine having an unlimited budget to redecorate your home! You'd surround yourself with colors, textures, and fragrances that reflect your spirit and delight your senses. You'd come up with a place both functional for you and beautiful to you.

Without constraints of any kind, God created a perfect world, both functional and beautiful. He formed the earth to provide air, water, and food for people. He shaped its hills and valleys, seas and prairies, forests and deserts as places of unparalleled magnificence. God added colors bright and startling, shaded and subtle; He showered blossoms with fragrance; He wrapped trees in engaging textures; He touched tall grasses with captivating grace.

The world around you still reflects His creative act. It's a world He made as a perfect place for you, a place He wants you to notice and enjoy and use with pleasure and thanksgiving.

A berry right off the vine, a walk through the park, a flower savored as the scent of summer—all this is the home God has created (and decorated) for you!

Lord, thank You for creating...

_____

_____

_____

_____

_____

_____

_____

_____

New Life in You

*Don't you realize that all of you together are the temple of God
and that the Spirit of God lives in you?*

1 CORINTHIANS 3:16 NLT

At some point in a healthy pregnancy, the mother will start to feel the baby moving inside the womb. How awesome, how marvelous, to experience the first stirrings of new life growing within!

As you progress in your relationship with God, you will begin to detect the stirrings of His Spirit in your heart. Perhaps you have already. His stirrings may come as a prompting to speak up where you know you would have remained silent before. Or you might find yourself thinking twice about an activity you had never questioned until now. At a certain point, you become aware of changes taking place in your choices, outlook, and perspective.

Signals of God's Spirit taking hold include an increased desire to find out more about Him. When you experience the warmth of His peace in the midst of chaos or step forward without fear to do the right thing regardless of the consequences, it's a sure sign of new life thriving in you.

How awesome to feel the stirrings of God within your expectant heart!

Dear God, I first noticed the stirrings of Your Spirit when...

_____

_____

_____

_____

_____

_____

_____

Take the Load Off

Give all your worries and cares to God, for he cares about you.
1 PETER 5:7 NLT

Enter a friend's house, and she invites you to sit down. Take the load off your feet, she says. Make yourself comfortable and stay awhile. Happily, you take her up on her warm and welcoming hospitality.

Like a hospitable friend, God has opened His door to you, urging you to take the load off—not your feet, but your heart. Sit down. Stay awhile. And in His presence, tell Him about your fears and frustrations, your distress and disappointments. If it's something that's causing you a problem, describe it to Him. Even if it's a nagging worry you can't readily explain, tell Him about that too. He'll know exactly what you're talking about.

As you speak, picture yourself handing each burden to God. Put your worries and anxieties into His outstretched hand. Then settle back and listen while He speaks words of comfort and reassurance to you. Open your spiritual arms to receive the strength He desires to give you. Rejoice in His lovely hospitality.

Then leave your burden behind and go in His peace.

Lord, I want to leave with You the burden of...

_____

_____

_____

_____

_____

_____

_____

_____

_____

How to Age Beautifully

Man looks at the outward appearance, but the LORD looks at the heart.
1 SAMUEL 16:7

As girls, we didn't understand it. As teenagers, we didn't believe it. As young adults, we gave it lip service. But now the more wrinkles we start to see, the more gray hair we begin to notice, the more cellulite we attempt to cover up, the more we realize that true beauty really does come from the heart.

A heart steeped in kind, gracious, and noble thoughts overflows with words of kindness, encouragement, patience, and understanding. A heart embraced in God's peace radiates serenity, and a heart invigorated by knowing and carrying out God's plan and purpose shows in actions designed to lift up and inspire others.

Your exquisite beauty comes not from possessing youthful features, nor from anything you can buy in a jar. It begins in your heart, and it increases as you release yourself to the splendor of His holiness. Invite His Spirit in and let Him restore, renew, and rejuvenate you with true, never-ending and ageless beauty.

It's the kind of beauty that makes you beautiful and lets others feel beautiful too.

Grant me true beauty, Lord, so I can...

_____

_____

_____

_____

_____

_____

_____

_____

_____

Answer to Prayer

Show kindness and mercy to one another.
ZECHARIAH 7:9 NRSV

To someone who knows little about God's ways with His people, answers to prayer must seem like little more than wishful thinking. So even though you may appreciate the dependability and wisdom of God's answers, you may find yourself hesitant to recommend prayer to a particular friend.

Instead, you opt to sit down with her and listen while she pours out her words to you. Through your gestures and responses, you let her know you empathize with her and with everything she's going through. Then you might gently share with her the Spirit-nourished thoughts of your heart. If the time feels right, you might invite her to listen as you lift up her needs and desires to God.

In doing so, you're extending God's caring and goodness, kindness and love to someone who has yet to learn about the power of prayer. She won't recognize that God heard the prayer she didn't even know how to offer, but His answer was sitting right across the table from her. His answer to an unspoken prayer was you.

Lord, teach me how to respond to the needs of others, especially...

On Your Side

If God is for us, who can be against us?
ROMANS 8:31

In friendships and in marriages, as in families and in groups that worship and work together, battles break out from time to time. It's her against him, him against her, us against them.

Even in our relationship with God, we'll occasionally step back and eye Him as our divine opponent. It happens when we doubt His presence, question His wisdom, disagree with His timing, or chafe under His gentle correction. But even when we see a situation as us against God, it remains God for us.

God's goodness makes Him incapable of doing anything to provoke a fight with any of His children. Instead, He does the opposite. If you have something against Him, He never squares off for battle, but arms you with His Spirit and strengthens you with His understanding. If there's a spiritual conflict raging in your heart, He's on your side, empowering you with His Spirit and fortifying your faith so you will emerge victorious.

When your battle is with God, you can always count on this one thing: He's on your side.

Dear God, here's what troubles me most...

Something to Brag About

Those who wish to boast should boast in this alone:
that they truly know me and understand that I am the Lord.
JEREMIAH 9:24 NLT

From an early age, we're warned against bragging about ourselves. Even so, the temptation persists because we want others to know about our accomplishments. After all, we worked hard to complete them, and we're justifiably proud to have gained the recognition for them!

In the Bible, the missionary-apostle Paul went through extraordinary trials and hardships to preach God's message of love throughout Asia Minor and beyond. If anyone had something to brag about, he did. Yet when he spoke of his accomplishments, he pushed the spotlight away from himself and shined it straight at God. The apostle knew that God alone enabled him to persevere in his work with remarkable, long-lasting results. Paul used his accomplishments as a way to brag on God's power and strength.

Your triumphs, too, have their source in the same power and strength. God makes possible the opportunities you have to succeed and gives you everything you need to do well. How sweet when someone brags on you! And how remarkable when you, like Paul, use the occasion to switch the spotlight to God!

Thank You, God, for the opportunity to...

All the Best

If you sinful people know how to give good gifts to your children,
how much more will your heavenly Father give good gifts to those who ask him.
MATTHEW 7:11 NLT

Rare is the mother who doesn't want the best for her child. To most women, anything else is unthinkable. For children, grandchildren, nieces, and nephews, we desire the best, choose the best, and pray for the best of everything. But because we're limited in resources and ability, we're unable to provide the best at all times. In some situations, we might not even know what the best thing is!

Your heavenly Father faces no limitations of resources or ability, and He has perfect knowledge of your needs. As His beloved daughter, you receive of His best at all times, even those times you might think you're getting His worst. Sickness, financial worries, job insecurity, loss of a loved one—even these things turn to your good because of His goodness and faithfulness to you.

Perhaps you already have seen His best at work in your life, and you're ready to say today: "God, You always give me nothing but the best!"

God, help me see the best in...

The Face of Graciousness

The Lord is gracious and compassionate.
PSALM 111:4

Do you have one special friend who always makes you feel right at home when you visit? She's the one who shows you to the most comfortable chair and offers you the beverage she knows you favor. She's easy to talk to, she's attentive to what you have to say, and you leave her home feeling good about yourself. She's someone you'd describe as gracious.

God is gracious to you in all these ways and more. He welcomes you with open arms and invites you to feel at home in His presence. For your thirsting soul, He serves the refreshing waters of His Spirit, and He nourishes your faith with His life-giving Word.

He's more than attentive to what you have to say, for He knows even those feelings you cannot express in words. As you go about your day, you carry with you His strength, energy, and compassion for others. You carry with you His graciousness.

In your relationships, you are the heart, hands, and voice of God's gracious care. Yours is the beautiful face of His great love.

Let me be Your heart, hands, and voice, Lord, so I can...

A Thoughtful Heart

There is not a word on my tongue,
but behold, O LORD, You know it altogether.
PSALM 139:4 NKJV

Most of us can recall a time when a private thought popped out in words! We didn't mean to share that critical remark or negative opinion, but it managed to jump from our heart to others' ears.

In a way, there's really no such thing as a private thought. What we truly think is expressed in our attitude toward others, even if it never slips out in words. Loud and clear, our inmost thoughts come out in the choices we make, the company we keep, and our perspective on the world around us. They're illuminated for all to see in the life we live.

As you grow increasingly aware of God's loving thoughts toward you, your own thoughts begin to take on new freshness and ring with genuine caring for others. Gentle, kindly thoughts—as abundant as summer's blooms in your heart—leave no room for anything but loveliness.

With God's thoughts as your thoughts, you never need to worry about the private one that pops out, because it's bound to brighten someone's day!

Lord, please cleanse my thoughts about...

_____

_____

_____

_____

_____

_____

_____

_____

God's Good Will

Our Father in heaven,
hallowed be your name, your kingdom come,
your will be done on earth as it is in heaven.
MATTHEW 6:9–10

Good mothers know this: children need clear, age-appropriate directions if they're to do what they need to do. God knows the same thing. No matter how old you are physically or spiritually, He never expects you to guess how to please Him or wonder exactly how you're supposed to follow in His way. Instead, God has given you His clear directions in the Bible, and He provides examples of how to proceed in the lives of your sisters in Christ and those who have gone before you.

God's directions are spiritually age-appropriate too. He never asks what you're not ready to give. Through His Spirit, you have received the insight and ability you need to carry out His will for you today, and He will supply you with ever-increasing wisdom as you need it to carry out His plan and purpose for your life.

He even sends reminders! Ever been prompted to extend a word of compassion and caring to a needy heart? That's your good God talking!

Lord, I sense that You're reminding me today to...

_____

_____

_____

_____

_____

_____

_____

_____

All by Design

Known to God from eternity are all His works.
ACTS 15:18 NKJV

Serendipity explains those chance meetings that blossom into a vibrant friendship; those happy accidents that spark a routine day with unanticipated joy; those coincidences so good that they seem the stuff of fiction. By contrast, the word "design" describes a planned event or something prepared ahead of time.

Those two words, opposite in meaning, come together in God's wisdom. Blessings you never could have expected come into your life seemingly by chance, but each one has been in God's mind for you from the beginning. Fantastic news arrives as if out of the blue, yet God, in His divine knowledge, has been planning it all along. Your serendipity has always been His design for you.

Think about the many times serendipity has blessed, brightened, and changed your life. Can you perceive God's design behind it all? Can you look back and see His fingerprint on your life?

Maybe later today, your warm smile, caring touch, or encouraging words will lift the heart of someone you just happen to meet. Serendipity? It's being designed right now by God's Spirit at work in you!

Lord, I can see Your fingerprint on my life in...

Blessing of His Beauty

Grow in the grace and knowledge of our Lord and Savior Jesus Christ.
2 PETER 3:18

It's common to those of us who travel the same route day after day: we're so familiar with the landscape that we don't even see it anymore. When we arrive home, if someone says, "It's all over the news, and you must have passed right by the place," we sheepishly admit we did but noticed nothing out of the ordinary.

The spiritual path, too, becomes more and more familiar as you daily look to God and His will. By now you may have fallen into a routine of spiritual practices that work for you, bringing you closer to God and increasingly at ease in His presence.

At the same time, you may be seeing the same signposts over and over. The thrill of newness you experienced at the beginning has dulled to ho-hum, and the discoveries so engaging at first have slipped into the expected.

Yet amazing things are taking place. Look deeply at how God has enhanced your life with the blessing of His beauty, right where you are and through what you do every day.

Open the eyes of my spirit, Lord, to see...

An Eye for Beauty

I am the rose of Sharon, and the lily of the valleys.
SONG OF SOLOMON 2:1 NKJV

Some women seem to have an eye for beautiful things. We admire their taste in clothes and makeup, and we might even try to emulate their elegance in the way we walk, speak, and present ourselves.

Spiritually, your eye for the Lord's beauty makes you the kind of woman others look up to. Like a well-chosen garment, God's beauty fits you perfectly as you move through your day, comfortable in knowing His presence goes with you wherever you go. Like a graceful gait, God's beauty allows you to walk in the world with ease and confidence, relying on His forgiveness, untroubled by the weight of guilt or fear.

Like a whimsical pin or a fanciful hat, God's beauty attracts smiles and lifts hearts. Like the right word at the right time, God's beauty speaks through you to inspire others, promote harmony, and point more people to the Lord.

When you discern His gifts among all the distractions of everyday life, your eye for beauty is at work. Some women—like you!—have an eye for beautiful things.

Dear God, the beauty I desire most is...

His Way of Working

If anyone is in Christ, he is a new creation; the old has gone, the new has come!
2 CORINTHIANS 5:17

Whether your responsibilities lie inside or outside the home (or both!), you probably have a preferred way of working. You might like to work alone, or in a group; according to plan, or by intuition; under guidelines, or without constraint.

Your heavenly Father, too, has a preferred way of working. While He sometimes intervenes dramatically in a person's life, most of the time He chooses to advance slowly, gently, and modestly into the hearts and minds of His loved ones. Day by day, His Spirit moves to clear confusion, lift regret, dry tears, and provide hope to the awakening soul. There's little fanfare when God works in His usual way, but there's subtle, significant, and long-lasting change taking place.

You may not notice all the spiritual growth taking place in you every day, but it's happening as you think more deeply about God and His presence in your life. It continues as you respond to His work by reaching out to others with kindness, thoughtfulness, and love.

Dear Lord, I have discovered You at work in...

With Overflowing Measure

Grace and peace be yours in abundance through the knowledge of God and of Jesus our Lord.
2 PETER 1:2

A cookie chock-full of chips, a slice of banana bread loaded with nuts, or a piece of pie piled high with ice cream is a taste of heaven for those of us with a sweet tooth! We have the extravagance of the baker to thank for such luxurious treats.

God's great extravagance surrounds you. He created not one star, but sprinkled the sky with an array of twinkling lights. He provided not just one sunset, but day after day splashes the horizon with lavish reds, pinks, and purples for all to see.

He's extravagant, too, in the measure of His love for you. He enfolds you in His comfort not sometimes, but whenever you turn to Him. He showers you with His blessings not one day, but every day of your life. He gives you not a single spiritual adornment, but a multitude of His gifts.

What can you return to Him except an overflowing measure of gratitude? How can you give to others, except extravagantly, in a measure spilling over with love and joy?

Lord, I see Your extravagant love to me in...

Just for You

The LORD loves the godly.
PSALM 146:8 NLT

It was a gift with your name on it: a set of monogrammed towels, a keepsake box inscribed with your initials, a book with a special message. Someone not only gave you a gift, but personalized it for you.

God's gifts—both spiritual and material—are personalized for you too. More than any gift-giver, God knows exactly what you need right now, and this is the gift He chooses and makes special for you. When He gives you your heart's desire, it's easy to thank Him for making a dream come true!

But what about hardship? What about setbacks and disappointments? These, too, are gifts. Used as He intends you to use them, these gifts lead you to experience His very real help in times of trouble. When you accept these gifts as your own, God builds in you strength, endurance, and integrity— all elements of personal holiness.

All the gifts God has given you are to bless you and to build you, and each one has your name on it—the name of a woman God loves.

Thank You, Lord, for the very personal gift of...

_____

_____

_____

_____

_____

_____

_____

_____

_____

Against the Grain

Do not conform any longer to the pattern of this world,
but be transformed by the renewing of your mind.
ROMANS 12:2

Do you want to see someone who's living a counter-cultural lifestyle? Then get the mirror and look at yourself!

Prevailing social norms would have you put yourself first, grasp at easy money, and glory in fame. But now you're learning about another way to live—a way that leads to true wealth and lasting distinction in God's eyes. Under His guidance, you have found that there's much more to life than your own desires. As God's characteristics of love and kindness, gentleness and compassion flower in the things you do and say, you are living a counter-cultural lifestyle.

As with anyone who dares to go against social norms, you'll probably receive your share of ridicule and rejection. But you can wear it as a badge of honor, because it means that others recognize the difference between what's accepted by the world and what's acceptable to God. A little chiding lets you know that who you see in the mirror is God's creation—a truly counter-cultural woman!

Dear God, I find it hard to go against the grain when...

_____

_____

_____

_____

_____

_____

_____

_____

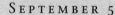

In the Details

In everything, by prayer and petition, with thanksgiving, present your requests to God.
PHILIPPIANS 4:6

If you want to do things exactly right, you know you need to pay attention to detail. A workable budget takes accurate numbers and a successful recipe calls for precise measurements, as does a prize-winning quilt or well-fitted garment. Without seeing to the details, the big picture won't come out as intended!

In the big picture of your life, details also matter. That's why God invites you to bring not only the heavy burdens of your heart to Him, but those small, niggling fears too. He opens His ears to whatever bothers you, from minor annoyances to major irritants. If it's important enough to occupy your thoughts, it's important enough to engage you in prayer.

The details of the lives of others are important to God, too, and He may use you to respond in precise and specific ways. One example: a friend's illness prompts you to bring her a meal. Another: a loved one's disappointment leads you to spend extra time with her. Small details? No, not to the ones you serve nor to God.

The small thing, Lord, that is bothering me today is…

A Precious Vessel

We are the temple of the living God.
2 CORINTHIANS 6:16

Many of us have an item we keep on a high shelf, well out of reach of children and pets. It might be a crystal vase handed down from a beloved grandmother or a glass figurine given to us by a loved one. Not only is it precious to us, but it's easily breakable.

Have you ever thought of your body in the same terms? No, not that you should sit on a high shelf, but that your body is the vessel of God's Spirit and, therefore, precious to Him. Yet He's well aware of the fragility of the human body and how susceptible it is to both spiritual and physical weakness.

For this reason, God extends His hand of forgiveness and reconciliation to renew and restore your spiritual health. He also invites you to maintain and enhance your physical well-being by making the best dietary and medical choices available to you.

Today, think about your body as God's precious vessel. Is there something you want to do differently from now on? Allow God's regard for your body to be your own as well.

Dear God, help me work toward change in...

_____

_____

_____

_____

_____

_____

_____

_____

_____

Love What You Do

Whether you eat or drink, or whatever you do, do all to the glory of God.
1 CORINTHIANS 10:31 ESV

What a blessing when you can do what you love! An even greater blessing, however, is to love what you do. There's a big difference!

To do what you love depends on circumstances, but to love what you do depends on the God-given privilege to understand your work as part of His plan and purpose for your life. Whether your work involves children or elders, a community or a corporation, or a combination of everything, it needs more than just your hands. It needs your heart as well.

Your work is the vehicle God uses to build the beauty of your character and to make His love visible in the world. Through what you do each day, you learn self-discipline and perseverance; you gain self-confidence; you discover God's hand in the direction of your life. What's not to love?

Yes, that seemingly thankless task might be hard to love, but it's worth trying to smile while you do it. Sooner than you may realize, you can know the blessing of loving what you do every day.

Strengthen my resolve, God, to...

_____

_____

_____

_____

_____

_____

_____

_____

_____

Facing the Truth

The word of God is living and active.
Sharper than any double-edged sword,
it penetrates even to dividing soul and spirit.
HEBREWS 4:12

When someone's in denial, she's unwilling or unable to face a hard truth. Often, intervention by trusted friends and family members can help the person deal with the fact she would rather avoid.

Spiritually, we may find ourselves shying away from certain truths about God or His purpose for our life when they are uncomfortable truths. Perhaps the knowledge God wants to share with us challenges long-held beliefs or would require a change in our daily routine that we don't want to make. When this happens, we hide in spiritual denial—yet God's truth remains, firm and unchanging.

If one of God's truths causes you to back up and turn away, please place yourself in His presence. While His truth may distress you, God would never share it with you without the presence of His Holy Spirit to lead you in a productive, life-enhancing, and God-pleasing response.

Perhaps you can discuss God's truths with others who are on a spiritual journey with you. Your conversation could yield a beautiful outcome.

Lord, I have trouble dealing with...

_____

_____

_____

_____

_____

_____

_____

_____

Smile of Peace

The one who comes to Me I will certainly not cast out.
JOHN 6:37 NASB

From childhood, we learned to expect punishment when we were discovered doing something wrong or when we admitted doing what we had been warned not to do. Even if we received no more than a disapproving look, we still did not want to get caught with our hands in the cookie jar.

Our early experience with chastisement carries over into adulthood and into our spiritual lives when we fear to admit our wrongdoing in front of God. Why? Because we expect to face His disapproval—or worse! Yet what we expect isn't what we get from God. Instead of an angry frown, we are the recipients of His smile—His smile of forgiveness and peace.

God smiles when you come to Him because He welcomes the opportunity to lift the burden of your guilt and ease the heaviness of your mistakes. Rather than a prelude to punishment, your confession brings God's reassurance of His continuing love and strengthening presence.

Trust God to deal lovingly with you. In God's smile, you can embrace the refreshing dawn of a brand new day.

Bring peace to my heart, Lord, about...

_____

_____

_____

_____

_____

_____

_____

_____

God of Help

My help comes from the LORD,
who made heaven and earth.
PSALM 121:2 NRSV

By now, no doubt you have come to realize that your God is a helpful God. Rather than sitting high in heaven and watching you struggle to follow Him, He gets right down where you are and clears the way ahead of you.

God's Son Jesus walked among people to prove the reality of God's presence here on earth. Jesus demonstrated God's concern for everyday women and men by healing, restoring, and renewing broken lives. He welcomed children and covered them with His blessing. Wherever He went, Jesus helped others discover and draw closer to His caring, compassionate Father.

Through His Holy Spirit, God stands ready to help you deepen your understanding of Him and His work in your life. Wherever you are, whatever challenges you face, and however many tears have fallen from your eyes, God is there to help you with His comfort and strength.

Open your arms to His help—and then keep them open for someone else. It's the way people come to know the reality of our very helpful God.

Today, Lord, please help me with...

_____

_____

_____

_____

_____

_____

_____

_____

_____

God of Hope

We are hard pressed on every side, but not crushed; perplexed, but not in despair.
2 CORINTHIANS 4:8

It might be said that the only true remedy for any disaster is hope. Without hope, a devastated landmark would remain in ruins forever, and a broken heart would never recover. Hope enables us to envision a better future, hope propels us forward, and hope motivates us to turn our dreams into reality.

God offers an even more remarkable hope. In the heart of the girl who has endured much, His hope enables her to imagine better and to take her place among survivors and achievers. In the heart of the woman who has been cast off and left alone, His hope enables her to believe in herself and walk with grace and dignity. His hope is for anyone who has known what it's like to cry, because His hope dries tears and comforts the downcast spirit.

In the world, as in your life, God has not promised to solve every problem, settle every conflict, or alleviate every injustice. But He does give this to you in abundance—life-giving, life-saving hope.

Lord God, I want to bring Your hope to...

_____

_____

_____

_____

_____

_____

_____

_____

_____

SEPTEMBER 12

The Whole Truth

Be not far from Me, for trouble is near.
PSALM 22:11 NKJV

If you have ever been hit with a stinging accusation or have found yourself the subject of a vicious rumor, you're well aware of the emotional trauma unkind words can cause. And one of the discoveries you might have made is who among your friends turned her back on you—and who did not.

Whether any gossip about you is partly true or entirely true or completely false, there's one whose back will never turn on you, and that's your heavenly Father. More than you know, He understands how you feel. In the person of His Son Jesus, He endured the sting of fabricated stories and malicious lies about His words and actions. Long before you walked this painful road, your Lord was there.

Rest, consoled by God's knowledge of the whole truth, and lean into the soothing comfort of His compassion. And while you're there, remember those who are suffering now under the tyranny of gossip. With your words of kindness and understanding, show them the beautiful face of God's understanding and love.

Heavenly Father, today I want to reach out to...

A Happy Result

Be sure of this: I am with you always, even to the end of the age.
MATTHEW 28:20 NLT

God designed us to live in relationship with one another. Yet, the sad fact remains that many family relationships disintegrate over time or are severed by death or divorce. Social relationships lose immediacy when someone moves, work relationships shift with the company's new goals, and community relationships fray in contentious struggles for power. The sad result? Loneliness.

Loneliness, caused by the innate weakness of all human relationships, affects most of us at one time or another. Not only does it damage our self-esteem and lead to depression, it even threatens our physical well-being when we lose sleep, eat carelessly, or become the victim of addiction in response to it.

The shadows of loneliness scatter when you lift the eyes of your spirit to the beauty of the Lord's constant, unchanging, and supportive presence in your heart. Your relationship with Him stands secure, and the happy result is this: you may be alone, but you need never be lonely, with Him in your life.

Cherish your relationship with Him—and with all others to whom you bring the gifts of companionship, support, and love.

God, I feel loneliest when...

_____

_____

_____

_____

_____

_____

_____

_____

The Smile of God

The LORD delights in you.
ISAIAH 62:4 NKJV

Is there a face that makes you smile? Perhaps it's the fresh-from-heaven face of an infant, the beloved face of your closest friend, or the wrinkled face of an elderly parent. Perhaps it's the heartwarming face of your adored cat or much-loved dog. When you look into that face, you can't help but break into a wide smile!

Imagine God gazing at your face—and smiling. Far-fetched? Not at all. God's adoration for you is complete, and His delight in you is infinite. Before you were born, He loved you, and today He reaches out to lead you. He opens His arms to hold you, and He yearns to hear the sound of your voice in prayer. Even more, He promises to love you forever. So why wouldn't He smile when He looks at your face?

Now imagine if you were to look at the face of others—and smile. Rest assured, they'll pass it on. Though they may not be able to put it in words, they'll know deep down inside that they've glimpsed the smile of God in you.

Lord God, Your smile makes me feel...

SEPTEMBER 15

A Dancing Lesson

*May God's grace be eternally upon all
who love our Lord Jesus Christ.*
EPHESIANS 6:24 NLT

If you have ever attended a ballet performance, you may have been awestruck by how gracefully the dancers moved. Experienced ballerinas turn, twirl, and glide with extraordinary elegance to the rhythm of the music, all the while balancing on the tips of their toes!

You don't need to undergo years of rigorous training, however, to dance with an even more astounding grace. A grace-full heart is all you need, and God's Spirit does all the work for you by inspiring you to think, speak, and act in harmony with His will. Where in the past you may have stumbled, now you are learning to glide smoothly toward gentleness, kindness, and thoughtfulness. Where before you may have slipped, now you are discovering how to step forward with God-given confidence and purpose.

Just as it's hard to take your eyes off the movements of a graceful ballerina, you might find others looking at grace-full you with awe and admiration. Accept the applause—it's God's way of attracting others to the beautiful art of dancing with a grace-full heart.

Grant me grace-full confidence, Lord, when I...

Sound in the Silence

The Spirit himself intercedes for us with groanings too deep for words.
ROMANS 8:26 ESV

At times of extraordinary joy or surprise, shock or sorrow, emotions are difficult to express. We just can't seem to find the right words to say how we feel.

Similarly, there may be times when you find it impossible to pray because you don't know what to say. You yearn to reveal your inmost thoughts to God, but the words that come to mind fall short of your true feelings and fail to get to the bottom of your anguish.

When you step into God's presence in prayer, think of yourself as sitting with a friend who has known you from before you can remember (He has), and who understands your deepest feelings and fears (He does). Silence is comfortable when you're with this kind of friend, and silence is comfortable with God. He can hear unspoken words, and He will respond to you in ways far beyond words.

A heart, buoyant with inexpressible joy or even burdened with indefinable sadness, is all you need to bring to Him. He will know exactly what you mean.

Lord, I want to sit in silence with You because...

_____

_____

_____

_____

_____

_____

_____

_____

_____

Room for New

Be made new in the attitude of your minds.
EPHESIANS 4:23

Have you ever looked in your closet and realized it's time to get rid of clothes you haven't worn in years and shoes that have long since gone out of fashion in order to make way for what's new?

It's the same in our relationship with God. By this time in your life, no doubt you have made significant progress in your relationship. Probably many things have changed. Perhaps even without your noticing it, you're no longer using the same tone of voice—or even the same words—when you speak to your loved ones. You don't even want to put on a me-first attitude, and you shifted your focus from your priorities to God's long ago.

If this describes you, it's time to make even more room available to God to work in your life. Mentally toss out any remaining thoughts or habits, actions or reactions, that no longer fit your new spiritual lifestyle. Anything unholy? Throw it out! Anything impure? Get rid of it! Anything ugly in the sight of God? You have no need for it now that God has opened a beautiful new life for you.

Lord God, help me get rid of...

_____

_____

_____

_____

_____

_____

_____

_____

_____

A Way to Grow

First a leaf blade pushes through, then the heads of wheat are formed, and finally the grain ripens.
MARK 4:28 NLT

Little by little, children grow and mature. They learn about colors and shapes and sounds, and then they become aware of connections, concepts, and ideas. Sounds smooth and easy, right?

Of course, it isn't. All along the way there are detours and setbacks, wrong turns and roadblocks. Unexpected problems crop up, and at the same time, amazing talents blossom. Far from a predictable process, physical growth is a unique flowering of body and mind.

Spiritual growth also is far from a humdrum affair. You can expect to make wrong turns and come face-to-face with roadblocks—it's all part of the being and doing, the learning, growing, and maturing process. But even more, you can look forward to discovering some amazing talents. A talent for patience and for kindness. A talent for giving and for listening. A talent for encouraging others and for understanding their true needs.

The more you learn about God, the more you can expect to grow in beauty of heart and soul.

Thank You, God, for giving me the spiritual talent for...

_____

_____

_____

_____

_____

_____

_____

_____

_____

Plan of Escape

The Lord knows how to deliver the godly out of temptations.
2 PETER 2:9 NKJV

Most of us have taken emergency workers' advice and thought about how we would get out of our home in case of fire. Though a house fire may never occur, we are wise to have an escape plan in place for our family and ourselves.

Spiritually, God has put an escape plan in place for you in case of temptation of any kind. His plan shows you the quickest way out of guilt and confusion and into the safety and security of His loving presence.

His plan is this: When tempted, leave immediately, whether from a physical place or an emotional state of mind, and run (not walk!) to your heavenly Father's arms. Take whatever troubles you to Him in prayer and then stay where you are until the way forward is clear. He may choose to soothe you with an outpouring of His Spirit, or with the strengthening words of Scripture, or with the counsel of a wise and spiritually mature friend.

Before you face temptation, know your plan of escape—He'll be there for you.

Dear God, I feel in spiritual danger when...

_____

_____

_____

_____

_____

_____

_____

_____

Thanks for Asking

Listen, my sons, to a father's instruction; pay attention and gain understanding.
PROVERBS 4:1

An ambitious project pops into your mind, or an exciting cause fills you with fervor. Is this God-ordained or isn't it?

God appreciates your asking (not everybody does). To answer your question, there are three tests for you to apply to any course of action.

First, the test of God's essence. Nothing He would ask you to do would go against His love for you and His love for others. His will is life-giving and life-enhancing.

Second, the test of God's law. God never contradicts Himself, and He would never require you to act contrary to His stated commandments.

Third, the test of God's gifts. God endows your heart with faith and joy, patience and gentleness, purity and kindness, godly strength and courage. Anything that would lessen or negate His gifts is not in His plan for you.

As you follow the Lord, many ideas are likely to come to your mind, but not all of them spring from His mind. When in doubt, please don't hesitate to ask.

Lord God, the idea I want to put to the test is...

_____

_____

_____

_____

_____

_____

_____

_____

The Ripple Effect

Dear brothers and sisters,
pattern your lives after mine,
and learn from those who follow our example.
PHILIPPIANS 3:17 NLT

As you recognize more clearly the beauty of the Lord and His love for you, His Spirit moves you to imitate His characteristics. His compassion for you inspires you to show more compassion to others, and His mercy toward your weaknesses enables you to deal gently with the frailties of others. Your knowledge of His presence in your life becomes the source of your genuine confidence, true security, and lasting joy.

His Spirit at work in you cannot fail to touch the lives of others. As a small pebble dropped into the middle of a pond creates ever-flowing, ever-widening ripples, the things you do make others want to imitate you—your thoughtfulness, your kindness, your gentleness, your joy in life. Their actions inspire more people, and so on!

You cannot imagine how many ripples you already have sent out among your loved ones and friends, and this side of heaven, you will never really know. But do know this: the world is a very big pond, and ripples can spread a long way out.

Praise to You, Father, because I sent out a ripple when...

_____

_____

_____

_____

_____

_____

_____

_____

Nutrition for the Soul

Jesus declared, "I am the bread of life. He who comes to me will never go hungry."
JOHN 6:35

At least to some degree, most of us are aware of basic facts about the foods we eat. We know, for example, that fruits and vegetables are more nutritious than candy and cake, and that a daily diet of desserts would lead to some serious health issues.

Yet we often find ourselves wanting nothing but a diet of desserts from God. We ought to be immune from troubles that afflict other people, our thinking goes, because, after all, God is our protector. Indeed He is! And nothing is more important to Him than our spiritual health.

God knows how spiritually strong you are, but He wants you to know; and that's why He may permit some adversity to come into your life. Adversity fortifies your faith and lets you exercise your spiritual muscles in real-life situations. It allows you to counter trouble with trust in God's continuing love for you.

Adversity is certainly not as tasty as a scoop of chocolate ice cream, but sometimes it's exactly what the spiritual body needs to stay in tip-top shape!

God, I want more than spiritual dessert, I want challenges that...

_____

_____

_____

_____

_____

_____

_____

_____

The Seasonal Difference

To everything there is a season, a time for every purpose under heaven.
ECCLESIASTES 3:1 NKJV

Autumn has arrived. Though we may have seen more autumns than we care to admit, we can say this: each one is different. To this year we're bringing more experience, more understanding, and more life-wisdom than we had last year. Even if this autumn were to mirror last autumn in its details, we would still see it differently because we are different people now.

As you study Scripture, you read the same stories repeatedly, and the history of God's people becomes familiar to you. Though the details of biblical accounts never vary, each time you approach them, it's a distinctive experience. You have lived another season, another month, another day, and you're not the same person you were the last time you read that story. You possess more experience and more life-wisdom now. You can discover something new or perceive a truth that was hidden from you before, or understand a passage that, not long ago, was incomprehensible to you.

God's story never changes, but you do. That's the beauty of every season you spend in Him.

Lord, thank You for coming to me in...

Your 20/20 Vision

Now we see things imperfectly as in a cloudy mirror,
but then we will see everything with perfect clarity.
1 CORINTHIANS 13:12 NLT

A new pair of eyeglasses can bring big changes. Suddenly, the world looks brighter, reading becomes easier, and everything appears clearer and sharper. What a difference!

As you continue to focus on God and His love for you, you will experience a change in your vision—your spiritual vision, that is. Increasingly, His presence brightens your outlook, and you can read His plans and purposes for your life more easily. A clearer, sharper image of God, His work in the world, and His attitude toward you begins to take shape, because now you can spiritually discern Him.

With a new lens prescription, it can take time for your eyes to adjust. A change in spiritual vision can take time, too, and you might find yourself slipping back to old ways of acting or thinking. When that happens, remind yourself that God has given you a new way to see yourself and the world, and He has enabled you to recognize His presence and His love in your life. What a beautiful difference!

I have seen this about You, dear God...

On a Dark Night

The light shines in the darkness, and the darkness did not comprehend it.
JOHN 1:5 NKJV

When the harvest moon sits low and bright in the autumn sky, it inspires tales and legends, as well as reflections, songs, and poems. Sure, astronauts have set foot on it and cameras have charted its surface, but the full moon continues to light the night with enchantment. The full moon remains a magnificent reminder of God's creative genius.

Always ongoing is God's willingness and ability to create. He still fascinates those who are attentive to Him as He shapes something from nothing, makes new from old. Through the power of His Spirit in the believer's heart, God shines the light of hope to dispel the darkness of despair; He pours the warmth of joy to chase away the chill shiver of sadness; He showers the blessing of abundance to satisfy a soul once wandering and alone.

Our Creator-God hasn't lost His passion to create beauty and loveliness, and His presence in your life never fails to enchant. And like the harvest moon, sometimes He's most visible in the darkest of nights.

Creator-God, please shine Your light on...

Love for Real

The LORD will command
His lovingkindness in the daytime,
and in the night His song shall be with me.
PSALM 42:8 NKJV

By now you've read it and heard it repeatedly: Your heavenly Father loves you. But ask yourself: Is His love real to me? Has the certainty of His love for me caused a fundamental change in the way I think about myself? About others? Because that's what it's meant to do!

God's love is more than merely a pleasant thing to believe or a good motto to remember in times of trouble. Rather, God invites you to make His love a living and breathing part of your life. He wants you to know His love as a daily, living, and ever-present reality.

The beautiful reality of your Lord's love enables you to humbly embrace yourself with nothing less than godly pride. His transforming love for you motivates you to reach out to help the hopeless, the distressed, and the discouraged discover how much they are worth in God's eyes.

It's a certainty: God loves you, and the reality of His love makes a beautiful difference wherever it lives and breathes.

God, Your love has changed how I think about...

_____

_____

_____

_____

_____

_____

_____

_____

So That's How

I want you to be wise about what is good, and simple concerning evil.
ROMANS 16:19 NKJV

Probably some of the most practical lessons you've learned in life came not from a classroom teacher, but from a parent, relative, neighbor, or friend. Perhaps your mother taught you how to bake lasagna, your neighbor showed you how to grow tomatoes, or a friend taught you how to dress with flair. Conversely, you may have learned from many of the same sources how not to do certain things!

You pick up practical spiritual dos and don'ts in the same way. As you observe how women and men in your life approach their hardships and challenges, you find some acting in ways corresponding with God's expressed will, and others in ways contradicting it. Many, in striving to obey God, serve as inspiring examples as you learn how to bring the beauty of God's presence into your life in practical ways.

At the same time, others watch you. From your God-inspired attempts to live in His presence, others learn how to say yes to God. In your gentleness and kindness, grace and gratitude, others discover how it's done.

Thank You, God, for sending to me special people like...

Life of Joy

The LORD your God will bless you in all your harvest
and in all the work of your hands, and your joy will be complete.
DEUTERONOMY 16:15

Along with His other spiritual gifts, God has planted in you the seed of genuine joy so that you can live a joyful life!

To nurture joy, give first place to things you love. When you go outside, ignore the weeds that need pulling and discover what makes you happy. Maybe it's how willow branches sway in the wind or the way a big fluffy cloud appears as cozy as a teddy bear. When you walk around your home, overlook the dust on your dining room table. Instead, feast your eyes on the face in a favorite photograph, the color you're so glad you painted on the wall, or the memento of a fantastic vacation.

The joy in your heart and mind flows out to lift your attitude, sweeten your words, and energize the things you do and say. Before you know it, people start asking you how you can be so joyful—people who don't yet know that God has more seeds of joy to plant in waiting hearts!

Fill me, Lord God, with Your joy when...

Beauty of God's Strength

Cast your burden on the LORD,
and He shall sustain you.
PSALM 55:22 NKJV

Most women carry a heavy load of responsibilities. They're responsible—sometimes single-handedly—for raising children, keeping house, earning enough to keep the family afloat, caring for elderly relatives, and maintaining their own health and well-being.

The beauty of God's strength is that it belongs to you. Your responsibilities are not yours alone, but His too.

First, God invites you to spend some quiet time with Him every day. During your time with Him, He refreshes your spirit, assuring you of His concern for everything that concerns you and His care for everyone you care about.

Second, God leads you into His presence, nurturing your awareness of His work in your life, along with His plans and purposes for all the responsibilities you bear.

Third, God opens the eyes of your spirit to show you the beauty of the gifts He is building in you—gifts like loyalty and faithfulness, selflessness and love for others.

Heavy loads—no matter how burdensome—lighten up when you carry them with the strength of God in you.

Heavenly Father, please help me carry the burden of...

_____

_____

_____

_____

_____

_____

_____

_____

Come In Gently

The wisdom from above is first pure, then peaceable,
gentle, willing to yield, full of mercy and good fruits.
JAMES 3:17 NRSV

You might have noticed something about the Lord: He knocks, but He doesn't beat down the door if you don't answer immediately. He enters, but He doesn't sit down until you invite Him.

When the Lord steps into your life, He does so gently. He wants you to feel safe with Him and relaxed in His presence. If you're not ready to handle one of His truths or attributes yet, He takes no offense, but waits with loving patience until you want to bring up the subject. If you aren't prepared for a committed relationship right now, He won't press you, but will speak to you with inviting words and affectionate phrases. Even if you choose to ignore Him for a while, He won't bolt the door, but you'll find Him when you're ready to look for Him.

With respect for your true feelings, the Lord reveals Himself and opens the way to a relationship with Him. He knocks on the door of your heart and waits until He hears your footsteps.

Lord, come to me with gentleness and...

_____

_____

_____

_____

_____

_____

_____

_____

_____

Faith of a Child

Jesus said, "Let the little children come to Me, and do not forbid them;
for of such is the kingdom of heaven."
MATTHEW 19:14 NKJV

God has a way of turning our ideas upside down. During the Lord's earthly ministry, He embraced children, praised them, and pointed to them as examples for grown-ups to follow in the way of faith!

Childlike faith is open and trusting, innocent of doubt and deceit. It is also teachable, eager to hear more and discover more about our heavenly Father. This is the kind of faith God would have you emulate, no matter how many candles might crowd your birthday cake this year.

As your relationship with God grows, your faith will grow as you remain open to hearing what He has to say. Your faith matures as you put your trust in Him in more areas of your life. You'll desire to follow Him in ever-expanding ways. The more of your life you surrender, the more childlike your faith becomes!

The next time the innocent eyes of a small child look up to you, imagine yourself looking to your heavenly Father with the innocent eyes of a childlike faith.

Lord, help me surrender in the area of...

A Well-Connected Life

Let us not give up meeting together, as some are in the habit of doing,
but let us encourage one another.

HEBREWS 10:25

When you keep in touch with people, you're doing yourself a big favor!

Whether you pick up a pen or a phone, tap on a keyboard, or visit in person, your willingness to share your stories, thoughts, and experience with others relieves stress, invites support and encouragement, and prevents social isolation. Engagement with others deepens your family ties and strengthens your relationships. Your connection with others in your line of work helps you advance in business, and friends who share your interests are natural sources of inspiration and motivation for you.

Even greater benefits come to you when you remain connected to God. By discovering Him in Scripture, you broaden your understanding of His way with people and His presence in your life. By speaking to Him in prayer, you open yourself to receive His soothing comfort and embracing peace. By responding to Him with godly thoughts, words, and actions, you find fulfillment, joy, and satisfaction in your day.

In turn, all these things make you the contact who truly benefits others!

Lord, I want to deepen my relationship with You. Help me to...

A Building Project

*Everyone who hears these words of mine and puts them into practice
is like a wise man who built his house on the rock.*

MATTHEW 7:24

If you have ever built a new house or remodeled your home, there's no doubt you learned something about construction materials. You found that some materials offered more durability than others and some were better suited to your needs than others. As well as function, you probably considered cost, appearance, and ease of upkeep.

You and God's Spirit are working together on a building project right now; that is, the building of your spiritual dwelling and the remodeling of your life according to His plan and purpose. As with building materials, durability matters in the values and principles you select. Let His Spirit provide you with the most long-lasting ones: faith, hope, and love. Let Him present to you the guidance, comfort, and wisdom you need. Trust Him to keep you in His embrace as He builds you up in spiritual strength and understanding.

And don't forget about appearance, because He hasn't. His spiritual gifts of kindness and gentleness, faithfulness and peace grow only more and more beautiful with time.

Today, dear God, enable me to build...

_____

_____

_____

_____

_____

_____

_____

_____

A Lasting Image

You have taken off your old self with its practices and have put on the new self.
COLOSSIANS 3:9–10

With a complete beauty makeover, we easily can change the way we look. While it's exciting and energizing to try out a new personal style, those of us who have done it know this: neither the excitement nor the energy it generates lasts very long. In fact, even its newness disappears with next season's fashions.

God's beauty makeover is completely different. He starts not on your body, but in your heart by generating wholesome and healthy self-love. Why? Because without self-love, you cannot love others the way God would have you love them. Flowing from God-given love, your words and actions have the power to encourage the weak and comfort the brokenhearted, to laugh with the lighthearted and rejoice with the blessed.

Rather than diminish, the excitement of being able to make a real difference in the lives of others escalates, and the energy you get from seeing positive change continues to grow. The time-honored quality of heart-deep love never goes out of style. It's your heart's new look that is designed to last forever.

Lord, give me a makeover that lasts forever so I can...

_____

_____

_____

_____

_____

_____

_____

_____

A Beautiful Pattern

We know that in all things God works for the good of those who love him,
who have been called according to his purpose.

ROMANS 8:28

If your home is in the northern or mountain regions of our country, you're probably ready to get out the winter bedding. Perhaps among your blankets is a patchwork quilt handmade by a dear aunt or grandmother—but if you don't have one, feel free to piece one together in your imagination! If you reflect on the years of your life so far, you may be surprised how everything fits together like an exquisitely designed patchwork quilt.

As a quilt's light colors appear brighter when paired with dark colors, hard-won triumphs stand out because they follow hard-fought struggles. Busy and quiet prints together add interest to the quilt's pattern, just as active days and restful hours keep you emotionally balanced and physically healthy. Various shapes and shadings of color are what make a quilt distinctive, and it's your thoughts, experiences, and responses that make your life uniquely yours, and lovely.

The Creator-God showers you with blessings and permits your struggles and challenges so that the pieces of your life fit together beautifully.

Lord, help me see how things fit together like...

_____

_____

_____

_____

_____

_____

_____

_____

_____

Faithful to You

The LORD is good; his steadfast love endures for ever, and his faithfulness to all generations.
PSALM 100:5 NRSV

Think back to times you acted out of overwhelming emotion. Perhaps you were elated to hear you had a new niece, nephew, or grandchild, and you let out a whoop of delight. At another point, perhaps you were struck by sudden loss, and you couldn't hold back the tears.

Feelings fluctuate, and because they do, God urges you not to believe in or doubt His presence based on them. After all, you may feel embraced by His presence as you happily dance in the light of His blessings, but feel abandoned by Him as you stand alone in the darkness. The truth lies not in your feelings, but in His unchangeable promise: God is always with you. God will never leave you.

Let the truth of His presence rest at the center of your heart, and hold to it when conflicting emotions threaten to tear you away from it. Then, accompany others not only in their emotional highs but in their emotional lows too. Let them know that your presence—and God's presence—hinges not on feelings, but on faithfulness.

Lord, I want to remember Your presence, especially when...

It's Highly Contagious

I have indeed received much joy and encouragement from your love,
because the hearts of the saints
have been refreshed through you.
PHILEMON 1:7 NRSV

If you've ever suffered with the flu, you haven't forgotten the headaches, muscle aches, fever, and chills that kept you homebound for days, or possibly longer. If at the same time, other members of your family or some of your friends started feeling bad, you realized how contagious the flu can be.

There's something else equally contagious, if not more so, and that's the influence of the friend who makes you feel good. Though a great listener when problems arise, this friend focuses on triumphs instead of troubles, on stories that lift up rather than drag down. Though not blind to weaknesses, this friend prefers to highlight your successes and strengths. Though caring, this friend never controls but gently suggests; never intrudes but dependably remains beside you.

You leave the presence of this friend feeling lighthearted and motivated to do your best and to try new things because you believe you can. Maybe you know this friend. Maybe you are this friend. In either case, God-given goodness is contagious in all the right ways.

Lord God, I feel really good about myself when...

_____

_____

_____

_____

_____

_____

_____

_____

OCTOBER 8

An Uncommon Blessing

[The Lord] said, "My grace is sufficient for you, for My strength is made perfect in weakness."
2 CORINTHIANS 12:9 NKJV

Most of us have a hard time seeing anything beautiful coming from our weaknesses! In fact, we're more likely to hide them rather than admit to them. Yet in God's hands, our weaknesses are a source of uncommon blessings.

Without weaknesses, you would have no reason to lean on God's strength, or to ask for His forgiveness. If you never needed to ask Him for forgiveness, you might never experience the depth of His love and compassion, and in turn never even glimpse God's ineffable characteristics.

An admission of weaknesses is the source of genuine humility of heart, one of the spiritual gifts God gives to those who come to Him. Your own ability to recognize your weaknesses enables you to empathize with the frailties of others and help them overcome them as a sister-traveler on the same road.

The more you think about all you have gained and learned and understood only because you can admit to being weak, the more you see just how strong, beautiful, and uncommonly blessed you really are.

Heavenly Father, show me how to use weaknesses like...

_____

_____

_____

_____

_____

_____

_____

_____

Season of Change

Praise be to the name of God for ever and ever; wisdom and power are his.
He changes times and seasons.
DANIEL 2:20–21

A rolling hillside draped in restful shades of green only a few weeks ago now swells in swathes of vibrant reds, purples, and golds. What a glorious reminder that change can be extraordinarily beautiful!

Even more beautiful is the change your Lord is working in you as you follow Him day by day. When you may have wondered who you are, your Lord has called you the daughter of His heart. Where there may have been skepticism or doubt, His Spirit has turned your misgivings into a growing certainty rooted in faith and trust. When you may have been searching for purpose, He continues to pour out His counsel and guidance.

The light of His presence transforms you. His Spirit dispels shadows of discomfort and shines with uncommon brilliance through your thoughts, words, and actions.

With the Lord as the creator and author of all good change, expect nothing short of spectacular—whether rippling across an autumn hillside in brilliant color or transforming the landscape of your heart, mind, and soul to reflect His love.

God, You make me feel beautiful when...

The Best Advice

Every word of God is pure: he is a shield unto them that put their trust in him.
PROVERBS 30:5 KJV

From how to navigate a sticky relationship to how to fix a leaky faucet, a reliable source of advice is essential to us. Without it, we're forced to learn by trial and error, and for most of us, that involves a lot of error.

In matters concerning your relationship with God, you need never rely on trial and error because God has provided you with fail-safe guidance and step-by-step directions to lead you to Him. In Scripture, He speaks of His unconditional love for you, and He shows you how to live according to His will in the life and ministry of His Son Jesus. Through Jesus, He made it clear that your salvation has been won and that you have been made His own.

You can find no advice more reliable about God than from God, so why learn about Him any other way? Let His Spirit open Scripture for you and in it discover all you need to know for the strengthening of your faith and your continued spiritual growth and well-being.

Lord, I need advice from You about...

A Guaranteed Profit

May the Lord make you increase and abound in love
to one another and to all, just as we do to you.
1 THESSALONIANS 3:12 NKJV

If you invest a portion of your money in the stock market, you're accustomed to the market's pattern of gains and losses. Sometimes insignificant and sometimes dramatic, stock market fluctuations can cause your money to double in value one day, dip precipitously the next, only to gain again the following week.

The same pattern of gains and losses does not hold true with investments you make in God's spiritual gifts. These investments continue to climb in value with the more time and effort you put into them—there's no other way for them to go but up. The more kindness you invest in your relationships with others, the more kindness grows within you. The more patience, forgiveness, and gentleness you pour out to the people you meet every day, the more patience, forgiveness, and gentleness blooms in your heart.

On Wall Street, there's no such thing as guaranteed returns, but in the spiritual realm, it's a different story. Why not increase your investments today?

Dear God, I want to invest more in...

_____

_____

_____

_____

_____

_____

_____

An Unbreakable Commitment

The eyes of the LORD range throughout the earth to strengthen
those whose hearts are fully committed to him.

2 CHRONICLES 16:9

When we commit ourselves to a relationship or job, we go into it with the intention of seeing it through. But for any number of reasons, we sometimes make a decision to break our commitment.

Even spiritual commitments can fail. Sometimes we lose our resolve, or we find we have over-committed ourselves, or we realize a particular spiritual practice is not drawing us closer to God. What then?

Unconditionally committed to you, your heavenly Father speaks no words of rejection. He has no wish to make you feel sad but only to help you grow in spiritual wisdom. The words you will most often hear from Him are "try again."

Try again with another book of devotions or a different Bible study group; change when or where you meditate and pray; adjust what you do to the time, energy, and resources God has made available to you today.

Fulfill your commitment to Him by putting your trust in His unbreakable commitment to you.

Dear God, I want to make spiritual commitments like...

_____

_____

_____

_____

_____

_____

_____

_____

Something to Do

*[Jesus said], "I tell you the truth, whatever you did
for one of the least of these brothers of mine, you did for me."*
MATTHEW 25:40

You know who they are—the women who help and serve, cheer and encourage, comfort and soothe without looking for praise or reward. They're more interested in offering solace to the bereaved than in bemoaning loss. They can be depended on to assist a victim rather than demand an explanation from God. Are you one of those women? Yes!

As the Holy Spirit blesses you with His spiritual gifts, He moves you to express them in practical, real-life, and often seemingly small ways. Perhaps the thought of thousands of people enduring famine makes you throw your hands in the air, but those same hands can serve hungry people who flock to your local soup kitchen. Though the sight of widespread destruction in another country makes you wonder what you can do, you know exactly what to do for your hospitalized friend, widowed neighbor, and elderly relative.

Yes, you're one of those women whose fervent prayers reach around the world, but whose loving service starts right where she lives.

Today, Lord God, I want to pray for...

Confident in Him

I am not ashamed,
because I know whom I have believed.
2 TIMOTHY 1:12

To some degree, most of us care what other people think about us. After all, our failure to make a good impression could lead to a loss of opportunity or a lackluster reputation. Trouble arises, however, when we lose confidence in who we are, in what we believe, or in what we're doing because we fear the disapproval of others.

A relationship with God puts less of your focus on what people think and more on what God thinks. When your conduct matches your Spirit-led heart, you owe no one an apology. When your words and actions emanate from God-given guidance, you need not worry about any criticism you may hear. When you're following God's will and purpose, the opinions of others can have the power to disturb you, but with God's help, not the power to dissuade you from doing what you know is right.

To not care at all what anyone thinks is unrealistic and unproductive—but to care more about what the Lord thinks, says, and does for you than what other people think is the source of true confidence.

Heavenly Father, help me to not worry about what others think but to instead...

_____

_____

_____

_____

_____

_____

_____

_____

Drawn to Him

You know that the Lord will reward everyone for whatever good he does.
EPHESIANS 6:8

Incentives come in handy. Moms use them to encourage good behavior or motivate children to complete their homework. Managers use them to stimulate product ideas and increase production numbers.

God uses incentives too. He uses them to attract you to Him, lead you to discover Him, and motivate you to apply His qualities to your life.

You may have been attracted to Him because you wanted to become more spiritual. Your incentive was God Himself—invisible but present. Spiritual but ready and willing to live in you.

As you learned more about Him, you may have been drawn by the awe you felt as you immersed yourself in the beauty of His characteristics, such as compassion, generosity, goodness, and love. Awe was God's incentive to draw you closer.

As you let His qualities shine through the things you do and say, the transformation you see in your relationships and the joy you feel inside are incentives to surrender even more completely to His divine will.

Incentives come in handy—and they work!

Lord, the incentive that draws me to You is...

_____

_____

_____

_____

_____

_____

_____

_____

Faith or Fate?

Be joyful always; pray continually; give thanks in all circumstances,
for this is God's will for you in Christ Jesus.
1 THESSALONIANS 5:16–18

Is it possible for you to change your fate? Let philosophers debate that one. Meanwhile, spend a few minutes thinking about God's perspective on the topic.

When you entered into your relationship with your heavenly Father, He assured you that He has known you from the beginning and that He has a plan and purpose for your life. Through the work of His Spirit in your heart, you learned to identify the good things you enjoy as blessings from Him and to give thanks for them.

At the same time, you discovered that adversities and challenges come into your life, not on account of some blind force of nature or random accident, but because God permitted them to happen. Though you may not know why they happened, you thank God for those things too, because you trust in His wisdom.

If you believe in fate, your question might be, "How can I change this?" But since you have faith in God and His care for you, your question becomes, "Why would I want to?"

Lord, because You're in control, I feel...

_____

_____

_____

_____

_____

_____

_____

_____

_____

_____

Greed to Grow

*[Jesus said], "If you remain in me and my words remain in you,
ask whatever you wish, and it will be given you."*

JOHN 15:7

We have a word for people who have much but ask for more—greedy! We warn children not to be greedy when they beg for yet another video game, and we may even silently chide ourselves for buying not one, but two or three pairs of shoes at a time.

God turns greed on its head, however, because He invites you—even encourages you!—to ask for more from Him. Yes, He has blessed you with spiritual gifts, and His Spirit continues to nurture His gifts in your heart. You find yourself putting His gifts to practical use in the things you do and say. You begin to notice the way you feel, the way people respond to you, and the way you respond to God. You realize you're changing for the better as the days, weeks, and months pass. Now God says, "Ask for even more, and I will give it to you."

A hunger for more of God's spiritual gifts is the kind of greed you can grow with!

Giver of all good gifts, please grant me more...

Circle of Love

Unfailing love surrounds those who trust the LORD.
PSALM 32:10 NLT

Have you ever gathered with friends and family around an outdoor fire on a cool fall evening? If so, the fragrance of burning logs, leaves, and twigs easily comes to mind, and maybe the sound of giggles as marshmallows were drawn from the flames more burnt than roasted. And as the evening chilled, everyone scooted a little closer together and nearer to the center of the fire's warming circle.

The soul-deep warmth of God's love reaches out to you like the welcoming radiance of a crackling fire. When you feel the chill of sadness or loss, He beckons you to draw even nearer to Him, the source of comfort and compassion. He wraps you in the warmth of His embrace, and the fragrance of His presence calms, soothes, and renews you in body and in spirit.

As you pull closer to God, the center of love's flame, you also pull closer to others who seek His warmth. Shoulder-to-shoulder with those whose eyes are on Him, encircled in His radiance, you find companionship and light.

Dear God, I feel surrounded by Your love when...

_____

_____

_____

_____

_____

_____

_____

_____

Under His Wings

He shall cover you with His feathers,
and under His wings you shall take refuge.
PSALM 91:4 NKJV

As women, most of us are concerned about our personal safety, and we take care not to put ourselves in harm's way. We may even have a plan in place so we know what to do in the event we need to defend ourselves.

Writers of Scripture frequently compared God to an eagle, a bird associated to this day with swiftness, strength, power, and protection. What an apt description of God's willingness and ability to come to your rescue when your spiritual safety is in danger!

Temptation will come into your life as long as you live, so God has set up a sure plan for your defense. When fear or doubt threatens your inner peace, you can depend on God's immediate presence. As the eagle symbolizes great might, so God's power overwhelms any assault against you, and under His broad wings He shelters your heart and soul.

A woman secure in her environment radiates confidence, and a woman whose spirit dwells safely under the shadow of His wings has nothing to fear. This woman is you.

Cover me, Lord, with Your wings, especially when...

_____

_____

_____

_____

_____

_____

_____

_____

All in One

The LORD is the true God, he is the living God,
and an everlasting king.
JEREMIAH 10:10 KJV

The days of the superwoman are over—at least that's the news some voices proclaim. Nonetheless, her image lingers, luring many of us to feel some measure of guilt if we're not an attentive mom, creative homemaker, prominent businesswoman, and generous volunteer, all at the same time. Ridiculous? Of course! Not one of us can be everything simultaneously; only God can, because He is.

When you first began exploring God's characteristics, one or two particular traits might have jumped out at you. Perhaps you were startled to learn how compassionate He is because at that time you thought no one cared. Or you were amazed to realize how generous He is when you were wondering what it meant to be blessed.

Now you're seeing and experiencing even more of who God is. His faithfulness sustains you, His presence assures you, His power protects you, His caring comforts you, and His love lifts you up to His heart.

God alone is everything, and He desires to be (and has the power to be) everything to you.

Lord, thank You for reminding me that you are everything when You...

_____

_____

_____

_____

_____

_____

_____

_____

_____

His Presence Granted

Draw near to God and he will draw near to you.
JAMES 4:8 NRSV

Isn't it comforting to have people you can count on? People like the woman next door who looks after your home while you're away, the stylist who knows exactly how you like your hair, the physician who can fit you in whenever you call. You almost take them for granted because they're so dependable.

For a time, the exciting newness of knowing God ripples through your spirit like a charge of electricity. Then, although you continue to discover more about Him, the fact of His presence in your life becomes something you routinely depend on each day. You wake up with it, go about the business of your day with it, and go to sleep in its peace. Beyond the time you spend in meditation and prayer, you may not even think about God. You might almost take Him for granted because you have learned you can trust His promises, and He has promised to hear you whenever you call.

Yes, you can count on Him—He will be there for you. Now that's really comforting!

Dear Lord, today I'm depending on You for...

His Heart's Delight

The LORD takes delight in his people.
PSALM 149:4

Who's the someone you're always delighted to see? Perhaps it's your spouse, your son or daughter, or your fun-loving girlfriend who makes your heart sing whenever you hear her knock on your door.

Just being in the presence of someone who delights you makes you feel happy. You're alive to the moment because for this moment all your cares have slipped away, and you're attentive to whatever would please your special guest. Lots of conversation? Maybe, or maybe not. As long as you're together—that's all that matters.

Have you ever considered yourself as someone special to the Lord—someone He delights to see? You can enter His presence silently, without saying a word, and He smiles with infinite warmth and unbounded pleasure. Or you can chat up a storm, pouring out your deepest thoughts and inmost anxieties, and He's still happy He asked you over. It's your presence that matters to His heart.

Anytime you want, you can knock on His door in prayer. It will open, and He'll be there to welcome you. Your gracious Lord will be nothing short of delighted to see you.

God, Your delight in me means that I...

_____

_____

_____

_____

_____

_____

_____

_____

A New Beginning in God

I will take away their stony, stubborn heart and give them a tender, responsive heart.
EZEKIEL 11:19 NLT

Every autumn, oak trees begin to lose their leaves. The green leaves of summer turn to brown, and then let go to float lightly to the ground, landing with a whisper on the wind. Wouldn't it be wonderful if we could let go as easily!

As your relationship with God progresses, there may be habits, thoughts, and perceptions that no longer serve your new ideals and principles. But old reasoning may still affect decisions, and the force of habit can hinder you from discovering better, more spiritually productive responses.

Your God of new beginnings invites you to reject those things that hold you back from new growth, from broader understanding and deeper wisdom. You no longer need to hold on to anything that keeps you from freely embracing God's love for you and His abundant spiritual gifts. With Him, you can let go.

The oak tree makes room for new buds only by losing last season's leaves. Today, release the thoughts, words, and actions that no longer serve your new beginning in the Lord.

Enable me, Lord, to let go of...

_____

_____

_____

_____

_____

_____

_____

_____

_____

_____

OCTOBER 24

If Only an Hour

Outwardly we are wasting away, yet inwardly we are being renewed day by day.
2 CORINTHIANS 4:16

How does one get to be an expert? By completing ten thousand hours of practice, according to some. But to get in ten thousand hours over the course of ten years, we would need close to three hours a day every day of the week devoted to attentive, dedicated practice.

While true expertise in the spiritual realm belongs to God alone, there's something in the ten-thousand-hour theory that we can apply to our spiritual growth and maturity. What if just an hour a day were spent consciously practicing one of God's spiritual gifts? What if today we focus our attention on being joyful? Whether we feel particularly joyful or not, we'll act joyfully, at least for an hour. What if tomorrow we turned to patience? No matter who pushes our buttons, we'll respond with patience and good humor. Even if it's only for an hour.

What if? In far fewer than ten thousand hours and far short of ten years, practicing God's gifts would be as natural as breathing—and as thinking and doing—all day long. That's real expertise!

Lord, today I want to practice...

No and Yes

I command you today to love the LORD your God, to walk in his ways,
and to keep his commands, decrees and laws.

DEUTERONOMY 30:16

Imagine raising a child without ever saying no. The first hindrance she encountered in the world would throw her into a tailspin! Though it can be one of the most difficult words to hear, no is often one of the most necessary.

The Lord intends for you to take the reflection of His Spirit into the real world where temptations, dangers, and pitfalls abound. Not only does He equip you to avoid hazards, but He prepares you to project His compassion, strength, and love on others. A big part of His equipping and preparation comes in one word: no.

With each no you say to the enticements that would carry you away from Him, you grow more able to say no to the next. With each yes to boundaries of thought, speech, and action He sets up to guard you, you mature in trust and grow in the wisdom of your heavenly Father.

God never sends you out into the world without telling you no. Why? Because He loves you way too much.

Lord, I'm struggling with no right now in...

Sky's Not the Limit

As the heavens are high above the earth, so great is His mercy toward those who fear Him.
PSALM 103:11 NKJV

A cool, crisp, clear fall day lends itself to sky gazing. Way above what we can see with our eyes, we know there are miles more sky, outer space beyond, and deep space farther out! Even using the most sophisticated instruments, no one has discovered the edge of the universe.

For us, the sky stretches to infinity, and explorations reveal that it's filled with mysteries beyond what we have charted. Though we have photographed remote planets and distant stars, there's still more out there for us to discover.

The sky provides some of the most amazing spectacles of nature too. Consider a sunrise. Take in a sunset. And the same sky covers us all, regardless of who we are or where we are.

Like the sky, God's grace—His compassionate, undeserved love—stretches way beyond our comprehension. His grace restores and renews, forgives and transforms wherever it finds a willing heart, and His grace covers everyone on earth.

Like the sky above, God's marvelous grace is yours, no matter who you are. No matter where you are.

To me, God, the beauty of Your grace shows in...

_____

_____

_____

_____

_____

_____

_____

_____

For Peaceful Sleep

The LORD gives strength to his people;
the LORD blesses his people with peace.

PSALM 29:11

Have you ever awakened in a cold sweat, realizing *it all depends on you?* You alone are responsible for keeping the household together, for the success of a highly visible project, for getting a report turned in on time. No wonder you spend the rest of the night tossing and turning!

Your spiritual growth, however, is one subject where you can rest at ease, because it doesn't all depend on you. God, who called you His daughter way before your mother knew there was a you, does all the work in your willing heart. He sent His Son to clothe you in the purity that pleases Him, and He sends His Spirit to keep you holy and perfect in His sight.

Once you release to Him the work He does so faithfully and so well, you realize there's help for those restless nights. With your God-given strength and confidence, you know you're more than capable of doing anything He asks you to do. You can go to sleep in His peace.

Dear Lord, I'm feeling anxious about...

_____

_____

_____

_____

_____

_____

_____

_____

_____

The Highest Purpose

He chose us in advance,
and he makes everything work out according to his plan.
EPHESIANS 1:11 NLT

Few things are done simply for their own sake. We earn money not for the sake of having money, but so we can buy the things we need. We clean house not for the sake of cleaning house, but to create a pleasant home. The things we do every day serve a higher purpose.

When we're able to see the higher purpose of our activities and responsibilities, we derive satisfaction from what we're doing. A higher purpose gives us the endurance to follow through when the going gets tough—or boring. It provides us with the motivation we need to overcome challenges and grab hold of opportunities.

As you reflect the beauty of God's love in your everyday words and actions, you're doing more than simply soothing one heart or drying one tear. In bringing His presence to others, you're praising Him by obeying His will for you; you're returning thanks to Him for all He has done for you; and, by serving one another, you're extending His compassion to the world. Yours is the highest purpose imaginable!

Lord, I have trouble finding my purpose because...

Picture This One

My words are plain to anyone with understanding,
clear to those with knowledge.

PROVERBS 8:9 NLT

If your relationship with God were pictured, it might look like this: a strong, straight pillar of light between heaven and earth—between your heavenly Father and you.

Bathed in the circle of His light, you are enabled to see the world around you with more clarity and understanding and with less fear and apprehension than ever before. Rather than look out to human thoughts and theories with your spiritual questions, you look up and receive the wisest of all answers. Instead of looking down at your feet to find your way, you look ahead and walk by the light illuminating your path.

If your relationship with others were pictured, it might look like this: a strong, straight crossbeam of kindness, gentleness, patience, and love embracing those to your right hand and those to your left. Pouring out from the heart of your relationship with God, your light draws others into relationship with you—and with Him.

If you were to draw a picture, it would surely resemble the shape of a cross.

Dear God, I would describe our relationship as...

_____

_____

_____

_____

_____

_____

_____

_____

Beauty of Faith

We walk by faith, not by sight.
2 CORINTHIANS 5:7 NRSV

Some say God's existence is like a circle, with no beginning and no end—yet our human understanding stumbles because, in our experience, someone has to draw the circle. Others compare God to a person, having a face and arms, hands and fingers; but He wears none of those features, for God is a Spirit. In describing His presence, we use the words *yesterday*, *today*, and *tomorrow*, but truly, our eternal God lives outside the confines of time.

While comparisons and illustrations may help us glimpse various aspects of God, each one ultimately falls short of bringing to our minds the entire truth of His being. Indeed, our human reasoning is limited and cannot fully comprehend everything God is. But where reason fails, faith steps in.

Your God-given faith releases you from the burden of explaining what cannot be explained in words. You don't have to understand what cannot be measured by human calculation. Faith offers you the comfort and excitement of knowing there's more—much more than you can imagine— to know about your Lord.

Lord, one of the things I'm wondering about is...

An Authentic Face

The Spirit himself testifies with our spirit that we are God's children.
ROMANS 8:16

Children enjoy pretending they're someone else—a princess or superhero, a race car driver or ballerina. Some adults enjoy pretending too. Though costume, mask, and makeup provide entertainment for some, they are precisely what God's Spirit seeks to strip away from your heart. He asks you to permit Him to remove the mask you may be tempted to hide behind—perhaps a mask of confidence where there is insecurity, or a mask of strength when you're numb with weakness and fear. He coaxes you to exchange any costume for His robe of genuine godliness, and become (for real!) the woman He knows you can be—and are.

God calls you His beloved daughter. With that kind of identity, who needs to pretend? His Spirit enables you to live in the world as your genuine self. With that kind of confidence, why hide behind a costume or mask?

Your authentic God invites you to be none other than beautiful you.

Empower me, Lord, to remove the mask of...

An Unreasonable Love

God has poured out his love into our hearts by the Holy Spirit,
whom he has given us.

ROMANS 5:5

What's the word for love that goes beyond reason? You've seen it in the love of a mother for her child who brings her nothing but grief. You've seen it in the love of a wife whose husband has proven unfaithful to her and their family. Though neither the mother nor the wife enables others to take advantage of her, the love she holds for her loved ones is like a candle's flame in the darkness in her heart.

You may understand this love because you know a woman who carries this kind of love with her wherever she goes. You may recognize this love because it is the same flame burning in your own heart, which has only intensified with the passage of time.

This is the love God has for you. Less like a candle and more like the sun, His love is intense, warming, and constant. It never permits disobedience, yet stands ready to forgive; it doesn't sanction defiance, but yearns for the day of reconciliation.

That is love. Unreasonable. Undeniable. Love.

Lord God, please increase my love for...

_____

_____

_____

_____

_____

_____

_____

_____

A Good Word

*[Jesus prayed,] "Sanctify them
by Your truth. Your word is truth."*
JOHN 17:17 NKJV

Though we've grown to rely on electronic background checks to verify personal information, there are still people whose word is all we need. Most of us can name a friend who tells the truth and does what she says she's going to do. We know we can take her at her word, because her word is good.

God speaks to you through the words of the Bible. In the Bible, you discover His promises to you, understand His attitude toward you, and realize what delights Him about you. These are the words He still uses to plant seeds of faith and joy in your willing heart. These are the words He speaks to you to lead you more deeply into a meaningful and purposeful relationship with Him.

But what about those parts of the Bible you find unreasonable or even irrational? And there are those parts! Though you may never understand the full meaning, these are also words God wants you to hear. They may be hard to understand, but they are for your good. His Word is always good.

Lead me, Lord, to understand...

Your Question, God's Answer

I know that You are well pleased with me.
PSALM 41:11 NKJV

During our growing up years, most of us yearned for the approval of the adults around us. We looked for praise from our parents and worked hard to get good grades from our teachers. In many ways, we asked, "What can I do to please you?"

We often approach God with the same question. Then, before waiting for an answer, we list dozens of things we think will impress God and earn the compliments we crave.

If you'd like to ask God what you must do to please Him, go ahead. It's a natural question. But His answer might surprise you, because He will give it to you in one word: nothing. Nothing, because you already please Him, and you always have! His goodwill is one thing in this world you don't need to do a thing to earn. It's His gift to you, and He gives it to you for free. That's the beauty of His indescribable love.

Enjoy His presence in your life and bask in the sunshine of His smile, because you please Him very much.

Dear God, I desire to respond to Your love by...

_____

_____

_____

_____

_____

_____

_____

_____

Blessing of Time

Be very careful, then, how you live—
not as unwise but as wise,
making the most of every opportunity.
EPHESIANS 5:15–16

Time: we just can't seem to get enough of it! When the alarm clock goes off in the morning, we yearn for a few more minutes under the comforter. When the calendar page overflows, we long for just one more hour to get everything done.

God, who exists outside of time, created time, and He placed each of us under its governance. We're unable to stretch a minute beyond sixty seconds, and no one can slip extra hours into a day. Long ago, God set the time between sunrise and sunset, placed the stars, and structured the seasons according to His wisdom.

He has made it so, and He invites you to live fully and attentively in the moment, neither regretting the past nor fearing the future. The blessing of time lies in the trust you place in His wisdom, believing He will give you enough time to fulfill the purpose He has in mind for you today.

Your time is His time, and He offers you the priceless gift of now.

Lord God, show me how to use my time today, not being bogged down by...

_____

_____

_____

_____

_____

_____

_____

_____

An Inclusive Invitation

The Word became flesh and dwelt among us.
JOHN 1:14 ESV

God's Son Jesus walked among us to show us the face of God in the flesh. The more we reflect on the things He said and did, the more one detail stands out through His life and ministry: Jesus invited everyone to join the family of God.

In a day much like our own, rife with religious and ethnic rivalries, He reached out with gentleness, kindness, and respect to all people. Despite entrenched gender and age discrimination, He welcomed women and children into the circle of God's love. Not subservient to social mores, He touched the sick, listened to the poor, and dined with whoever kindly invited Him in. In an atmosphere of political oppression, He spoke God's message of mercy and compassion to the oppressed and the oppressor alike.

As a woman, you may have faced unjust discrimination in your life, or know a woman who has. The pain goes deep, and the wound remains tender for a long time. With God, Jesus' inclusive invitation still stands, and now it rests in your hands. Will you reach out?

Lord, open my heart to welcome...

His Effective Gifts

Each man has his own gift from God; one has this gift, another has that.
1 CORINTHIANS 7:7

Where women and men with diversity of talents and skills contribute to the overall good, corporations, communities, and households thrive. People bringing their strengths together accomplish more than any one of them could alone, and with far more effectiveness.

When you entered your relationship with God, you brought with you certain skills and talents, interests and abilities. These are exactly the gifts He will use for the good and well-being of His family, your spiritual sisters and brothers. Whether your particular gifts have brought you prominence in the world or are generally unnoticed by others, God sees them and holds them in high esteem.

God the Creator has blessed you with gifts needed by and necessary to His family right now where you are. He may call you to work alongside someone else to lighten the common burden, or He may direct you to a unique task only you have the ability to do. However it turns out, you may be surprised how effectively He uses you—and how great you'll feel inside!

Dear God, please show me what gifts I can contribute when...

_____

_____

_____

_____

_____

_____

_____

_____

_____

A Gift Best Shared

Our mouths were filled with laughter, our tongues with songs of joy.
PSALM 126:2

The carefree giggles of girls bring back memories of being their age, laughing at everything. And the humor that leaves parents completely clueless only ignites more hilarity!

For many of us, the desire to laugh slips away as we strive for maturity and to be taken seriously by those around us. Sometimes the duties and responsibilities of adulthood remove amusements far from our mind and blind us to common, everyday humor that used to make us smile. And as we realize how hurtful some humor can be, some of us choose to avoid it all together.

Perhaps it's time to redefine humor from God's perspective. He blessed us with the ability to laugh heartily, and for laughter to lighten our hearts, ease our sorrows, and comfort our minds. Godly giggles, which do not hurt, offend, or exclude, draw us together and even spread the joy.

If the lilting sound of another's laugh has ever started you laughing too, you have found the beauty of true, God-blessed humor. It's a gift that's best when it's shared.

Open my heart, Lord, to true laughter, especially when...

The Presence of Love

I am my beloved's, and my beloved is mine.
SONG OF SOLOMON 6:3 NKJV

When you're in love with someone, a walk in the rain becomes a welcome chance to share an umbrella. An unexpected snowstorm provides the setting for a quiet afternoon snuggled in front of the fireplace together. What could be bad times are good when you are with the one you love.

In the same way, a growing love for God and appreciation for His presence beside you can give you a whole new outlook on life's storms. From a short-lived cloudburst to a long and difficult winter, adversity offers yet another occasion to draw closer to the Lord you love—and who loves you even more. Nothing can happen to you that would be too small for His protective hand. Nothing you will ever face could be too serious, too difficult, or too long-lasting to keep the warmth and closeness of His comfort away from your heart.

When you're in love with someone, suddenly nothing matters quite so much as the fact that you are with your beloved and your beloved is with you.

Lord, let me sit at rest in Your love, especially when...

Blessed to Give

God shall bless us, and all the ends of the earth shall fear Him.
PSALM 67:7 NKJV

We may smile to notice the change. While shopping, we see an outfit we would have bought for ourselves years ago, but now we buy it for a daughter, niece, or sister. Why? Because the delight in her eyes when she receives it brings us more joy than taking it home and hanging it in our own closet.

Perhaps a similar dynamic is at play when your heavenly Father showers you with His abundant blessings and spiritual gifts. Imagine Him sitting back and smiling with pleasure as you reflect on all He has provided for you, from the earth and sky outside to the inmost blessings of your heart.

Think how He must feel when your soul swells with delight when you recognize His Spirit at work in you. Reflect on His satisfaction when you clap your hands in gratitude because you were able to help, encourage, and comfort someone in need.

Certainly there's happiness in receiving, but there's joy and contentment in giving. Maybe that's why the Lord does so much of it.

I thank You, heavenly Father, for...

_____

_____

_____

_____

_____

_____

_____

_____

_____

Lend a Hand

Do not let your hands be weak, for your work shall be rewarded.
2 CHRONICLES 15:7 NRSV

Think for a minute about your hands. Chances are, they're busy! They scrub and vacuum, wash and fold. They pick up groceries and bed down children, flit across keyboards and pick up phones, plant flowers and set tables. They rub backs, soothe hurts, tighten hugs, and hold other hands in affectionate love.

Imagine God's hands at work in your life. Extended to you, His hands are ready to mend your broken heart, strengthen your tired spirit, and ease your troubled soul. His hands are able to draw you closer and lead you further, to guide you safely and provide for you richly. They're strong enough to carry you through the toughest hardship, yet gentle enough to touch the deepest wounds of your heart.

God's hands use many hands, as you may have noticed—the hands of parents and children, doctors and nurses, friends and coworkers. His hands come in all colors, some soft and smooth, some wrinkled with age, and some cracked with wear and labor. And two of the hands God uses even look like yours.

Lord God, thank You for the work of my hands, especially...

A Double Freedom

The Lord is the Spirit, and where the Spirit of the Lord is, there is freedom.
2 CORINTHIANS 3:17

Though many are afraid a relationship with God would limit them, the opposite is true. The more you learn about God, the more you find Him a God of two freedoms: freedom *from* and freedom *to*. If you have one without the other, you're living with only half the freedom God has in mind for you!

God's first freedom is freedom from those things that would disturb your spirit—things like fear and guilt, sadness and despondency, hopelessness and despair. In Him, you possess the light of His presence to scatter shadows of mind and heart and the reality of His love to release you from anything that would threaten your spiritual serenity.

God's second freedom is freedom to make peace with your past, knowing that your new life has begun in Him. You're free to take delight in the present moment, which opens you to the blessings, opportunities, and miracles around you. And no matter who would tell you differently, in Him you're free to look forward to the future with God-given hope and confidence.

Lord, I thank You for my freedom from and to…

_____

_____

_____

_____

_____

_____

_____

_____

It's Only Natural

You were once darkness, but now you are light in the Lord.
Live as children of light.
EPHESIANS 5:8

Whether biological or adopted, young children pick up the traits and mannerisms of their parents. The values they live by reflect the principles their parents model, and their behavior is informed by their parents' rules and expectations.

It's no wonder then that the more time you spend in the company of your heavenly Father and the better you get to know Him, the more you mirror His characteristics and attributes! For instance, you become accustomed to receiving His welcoming smile every time you approach Him. How could that not shape the way you greet others and respond to their needs? More and more, you rely on His compassion to embrace your heartfelt desires, and so you naturally find yourself leaning forward to listen when another's voice cries out for understanding.

God's eternal values—honesty, integrity, generosity, humility, to name a few—form your thoughts, and they're at the core of the things you do and say. It's only natural that this should happen, because He has brought you into His beloved family.

Heavenly Father, I love belonging to You because...

Compassion in Action

Be kind and compassionate to one another, forgiving each other, just as in Christ God forgave you.
EPHESIANS 4:32

Compassion is far from free for the one who practices it. If you have raised a child, cared for elderly relatives, or spent long hours as a volunteer, you know what compassion costs. Though it has taken time, money, energy, and other personal sacrifices to put compassionate feelings into compassionate action, you were willing to do it. Not only willing to do it, but chances are, you were glad to.

The compassion you have shown in your life and the compassionate things you do for others reflect what your Lord has done for you. Because of His compassion for you, He has promised to care for you and protect you as you walk your life's path. He has poured out His presence on you and blessed you with countless gifts for your pleasure, comfort, and well-being. He even was born for you as God in the flesh to bring you what you could not bring yourself: a present and eternal relationship with Him.

He was willing to do it for you. In fact, He was glad to.

Thank You, Lord, for Your compassion. Help me to be more compassionate toward...

A Strong Relationship

Let your lives be built on him.
Then your faith will grow strong in the truth you were taught.
COLOSSIANS 2:7 NLT

You know you're in a strong relationship when love overcomes all obstacles. You and your beloved communicate daily even though distance may come between you. You find time for him, even though your calendar is full. Sure, the two of you have your differences—even a spat now and then—but you both make up and go forward hand-in-hand.

Your relationship with God gets strengthened in the same way. Daily communication is the key to keeping His presence fresh in your mind and alive in your heart. You desire to hear His voice in Scripture and speak with Him in prayer today and every day, even though many other things call for your time and attention.

Even spiritual spats work to strengthen your relationship with God. Times when you feel He has abandoned you, you're up against hard choices, or you wonder if what He says is true—those are testing times. Not one test passes by, however, without God's outstretched hand ready to clasp yours and lead you forward with Him.

Lord God, I keep our relationship alive by...

Real-Life Family Love

God was pleased to have all his fullness dwell in him,
and through him to reconcile to himself all things.
COLOSSIANS 1:19–20

The Thanksgiving season highlights family relationships and how much they mean. Though ideal families exist in classic TV shows and perhaps in our own imagination, they don't exist in the real world. And sometimes the gap between the ideal and the real keeps us from appreciating those around us. We focus more on what they ought to be than on who they are.

As you learn more about your Father, you begin to realize how far His infinite majesty, His indescribable loveliness, and His complete perfection set Him apart from you and from anyone imaginable. Yet no gap exists between the Lord and you, because He reaches out to you with unbounded compassion, understanding, and love. He allows no shame, irritation, or judgment to mar the family relationship He has created with you, and when you come to visit, it's always a reason to give thanks. Why? Because you're family.

The Lord accepts you just the way you are, and proudly calls you His daughter. That's the beauty of His real-life family.

Dear God, help me truly accept...

_____

_____

_____

_____

_____

_____

_____

_____

Beauty of Being Needed

We are His workmanship, created in Christ Jesus for good works,
which God prepared beforehand that we should walk in them.
EPHESIANS 2:10 NKJV

Imagine living a life of carefree leisure, with no attachments or demands on your time and energy. Do you think you would be happy? Probably it would not be long at all before you started looking around for something to do and began reaching out to others. There's beauty in being needed!

Perhaps your need for spiritual meaning, fulfillment, and beauty was what opened you to a relationship with God. Maybe you have discovered how willing and able He is to meet those very needs.

God's desire rests in doing the work of nourishing the faith now planted in your heart and in being needed by you to strengthen the trust you have in Him. He invites you to recognize your need for His wisdom and counsel, and He consents to walk with you every step of the way—not *if* you need Him, but *because* you need Him.

There's meaning, fulfillment, beauty in being needed—and in embracing your very real need for everything your Lord has to give to you and desires for you to share with others.

Lord, I want to better meet the needs of...

_____

_____

_____

_____

_____

_____

_____

_____

An Appeal for Help

The LORD longs to be gracious to you;
he rises to show you compassion.

ISAIAH 30:18

This time of year, appeals for money flood our mailboxes. Through heartrending photos and poignant stories, we're reminded of our responsibility toward those less fortunate than ourselves. Though financial donations help the needy, there's a kind of poverty around us—perhaps within our own family or circle of friends—that money can't begin to conquer.

Poverty of spirit is felt by those who can't imagine a God who hears them because they've never met a person willing to listen to what they have to say. It's endured by anyone for whom kindness is only a high-sounding concept because they have never experienced the reality of compassion right here on earth. It's suffered by those who can't focus on God's beauty because they see so little beauty in their day-to-day life.

Especially at this time of year, spiritual poverty affects people, even those you meet every day. The only kind of currency able to change it is love and gentleness and compassion and understanding, and that's the kind of currency you carry in your Spirit-gifted heart.

Dear God, help me take time today to...

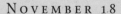

To Please You

The eyes of all look expectantly to You, and You give them their food in due season.
PSALM 145:15 NKJV

If you were to plan a menu for Thanksgiving dinner, it's likely you would choose dishes suited not only to the dietary needs of your guests, but dishes also prepared for their pleasure. It might be the pecan pie your daughter loves or the candied yams that your aunt adores.

Though your heavenly Father supplies everything you require for your spiritual health and well-being, did you realize that He prepares certain blessings just to please you? Perhaps He has endowed you with a talent that brings you special joy, or has put people in your life you cannot imagine never having known. Perhaps your Creator-God saw to it you were born in a place you have found to be the best spot on earth, or at a time when you could take advantage of exciting opportunities and adventures.

If you were to peek inside the menu your heavenly Father has planned for you, you would find on it everything you need, along with many things He prepared just to make you happy.

Thank You, Father, for blessing me with...

_____

_____

_____

_____

_____

_____

_____

_____

_____

_____

A Cornucopia of Blessings

God is able to provide you with every blessing in abundance.
2 CORINTHIANS 9:8 NRSV

It's a common display around this time of year: a cornucopia overflowing with apples and pumpkins, squashes and pears, bananas and nuts, and flanked by sprigs of wheat artfully tied together with ribbons of raffia. The festive decoration represents harvest time and reminds us of the abundance and variety of foods we receive every day from the good earth and from those who work the land.

The Lord's hands hold a cornucopia brimming over with blessings of the spirit, blessings He desires to pour out on you. As food from the earth feeds your body, so food from heaven feeds, nourishes, and strengthens your soul. He gives in abundance—wherever He has given, He has more to give. And He showers His people with untold varieties of gifts and abilities—to carry His message of hope, to offer His touch of comfort, to share His heart of kindness—yet all pour out from the same Spirit.

A cornucopia is the perfect symbol for the Thanksgiving season—and for the work of God's Spirit all year round.

In gratitude I come to You, God, for...

_____

_____

_____

_____

_____

_____

_____

_____

A Powerful Friend

He saved them for His name's sake,
that He might make His mighty power known.
PSALM 106:8 NKJV

Sometimes power evokes fear. We're afraid of power that dictates or dominates, or power wielded solely for personal gain, or power exerted to rob others of power. Yet one of God's attributes is power—infinite, insurmountable, overwhelming power. Does the thought make you fearful? If so, consider for a moment what God's power means to you.

Your all-powerful God, who is not subject to the misuse of any of His attributes, is your all-powerful Friend. With Him, nothing is impossible and that's why He invites you to ask Him for anything you need or desire, believing He has the will and ability to respond to your prayers.

Because He has the power to hold you up, He encourages you to lean on Him for strength and comfort, consolation and rest. Because He alone has the power to renew and restore your spirit, He opens His arms to you and yearns to give you peace.

God's power means you need never fear anyone else's power over you, because in Him, you have an all-powerful Friend.

Lord God, grant me Your power to...

Giver and Receiver

Give to the LORD the glory due His name;
bring an offering, and come into His courts.
PSALM 96:8 NKJV

What makes some relationships so pleasurable? Among the qualities you might mention is this one: your relationship with this person allows you to be both a giver and at the same time, a receiver.

In healthy relationships, the other person responds to your gifts with genuine gratitude; and you feel blessed to receive from them because you know the gifts are offered with unfeigned love.

In your relationship with the Lord, the same principle holds true. Your Lord desires a relationship marked by your ability to not only receive from Him, but to give to Him also. Yes, God is the most generous giver you will ever know, but He delights in receiving your words of gratitude and your prayers of praise. His Spirit builds you up as a giver of devotion to Him and of His love to others.

The pleasure of your relationship with Him comes from giving Him thanks and praise, receiving His love, and sharing the beauty of His ever-giving Spirit.

Dear Lord, today I want to give...

_____

_____

_____

_____

_____

_____

_____

_____

_____

An Aha Moment

*Those who do what is true come to the light,
so that it may be clearly seen that
their deeds have been done in God.*

JOHN 3:21 NRSV

Those *aha* moments come when a concept finally clicks. And once we see the logic, we wonder why it took us so long to figure it out! Very often, we inadvertently bury what's clear and simple beneath layers of preconceived notions, intricate rules, and roundabout reasoning.

Human-devised reasoning and preconceptions work to hide the light of God's pure love for all people, sending innocent souls on long, torturous searches for truth and promising peace that never lasts for long, if it ever comes. False teachers guide others to where they have never been themselves and along routes God has not laid out for His daughters and sons.

The simple, uncomplicated, and pure beauty of God's love for you comes in one Spirit-given *aha* moment, and from then on, you desire no other way but His. It's so clear you wonder why everyone doesn't see it, believe it, and bask in it! Yet as you share it in word and action, you might find yourself the source of someone else's spiritual *aha* moment.

Lord, please help me see You clearly in...

A Good Apple

Charm is deceptive, and beauty is fleeting;
but a woman who fears the LORD is to be praised.

PROVERBS 31:30

If you've found time lately to bake homemade apple pies, you've peeled, cored, and sliced quite a few apples. In doing so, you might have come across an apple shiny and blemish-free on the outside, but brown and mushy at the core. It looked good, but it was spoiled inside.

Genuine spiritual goodness begins at the core—the human heart. God's Spirit at work in you steeps your heart in His purity and holiness, because real goodness flows from the inside out. Your heart, where your intentions and motivations have their genesis, is where God directs His eyes.

On the outside, each one of us has her blemishes—our faults and foibles, our false starts and misdirected plans. But God's focus rests where no one else can see, and His attention lies with what we're like inside. Not interested in good things done for bad reasons, He searches the heart for all things done in response to His love.

What comfort to know God's eyes reach beyond the outside and right into the place where it really counts!

Search my heart, Lord, and see my...

_____

_____

_____

_____

_____

_____

_____

_____

Holy, Holy, Holy

Put on the new man which was created according to God, in true righteousness and holiness.
EPHESIANS 4:24 NKJV

If you want to whip egg whites for the perfect meringue, even a few dribbles of yoke will wreck the full bowl. If you simmer a pot of apple cider, even a small drop of dirt will ruin the entire batch. Sometimes, all it takes is a little bit to change the character of the whole.

In a similar way, the beauty of God's holiness rests in its absolute purity. If even a speck of fault could be attributed to Him, He would no longer be holy. If even a minuscule amount of malice, weakness, or wickedness could enter His mind, He would no longer be God, holy in essence, but human in thought, speech, and action.

Holiness in its purest form is hard to imagine in a world of concessions and compromises, in a world that allows a little bit of wrong and winks at minor offenses. Yet attempting to contemplate God as your all-holy God without the merest hint of spot or stain is to glimpse the glory of pure, complete, unadulterated holiness.

Dear God, I think of Your holiness as...

Succeed in Faithfulness

Remember now, O LORD, I pray, how I have walked before You in truth and with a loyal heart.
ISAIAH 38:3 NKJV

When we put our hands to a task, we work for success. If we're able to reach a good outcome, we feel good about ourselves and our effort, and we're likely to head into the next task believing we can complete that one too. If, however, we don't succeed, we're disappointed and maybe not so eager to try again.

Your relationship with God provides you with God-given tasks. These tasks spring from your response to all of the spiritual blessings God has put in your heart. They're accomplished when you reach out to others with caring and compassion, speak words of kindness and gentleness, and offer practical help to those around you. But as with tasks of all kinds, some may not get done to your satisfaction. You may set out to build something positive, but it ends up crumbling at your feet.

God remains faithful, and all He asks is for you to remain faithful too—to Him, and to whatever you do. He will work success for you in ways beyond your wildest imagination.

Dear God, grant me faithfulness in...

His Work at Work

[God] does great things beyond our understanding.

JOB 37:5

Can you explain how your computer works? Unless you're an IT expert, you probably can't, but you know it works (at least most of the time). For more things you know work but can't explain how, just look around your home, office, and community!

God's activity in your heart defies human explanation, but what He works, works. You know it, because you're taking time out of your day to contemplate His characteristics and your relationship with Him. You can't exactly tell how, but you realize His spiritual gifts really work when you find yourself thinking, feeling, and acting just a little bit differently now than you might have before. You're able to pray with less apprehension than you had when prayer was not a part of your daily routine. That is an effect of His continuing, though incomprehensible, work in you.

You may not be able to explain exactly how He goes about His work in your heart, but you don't need to. You are all the proof you need that His work really works.

Lord God, let Your Spirit work in me to...

He Does It All

The Spirit gives life; the flesh counts for nothing.
JOHN 6:63

Many women have become proficient do-it-yourselfers. These are the women you see walking the aisles of home improvement centers with easy confidence, unfazed by rows of drill bits, nail bins, and caulking tubes. Among their friends, they're the go-to gals for how to tile a floor, replace a faucet, or patch a wall.

As your relationship with God grows, deepens, and broadens in strength and beauty, some of your friends might think you're in the middle of a do-it-yourself life improvement project. And why wouldn't they? They see in you a newfound peace and understanding, and they come to you for a listening ear and helping hands. Evidence of change lies no further than your words and actions, your opinions and ideas. You couldn't blame them for looking to you as the go-to gal for inner transformation!

How good to know there's no need for you to come up with a do-it-yourselfer's guide to spiritual repairs. The only thing needed is directions to the One who's doing all the work—your all-proficient heavenly Father.

Lord God, I come to You to help me repair...

NOVEMBER 28

Help in the Kitchen

You prepare a table before me.
PSALM 23:5 NKJV

Imagine hosting a holiday dinner for twenty. The dining room table is set for adults, card tables assembled for kids, the food smells delicious, everyone's present, and only last-minute stirring and pouring remain to be done in the kitchen—but you're in there all alone. Fair? Of course not!

If God's Spirit were to fill your heart with His gifts but then leave you to practice them without His help, you would find yourself in a similarly uncomfortable situation. Surrounded by the fragrance of goodness, kindness, compassion, and gentleness, you want to reach out to others with your love. Having received His spiritual nourishment, you long to bring the fruits of your knowledge and experience to friends and family. But can you do it alone? Fortunately, there is no need to even consider it.

God's spiritual gifts are like a festive meal with all the fixings, and mouth-watering aromas are drawing others to the dining room. You have everything required at the ready, including help with the work. God's Spirit is ready, willing, and able to serve alongside you as you bring spiritual food to your loved ones.

Dear God, please help me serve others by...

Knowledge of Wisdom

Let the wise also hear and gain in learning,
and the discerning acquire skill.
PROVERBS 1:5 NRSV

Surely we are unable to fully comprehend the depth or breadth of God's wisdom! Some of its mysteries we can glimpse and some elude us completely, yet we can appreciate the overwhelming loveliness of God's astounding wisdom.

God's wisdom is lovely because it whispers in your Spirit-fed thoughts and feelings and assures you that everything will work out in time. His wisdom gives hope. Its loveliness embraces you when you accept your real-life identity and circumstances, knowing that by God's wisdom, you are here at a specific time and in a particular place for a reason and a purpose. God's wisdom encourages you even when you don't know the answers—but you know He knows, and that's enough to see you through.

Even if you can understand many things, God's wisdom comprehends more. In fact, His wisdom comprehends all. Even if others have said you can't learn, God's wisdom infuses your heart, soul, and mind with understanding far greater than anything taught. That's the loveliness of God's wisdom: it's open to us all.

Open Your wisdom to me, Lord, and show me...

A Spiritual Fund

Walk in all the way that the LORD your God has commanded you, so that you may live and prosper.
DEUTERONOMY 5:33

All year long, many of us set aside a certain amount of money for the holidays. When it comes time to shop for gifts for our friends and loved ones, we have our little nest egg at hand, and we can avoid the anxiety associated with overusing credit or incurring debt.

In a similar way, the spiritual habits you are practicing today add to your spiritual storehouse, preparing you to meet tomorrow's needs ably and without fear. As looking to God's plan and purpose in your life becomes an integral part of your thinking, you gain the habits you need to handle upcoming decisions and evaluate future opportunities. Each day that you rely on His presence and trust in His strength adds just a little more to your fund of spiritual experience. No matter what tomorrow brings, you will have what you need to handle it already built up in your heart.

Unlike your Christmas nest egg, however, your spiritual account will never run dry, no matter how many times you dip into it!

Lord, store up in my heart a spiritual fund, so I can...

_____

_____

_____

_____

_____

_____

_____

_____

_____

A Simple Story

May the words of my mouth and the meditation of my heart be pleasing in your sight, O Lord.
PSALM 19:14

You heard what sounded like a simple story, yet it lingered in your mind for days. Only after visiting it repeatedly did you begin to perceive its deeper meaning and the importance of seemingly minor details. What wasn't apparent at first became clear after you thought about it for a while.

The story of God's creation is simple, but He invites you to quietly ponder its details and carefully search for its hidden truths and its profound significance. Guided by His Spirit, you will discover a world intentionally called into being and purposefully set in motion as a home for humankind. Given this understanding, you come to realize that the world's blessings are gifts from your generous God, given to you for your use, enjoyment, and appreciation.

Who would have thought to make something so fleetingly lovely as a snowflake, as intricately textured as an evergreen tree, as warmly reassuring as the touch of a loved one's hand? Yes, creation is a simple story, yet a story that continues to astound the more you think about it.

Creator-God, thank You for the simple beauty of...

He Never Gives Up

Let us run with perseverance the race marked out for us. Let us fix our eyes on Jesus.
HEBREWS 12:1–2

Perhaps you have read the biographies of heroic women of American history. Against all odds, some women defeated discrimination and injustice, while others ventured west and established homes in harsh and unforgiving territories across the country. Beyond even the remarkable fortitude and firm perseverance of these women, however, stands the Lord's infinite strength.

Your Lord is stronger than your fear or insecurity, despair or depression, even though these things can hold you down with seemingly insurmountable power. You may know your own weakness, but your Lord's strength can lift you up and out of your enemy's grasp. No matter how many times you may slip back, your Lord will never stop rescuing you.

Your Lord is stronger than your doubt or skepticism, uncertainty or disbelief, even though these things continually threaten to conquer faith. Despite any hindrance, your Lord perseveres to establish a dwelling place wherever the seed of faith has been planted.

Long after others have given up, the Lord's fortitude and perseverance remains. His strength is forever, and He will never give up on you.

Help me persevere, Lord, in...

_____

_____

_____

_____

_____

_____

_____

_____

The Right Amount

As newborn babes, desire the pure milk of the word, that you may grow.
1 PETER 2:2 NKJV

Too much information! Those words go through our heads when someone we barely know reveals her life's story to us or recites the minute details of her recent crisis. Often, rather than drawing us close to the person, too much information makes us want to pull back.

Perhaps "too much information" explains why the Lord sometimes chooses to approach you slowly, revealing only bits and pieces of His characteristics as your relationship grows. If, when you first began to explore His being, He immediately appeared to you in His full glory, majesty, and power, you could have been overwhelmed—perhaps to the point of retreating in shock.

Little by little the Lord opens to you His infinite beauty. Your enduring friendship with Him is more important to Him than your knowing everything about Him now. A glimpse of His presence in your life works to invite you to come closer to Him than an onslaught of His attributes ever could. And, as you get to know Him better, you'll find there's more information to come!

Dear God, today please share with me...

_____

_____

_____

_____

_____

_____

_____

_____

_____

Food at His Feast

You do not have, because you do not ask God.

JAMES 4:2

Dieters beware: Trays of mouthwatering appetizers, dips, desserts, and homemade Christmas cookies are coming your way! Food is a big part of the season's festivities, and the meals we share bring family and friends closer together, often becoming part of our fondest holiday traditions.

Receiving God's spiritual blessings is like sitting at His banquet table. Imagine a festive meal with steaming, aromatic foods piled high in front of you. Picture God, as your attentive host, offering you spoonful after spoonful of whatever you choose. Take in the laughter of others all around you who have come to His wonderful feast and experience the joy of His celebration. Taste the sweetness of it all.

God's spiritual blessings are yours for the asking simply because He desires to give them to you. So go ahead—take seconds, thirds, and more. Share His blessings with others, and invite them to join you at His feast.

What's more, at this table you don't need to worry about calories: the only thing that's sure to get bigger is your joy in Him!

Lord God, today I'm reaching for more of Your...

_____

_____

_____

_____

_____

_____

_____

_____

DECEMBER 5

A Certain Hope

No one whose hope is in you will ever be put to shame.
PSALM 25:3

Around the holidays, there's hope in the air. Travelers hope for good weather and hostesses hope all their decorations will be up before their first guests arrive. Children hope to get what's on their Christmas list, and maybe you do too. Hope is all around!

Among the many beautiful gifts the Lord holds out to you is the gift of hope. His hope, however, differs from the hope of favorable weather, a sparkling tree, and Christmas gifts, because His hope is certain hope. Your God offers you the hope of seeing Him in His full glory, the hope of worshiping Him fully and completely, and the hope of remaining with Him for eternity. Far more than a wish or expectation, your hope is certain, because it's based on your Lord's promise. Your Lord, whose knowledge reaches into the future, has told you.

Will your hopes for the holidays come true? Maybe, maybe not. But the hope you have in the Lord is certain. It's the certain hope you can carry with you all year long!

Dear God, please set my hope firmly on...

Easy to See

Those who are wise will shine like the brightness of the heavens.

DANIEL 12:3

You might find it on the cover of a greeting card or right outside your window: in the middle of a snow-covered landscape, a bright red cardinal sits serenely on the branch of a tree. Even if you know only a little about birds, it's easy to pick out a cardinal in a winter scene!

Like a redbird against a backdrop of snow, God's beauty is clearly evident in a world marked by weakness, adversity, and troubles. His compassion stands in stark contrast to indifference, and His presence cannot be missed when He enters a heart willing to receive Him.

The work of His Spirit is nothing short of obvious too. Against a backdrop of people too busy to care, your concern for others is like a shining light in a dreary day. Your gentleness stands out when a friend needs a word of encouragement, and your everyday joy breaks through the unremitting gray of gloom and sadness.

In a winter world, it's easy to pick out the woman who has been touched by the beauty of the Lord!

Dear God, let me show more of Your...

_____

_____

_____

_____

_____

_____

_____

_____

Behind the Scenes

The LORD will go before you, and the God of Israel will be your rear guard.
ISAIAH 52:12 NKJV

The more spectacular the show you watch on stage, the more complex the work going on behind the scenes. Though sets are changed, cues given, and spotlights managed out of the audience's view, there's no doubt that all this is going on, and much more besides.

Out of view, too, are many of the ways your Lord is working in your life. More times than you could realize, He has delivered you out of harm's way, even harm that you never knew was there. More often than you could ever know, He has removed from you a threat to your physical or spiritual well-being, a threat you didn't even see coming. He doesn't tell you each time He shelters you from a storm, but He has shielded you from many. He makes no noise when He leads you to safety, but He continually does so.

His presence may be the main attraction, but there's no doubt His care and concern, protection and guidance, grace and love are always at work behind the scenes.

Thank You, Lord, for all the times You...

DECEMBER 8

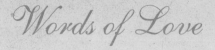

Let everything you say be good and helpful,
so that your words will be an encouragement
to those who hear them.
EPHESIANS 4:29 NLT

How sweet to hear words of endearment! They're welcome at any time, but most especially when we're least expecting them—perhaps in the middle of a busy day or at the end of a tiring week. It feels good to be told we are loved, even though we already know.

How about the Lord? Of course He is God and He knows everything, even the breadth and depth of your love for Him. But how sweet it must sound to His ears when words of endearment flow spontaneously from your heart! Yes, it is necessary to approach Him with your needs and desires, yet how sweet to say "Hi" simply because you're thinking of Him. How right to say you love Him in your prayers, yet how doubly sweet to say those words for no other reason than "just because."

In your relationships with others, words matter, and none more so than those words uttered from a heart overflowing with genuine love, caring, and gratitude. Your relationship with your Lord could be no different.

Dear Lord, I want to tell You about...

_____

_____

_____

_____

_____

_____

_____

_____

Found in Him

May the righteous be glad and rejoice before God;
may they be happy and joyful.
PSALM 68:3

If you've ever searched your house, top to bottom, looking for something, you know how frustrating it is not to find it. Imagine if you weren't even sure what it looked like, and then you know the problem of searching for happiness.

On our own, we don't know what happiness looks like and so we uncover things we think will bring us happiness. We come up with ideas and activities we identify as just what we need for happiness, but soon—and often sadly—we realize the happiness was temporary and the excitement didn't last.

God is the source of all true happiness. As your Lord steps into your life, He shows you what happiness looks like in the beauty of His peace and joy, His caring and compassion, and His willingness to gladly serve His loved ones as they serve Him. His kind of happiness doesn't depend on circumstances but on trusting and relying on Him.

Instead of searching for happiness, search for Him. Trust in Him. That is where true happiness can be found.

Dear God, I feel happiest when...

_____

_____

_____

_____

_____

_____

_____

_____

A Faithful Love

The LORD your God, He is God, the faithful God,
who keeps His covenant and His lovingkindness to a thousandth generation.
DEUTERONOMY 7:9 NASB

If you have been in a romantic relationship for a long time, you know what most young women have yet to realize: The ties of love grow stronger not because of intensified feelings, but as the result of practiced faithfulness.

The ties of spiritual love are strengthened the same way. God's faithfulness to you shows in His refusal to step away from you, no matter who you are, where you are in your life, or even how many times you might have stepped away from Him. He has bound you close to Him with eternal love.

As your relationship with God grows, your feelings may not necessarily intensify, but the strength of your ties to Him will. Rather than responding solely with emotion, you may find yourself responding to His faithfulness with acceptance of His will and with renewed gentleness toward others. You may discover a new delight in helping and encouraging, and new joy in serving others' needs.

Faithful love nurtures the bonds that bring—and keep—two hearts together.

Enable me, dear Lord, to show my love by...

Serenity of Soul

I am the Lord who heals you.
EXODUS 15:26 NRSV

Whenever we receive exciting news, the first thing we want to do is pass it on! All we have to do is tell a few friends, and soon everyone has heard all about it.

News traveled quickly in Jesus' time, too, even though there were no phones and certainly no e-mail—only a word from one person to the next. No sooner had the Lord healed a person in one town than a crowd from the next town poured out to meet Him, and with each healing, the crowds grew larger and larger. What to some was a blessing and to others a spectacle, Jesus' healing miracles reflected God's desire and ability to heal.

Though He generally works through physicians, surgeons, and counselors to treat our wounds of body and mind, there are some wounds too deep inside the heart for anyone to reach. These are the wounds God soothes with His presence and eases with Spirit-sent gifts of patience, faith, and hope.

Though a heart-deep wound may yet leave a scar, with Him a scar can serve as the foundation for serenity of soul.

Healer-Lord, please touch my wound of...

_____

_____

_____

_____

_____

_____

_____

_____

His Beloved Daughter

After you have suffered a little while,
[God] will himself restore you and make you strong, firm and steadfast.
1 PETER 5:10

When God formed the world, He created something out of nothing. What's hard to fathom for many of us is easy for a woman who believed herself nothing until her Lord spoke her name and called her His *Beloved Daughter*.

For a woman like that, who has had the eyes of her heart opened, something out of nothing is believable. She perceives His love and compassion toward her. She begins to see His hand at work in her life, and in time she finds herself not only something, but someone of worth and value, with talents, interests, and skills, and the God-given ability to serve.

Many women don't even notice the times He renews and restores them with the blessing of a good friend, an encouraging mentor, or a faithful spouse. But if we stop to consider how we came to be refreshed, chances are we will discover He uses others to help us go from nothing to something. Through others, He reminds us, "You are my beloved daughter."

Restore my spirit, Lord, when I feel...

Whatever It Is

I wait for you, O LORD; you will answer, O Lord my God.
PSALM 38:15

There's a gift under the tree, and it's for you. You have no idea what's inside, and you can't wait to open it. Whatever it is, you know it's going to be something absolutely wonderful, not from the size, shape, or weight of the box, but because of the person it's from. Like a little kid, you can hardly wait until Christmas morning to find out what it is!

When you ask God in prayer to grant your petitions and desires, you know He will answer with a gift especially for you. What you don't know, however, is what the gift will be, or what it might look like or what shape it may take, or even when it might come into your life. But because you know the giver, you know it will be exactly what's best and needful for you.

Answered prayer comes from your Lord who loves you deeply and takes pleasure in delighting you with His gifts. From Him, whatever it is, you know it's going to be absolutely wonderful.

Grant me patience, Lord, to wait for...

_____

_____

_____

_____

_____

_____

_____

_____

_____

Beauty of Music

Let us come before [God's] presence with thanksgiving,
and make a joyful noise unto him with psalms.
PSALM 95:2 KJV

Perhaps you have fond memories of caroling house to house as a child or of attending holiday songfests with your family. Maybe there's a tradition in your family of seeing a Christmas musical every December. At this time of year, seasonal music is everywhere—in churches and concert halls, on television and on the radio, and even piped over the sound system at your local supermarket.

A beautiful gift from your gracious Lord, music has the power to take your mind from the humdrum of everyday routine and into a world of reflection and optimism. A joyous melody can lift your spirits when you're feeling down and can soothe your soul when you're troubled. A familiar song can bring to mind a sweet season of life, a beloved face, a treasured voice.

It's almost impossible to read Scripture and not hear the melodic praises of the psalmist, the joyous songs of angels, the worshipful hymns of the first Christians. It's just as impossible to imagine standing in the presence of the Lord without being surrounded by beautiful music.

Thank You, dear God, for the music of...

_____

_____

_____

_____

_____

_____

_____

_____

More and More

The LORD directs the steps of the godly.
He delights in every detail of their lives.
PSALM 37:23 NLT

As you continue to contemplate God's presence, you become more and more aware of His activities. You recognize Him as the source of all the things you may have taken for granted before, such as home and family, friends and coworkers, food and comforts, pleasures and gifts.

Yet God's activities don't stop there! Perhaps you have seen with your mind's eye how His hand guided you to a particular person or place at just the right time, and there you found a special blessing waiting for you. Maybe you have realized how close you came to a dangerous decision but heard Him call you back to safety. More and more, the shadows of happenstance melt away, revealing the glorious goodwill of your all-powerful God.

God sits in His heaven, and He also lives in the lives of His beloved daughters on earth. The more you think about it, the more you want to bless Him for blessing you in all He says and does.

Dear Lord, thank You for blessing me with...

_____

_____

_____

_____

_____

_____

_____

_____

_____

Source of Love

We love Him because He first loved us.
1 JOHN 4:19 NKJV

If you have known true love, lift up your heart in thanksgiving to the source of all love, your gracious Lord. If you have been disappointed in love, lift up your heart in petition to the source of all love, your same gracious Lord.

His is the love that can never be quenched with time, because His love extends beyond the boundaries of time. It cannot be bought and cannot be earned by anyone, because He freely showers His love on all. His love is never feigned, for the God of all truth is incapable of lying; neither are we forced to return it, but invited, welcomed, and cherished by God, whose essence is love.

If human love has failed you, rest your head on the shoulder of the Lord who has known you and has loved you since before you were born. If human love has blessed your life, rest your eyes on His face, whose love not even time can end. To understand love, there's no better source than love itself.

Lord God, to me Your love is like...

_____

_____

_____

_____

_____

_____

_____

_____

Worth the Cost

Anyone who does not carry his cross and follow me cannot be my disciple.
LUKE 14:27

Is it worth the price? That's the question when a favorite brand or often-purchased item becomes more expensive. We might decide to pay the higher price, or we might leave it sitting on the shelf.

Though God's love is free to you, you may have noticed that sharing it is not always cheap. Your response to His love has cost you time as you attentively and deliberately reached out to others with kindness and compassion. It has cost you effort as you tried to be more patient with a difficult family member or demanding coworker, and it cost you personal resources as you volunteered hours and gave a portion of your income to help the less fortunate.

What's more, you might have realized that, as with items you buy, the price keeps going up. People know they can rely on you so they ask for more of your time and effort. They know you will stop and listen, so they come to you when they need someone to care. Is it worth the price?

There's only one answer. Absolutely!

Lord, You are worth the cost because...

An Awesome Guest

*Be still,
and know that I am God.*
PSALM 46:10

It could be a long-lost friend or admired dignitary, a well-known saint or popular celebrity. If you found yourself in the same room with this person, all you would do is stare in awe. Rather than speak, you would strain to catch every word uttered by your eminent guest.

Something similar happens when God moves the eyes of your spirit toward Himself. What words could possibly express how you feel or describe the movements of your heart? Besides, what if in speaking you should miss even one word to come out of His mouth? So you stand in His presence, not moving your eyes off His face and ever leaning forward to listen to His every breath.

Now you have a sense of what it's like to gaze upon the beauty of your Lord. You stand in awe, even though earthly comprehension allows only a fleeting glimpse of His glory and offers a mere peek at His majesty. Words cannot begin to explain it; only in your heart you will know the One you have met.

Open the eyes of my spirit, Lord, to see...

His Extravagant Gifts

*[God] has shown kindness by giving you rain from heaven
and crops in their seasons; he provides you with plenty of food
and fills your hearts with joy.*

ACTS 14:17

Some of us tell our loved ones not to spend a lot on a gift for us at Christmastime (though we're secretly pleased if they do).

Every day, most of us tell God not to spend a lot on us by neglecting to ask Him for our deepest desires or by not expecting Him to come through. But what does our Lord do? He goes ahead and blesses us anyway!

Whether you ask Him to or not, He showers you with such extravagant gifts as the assurance of His presence and the promise of His protection and guidance. He sends His Spirit into your heart even without your pleading. He picks out special blessings to bring you pleasure and comfort, laughter and joy, not just at Christmastime—it's something He does all year round.

It's true: you don't have to request anything from God, and you will receive from Him. But how much more could He have waiting for you, simply for the asking?

Dear Lord, I ask this of You...

_____

_____

_____

_____

_____

_____

_____

_____

Center of Serenity

You who dwell in the gardens, with companions listening for your voice; let me hear it.
SONG OF SOLOMON 8:13 ESV

Imagine stepping through the gate of an exquisite garden of winding paths bordered by bright, fragrant flowers. Your pace slows as you savor the rustle of leaves, the chirping of birds. You stop to let a butterfly light on your shoulder and stoop to cup a blossom in the palm of your hand.

You wander to where shade trees shelter the banks of a serene, sun-dappled pond. You had been rushing only an hour ago, you don't remember why. If then you were tense, now you feel relaxed and serene. You spy a bench and sit down.

The garden is like the whisper of your Lord enticing you with the fragrance of His gentleness and the beauty of His faithfulness. The pond is like His heart, a place for you to quietly contemplate the living waters of His love. It's a place of restoration, renewal, and rest.

As you leave your imagined garden and go back to your work and responsibilities, let the fragrance of His serenity linger long in your mind and heart.

Lord, I seek serenity in You to help me...

Light in Darkness

The people who walked in darkness have seen a great light.
ISAIAH 9:2 NKJV

For those of us living in the Northern Hemisphere, today is the shortest day of the year, the time of the longest night. Most of us will get up in the dark, and it will get dark before we finish our errands or return from work.

We're more conscious of light when it's dark—the lamp that brightens our room, the headlights that shine ahead on the street, the twinkle of buildings in the distance—and we appreciate light more too. We realize we'd be trying to find our way in the dark without it.

At times, you may be plunged into the darkness of anguish, fear, or hopelessness, helpless against the blinding pain of heartache and loss. In these dark times God enters with the light of His caring and compassion, leading and guiding you when you don't know where to turn. These are the times you perceive His love most clearly, appreciate it most heartily, and experience it most powerfully.

Like a shining lamp, His presence bathes your spirit in life-giving light.

Lord, please shine Your light on…

Most Beautiful Woman

The King will greatly desire your beauty; because He is your Lord, worship Him.
PSALM 45:11 NKJV

Who's the most beautiful woman in the world? It all depends on whom you ask and when! Standards of feminine beauty vary widely from culture to culture, and within cultures, each generation defines beauty anew.

No matter when or where you live, your supremely beautiful Lord does nothing less than shower you with beautiful features, inside and out. Unlike cultural measures of beauty, however, His standards remain the same throughout the ages and alike for all women of God. Your Lord sees the same beautiful smile of gratitude and contentment in you as He saw in believing women from centuries ago. Today, the timeless beauty of your helping hands graces the hands of your spiritual sisters in all lands, and the enduring beauty of your loving heart defies the boundaries of time and place.

Because He is the essence of beauty, your Lord is the best one to talk to about beauty and who has it. When you do, you just might find yourself feeling like the most beautiful woman in the world!

Lord, I feel beautiful in Your eyes when...

Not Just for Christmas

He has clothed me with the garments of salvation, He has covered me with the robe of righteousness.
ISAIAH 61:10 NKJV

If you like to wear sparkly T-shirts, sequined sweaters, and Christmas-themed accessories, now is your time of year! What fun to get into the holiday spirit by wearing something guaranteed to attract cheerful smiles wherever you go.

A few other attention-getting garments are the ones your Lord has ready and waiting for you. He desires to drape your heart and mind with His truth and to establish His holiness at the center of your spirit. He yearns to slip spiritual shoes on your feet so you may walk in serenity and to cover you with a robe of His wisdom. Your head He wants to adorn with His promise of eternal life. And to keep you so beautifully clothed, He opens to you the words and promises of Scripture.

His garments, while inner garments, can be seen in how you act and speak—in the things you do that bring smiles of appreciation wherever you go. And His garments—they're not just for Christmas, but for every day of the year.

Lord, put on me Your garment of...

_____

_____

_____

_____

_____

_____

_____

_____

_____

_____

Follow the Star

We have seen His star in the East and have come to worship Him.
MATTHEW 2:2 NKJV

The subject of hymns and carols over the centuries, the star of Bethlehem remains a symbol of God's guiding light to this day. Have you seen it?

You find it shining brightly when you look up to God for His wisdom and counsel, rather than limit yourself to the confines of human understanding. The star's radiance floods the heavens when you seek God's will, and its rays illumine your path as you walk in His way.

Your patience, kindness, and gentleness point to the star of Bethlehem, showing others how to discover God's beauty in their own lives. Just like the guiding light of song, your Spirit-blessed words and actions cause others to look up and see His goodness and go to where He may be found.

As you follow the star in your relationship with your Lord, don't be surprised if soon others are joining you on the same path, all of you looking toward the true light of the world.

It's still shining, still inviting, still leading. Have you seen it?

Lord, please lead me, illuminate my path as I...

_____

_____

_____

_____

_____

_____

_____

_____

_____

_____

_____

_____

Inside the Box

May you have the power to understand...
how wide, how long, how high, and how deep his love is.
EPHESIANS 3:18 NLT

While many gifts under the tree were wrapped in beautiful paper and topped with elegant bows, today the gifts are opened and the paper and bows discarded. No matter how exquisite the package, the best part of the gift lies inside the box!

To begin to get to know the Lord is like suddenly being surrounded with dozens of gifts, each one lovely and inviting—and marked especially for you. His attributes amaze you, and you might spend some time looking at them and wondering what His holiness means or pondering the depth of His compassion. If you were to stop there, however, it would be like leaving a stack of gorgeous gifts unopened. You're missing the best part!

Continuing your relationship with your Lord opens the eyes of your spirit to a fuller appreciation of His love for you and to a broader understanding of who He is. As taken as you are with the beauty of His attributes, even more beautiful are His attributes at work in your life.

The best parts of His beautiful gifts lie inside your heart.

Dear God, open to me Your special gift of...

To Cherish Forever

As for me, I shall behold your face in righteousness;
when I awake I shall be satisfied, beholding your likeness.
PSALM 17:15 NRSV

Today there will be many exchanges. In front of customer service counters across the country, people are waiting with armloads of bags and boxes to swap what they received for what they really want.

The customer service counter staffed by the Holy Spirit can be a busy place too. We come to exchange our spiritual gifts for something we think we really want—perhaps a dress that fits us right now, instead of the robe the Lord knows we have the potential to grow into given His help and strength. Or perhaps we would prefer a gem with more sparkle and shine to impress our girlfriends, rather than the jewel of humble service and quiet obedience He has selected for us with great care. Or maybe we were expecting some new household décor and not the plain, practical gifts of courtesy and kindness, patience and goodness.

The day after Christmas sends many of us to the stores, eager to find something else. Yet there are some gifts the wisest among us will cherish, as we cherish the giver.

Dear God, thank You for giving me...

New Year Predictions

"I know the plans I have for you,"
declares the LORD, "plans to prosper you and not to harm you,
plans to give you hope and a future."
JEREMIAH 29:11

By now the commentators and comedians are in full swing, announcing their forecasts for the new year. While some of the more levelheaded may speak with caution, many have no qualms predicting sensational events and devastating ruin.

Isn't it interesting to note that God, who knows what will happen every day of the coming year, is silent on the subject? Instead of giving you times and dates for future disasters, He provides you with far more useful information. For starters, He assures you He is in control of the world and everything in it, and He invites you to trust His wisdom. Then He begs you to put your fears and anxieties in His hands, and He tells you once again to lean on Him for your strength. Always, He promises you His presence, no matter what happens in the world or in your life.

His is the kind of information you can depend on. It's reliable information you can take with you today and every day ahead.

Lord God, please calm my fears about...

Learning to Love

Do not fear, for I am with you; do not be dismayed, for I am your God.
I will strengthen you and help you.

ISAIAH 41:10

God's presence in your life compares to the presence of a loving mother. In love God brought you into this world, and in love He raises you up. God opens His beauty to you as you grow in knowledge and experience, leading you to discover the loveliness of birdsongs and rainbows and the splendor of kindness and grace.

He embraces you in understanding when you are afraid or ashamed or bewildered, and opens His arms to gather you in when you need to cry. He guides you when you ask Him for direction, and He intervenes to protect you from all that would harm the sacred bond between you.

With each year that passes, you trust more confidently because He has never failed you; you pray more often because you have found His ear near to you whenever you call. You listen more intently because you know He speaks the truth.

You have given Him joy with the sound of your laughter and the voice of your speaking, and from Him you have learned how to love.

Teach me, Lord, to be like You and love...

Promise of Light

*God has rescued us from the dominion of darkness
and brought us into the kingdom of the Son he loves.*
COLOSSIANS 1:13

With every day comes another few seconds of light before the sun sets and night begins. Unless you study the skies, however, it's unlikely you will notice until the seconds become minutes and the minutes extend to half an hour. Then daylight and darkness are obvious, and you realize that change was taking place all along, even though you were unaware of it.

In your relationship with God, there may be times you feel stuck in darkness—the first flush of knowing Him has passed and you seem to be making no discernible progress in your spiritual growth. You might wonder about the seeming silence of the Lord and may even wonder if you're on the right spiritual path.

In the dark early evening of a cold winter day, it's easy to wonder if spring will ever come. But then one day you will notice that the day is just a little longer, the sky a bit brighter, the grip of winter slightly less firm. You will smile, because you will know that spring will come again.

Help me see progress, Lord, in...

A Lively Interest

*I will tell of the kindnesses of the LORD, the deeds for which
he is to be praised, according to all the LORD has done for us.*

ISAIAH 63:7

When you're attracted to someone, you want to find out more about the person—his likes and dislikes, his interests and passions, where he works and what he does. If you were to meet one of his friends, your ears would perk up at the mention of his name, and you would hope to glean a tidbit of information about him as the conversation continued. It's only natural, because attraction sparks lively interest and intense curiosity.

Spiritual women who have welcomed God into their lives leave tidbits of information concerning Him wherever they go. From these women, others learn that the Spirit of the Lord transforms the heart, turning selfish desires into willing service, bitter memories to forgiving words, nervous fears to quiet confidence and trust. What could be more attractive?

You cause the eyes of those around you to look to God and find out more about Him. It's only natural when you're the friend who kindles their lively interest and can speak to their intense curiosity.

Lord, enable me to speak to others about Your...

Past, Present, and Future

I am the Alpha and the Omega,
the Beginning and the End.
REVELATION 21:6 NKJV

Many of us choose the beginning of a new year to set fresh goals. Perhaps your goal might be to exercise more, save money, or get better organized. Your goal is based on what has gone before, where you are today, and where you want to find yourself tomorrow.

You have a past, present, and future with God. Before you became interested in discovering Him, you might have sensed something missing in your life. God whispers in tiny places and even a little emptiness is enough to draw Him in. Now you know about Him, His love for you, and you have seen the difference He has made in your heart.

He invites you now to receive His guidance as you visualize yourself in the coming year. Perhaps you see yourself reading or praying more; reaching out to others more; accepting more of His spiritual gifts into your thoughts, words, and actions.

He has been your light in the past, and He is your light today. Invite Him into your future, and walk in His light forever.

Dear God, guide me as I make plans to...

_____

_____

_____

_____

_____

_____

_____

_____

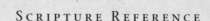

SCRIPTURE REFERENCE

A plan for Bible reading to take readers through the New Testament and
Psalms twice a year, and through the rest of the Bible once each year.

January

1st	Genesis	1	Matthew	1	Ezra	1	Acts	1
2nd	Genesis	2	Matthew	2	Ezra	2	Acts	2
3rd	Genesis	3	Matthew	3	Ezra	3	Acts	3
4th	Genesis	4	Matthew	4	Ezra	4	Acts	4
5th	Genesis	5	Matthew	5	Ezra	5	Acts	5
6th	Genesis	6	Matthew	6	Ezra	6	Acts	6
7th	Genesis	7	Matthew	7	Ezra	7	Acts	7
8th	Genesis	8	Matthew	8	Ezra	8	Acts	8
9th	Genesis	9–10	Matthew	9	Ezra	9	Acts	9
10th	Genesis	11	Matthew	10	Ezra	10	Acts	10
11th	Genesis	12	Matthew	11	Nehemiah	1	Acts	11
12th	Genesis	13	Matthew	12	Nehemiah	2	Acts	12
13th	Genesis	14	Matthew	13	Nehemiah	3	Acts	13
14th	Genesis	15	Matthew	14	Nehemiah	4	Acts	14
15th	Genesis	16	Matthew	15	Nehemiah	5	Acts	15
16th	Genesis	17	Matthew	16	Nehemiah	6	Acts	16
17th	Genesis	18	Matthew	17	Nehemiah	7	Acts	17
18th	Genesis	19	Matthew	18	Nehemiah	8	Acts	18
19th	Genesis	20	Matthew	19	Nehemiah	9	Acts	19
20th	Genesis	21	Matthew	20	Nehemiah	10	Acts	20
21st	Genesis	22	Matthew	21	Nehemiah	11	Acts	21
22nd	Genesis	23	Matthew	22	Nehemiah	12	Acts	22
23rd	Genesis	24	Matthew	23	Nehemiah	13	Acts	23
24th	Genesis	25	Matthew	24	Esther	1	Acts	24
25th	Genesis	26	Matthew	25	Esther	2	Acts	25
26th	Genesis	27	Matthew	26	Esther	3	Acts	26
27th	Genesis	28	Matthew	27	Esther	4	Acts	27
28th	Genesis	29	Matthew	28	Esther	5	Acts	28
29th	Genesis	30	Mark	1	Esther	6	Romans	1
30th	Genesis	31	Mark	2	Esther	7	Romans	2
31st	Genesis	32	Mark	3	Esther	8	Romans	3

February

1st	Genesis	33	Mark	4	Esther	9–10	Romans	4
2nd	Genesis	34	Mark	5	Job	1	Romans	5
3rd	Genesis	35–36	Mark	6	Job	2	Romans	6
4th	Genesis	37	Mark	7	Job	3	Romans	7
5th	Genesis	38	Mark	8	Job	4	Romans	8
6th	Genesis	39	Mark	9	Job	5	Romans	9
7th	Genesis	40	Mark	10	Job	6	Romans	10
8th	Genesis	41	Mark	11	Job	7	Romans	11
9th	Genesis	42	Mark	12	Job	8	Romans	12
10th	Genesis	43	Mark	13	Job	9	Romans	13
11th	Genesis	44	Mark	14	Job	10	Romans	14
12th	Genesis	45	Mark	15	Job	11	Romans	15
13th	Genesis	46	Mark	16	Job	12	Romans	16
14th	Genesis	47	Luke	1:1–38	Job	13	1 Corinthians	1
15th	Genesis	48	Luke	1:39ff	Job	14	1 Corinthians	2
16th	Genesis	49	Luke	2	Job	15	1 Corinthians	3
17th	Genesis	50	Luke	3	Job	16–17	1 Corinthians	4
18th	Exodus	1	Luke	4	Job	18	1 Corinthians	5
19th	Exodus	2	Luke	5	Job	19	1 Corinthians	6
20th	Exodus	3	Luke	6	Job	20	1 Corinthians	7
21st	Exodus	4	Luke	7	Job	21	1 Corinthians	8
22nd	Exodus	5	Luke	8	Job	22	1 Corinthians	9
23rd	Exodus	6	Luke	9	Job	23	1 Corinthians	10
24th	Exodus	7	Luke	10	Job	24	1 Corinthians	11
25th	Exodus	8	Luke	11	Job	25–26	1 Corinthians	12
26th	Exodus	9	Luke	12	Job	27	1 Corinthians	13
27th	Exodus	10	Luke	13	Job	28	1 Corinthians	14
28th	Exodus	11–12:21	Luke	14	Job	29	1 Corinthians	15

March

1st	Exodus	12:22ff	Luke	15	Job	30	1 Corinthians	16
2nd	Exodus	13	Luke	16	Job	31	2 Corinthians	1
3rd	Exodus	14	Luke	17	Job	32	2 Corinthians	2
4th	Exodus	15	Luke	18	Job	33	2 Corinthians	3
5th	Exodus	16	Luke	19	Job	34	2 Corinthians	4
6th	Exodus	17	Luke	20	Job	35	2 Corinthians	5
7th	Exodus	18	Luke	21	Job	36	2 Corinthians	6
8th	Exodus	19	Luke	22	Job	37	2 Corinthians	7
9th	Exodus	20	Luke	23	Job	38	2 Corinthians	8
10th	Exodus	21	Luke	24	Job	39	2 Corinthians	9
11th	Exodus	22	John	1	Job	40	2 Corinthians	10
12th	Exodus	23	John	2	Job	41	2 Corinthians	11
13th	Exodus	24	John	3	Job	42	2 Corinthians	12
14th	Exodus	25	John	4	Proverbs	1	2 Corinthians	13
15th	Exodus	26	John	5	Proverbs	2	Galatians	1
16th	Exodus	27	John	6	Proverbs	3	Galatians	2
17th	Exodus	28	John	7	Proverbs	4	Galatians	3
18th	Exodus	29	John	8	Proverbs	5	Galatians	4
19th	Exodus	30	John	9	Proverbs	6	Galatians	5
20th	Exodus	31	John	10	Proverbs	7	Galatians	6
21st	Exodus	32	John	11	Proverbs	8	Ephesians	1
22nd	Exodus	33	John	12	Proverbs	9	Ephesians	2
23rd	Exodus	34	John	13	Proverbs	10	Ephesians	3
24th	Exodus	35	John	14	Proverbs	11	Ephesians	4
25th	Exodus	36	John	15	Proverbs	12	Ephesians	5
26th	Exodus	37	John	16	Proverbs	13	Ephesians	6
27th	Exodus	38	John	17	Proverbs	14	Philippians	1
28th	Exodus	39	John	18	Proverbs	15	Philippians	2
29th	Exodus	40	John	19	Proverbs	16	Philippians	3
30th	Leviticus	1	John	20	Proverbs	17	Philippians	4
31st	Leviticus	2–3	John	21	Proverbs	18	Colossians	1

April

1st	Leviticus	4	Psalms	1–2	Proverbs	19	Colossians	2
2nd	Leviticus	5	Psalms	3–4	Proverbs	20	Colossians	3
3rd	Leviticus	6	Psalms	5–6	Proverbs	21	Colossians	4
4th	Leviticus	7	Psalms	7–8	Proverbs	22	1 Thessalonians	1
5th	Leviticus	8	Psalms	9	Proverbs	23	1 Thessalonians	2
6th	Leviticus	9	Psalms	10	Proverbs	24	1 Thessalonians	3
7th	Leviticus	10	Psalms	11–12	Proverbs	25	1 Thessalonians	4
8th	Leviticus	11–12	Psalms	13–14	Proverbs	26	1 Thessalonians	5
9th	Leviticus	13	Psalms	15–16	Proverbs	27	2 Thessalonians	1
10th	Leviticus	14	Psalms	17	Proverbs	28	2 Thessalonians	2
11th	Leviticus	15	Psalms	18	Proverbs	29	2 Thessalonians	3
12th	Leviticus	16	Psalms	19	Proverbs	30	1 Timothy	1
13th	Leviticus	17	Psalms	20–21	Proverbs	31	1 Timothy	2
14th	Leviticus	18	Psalms	22	Ecclesiastes	1	1 Timothy	3
15th	Leviticus	19	Psalms	23–24	Ecclesiastes	2	1 Timothy	4
16th	Leviticus	20	Psalms	25	Ecclesiastes	3	1 Timothy	5
17th	Leviticus	21	Psalms	26–27	Ecclesiastes	4	1 Timothy	6
18th	Leviticus	22	Psalms	28–29	Ecclesiastes	5	2 Timothy	1
19th	Leviticus	23	Psalms	30	Ecclesiastes	6	2 Timothy	2
20th	Leviticus	24	Psalms	31	Ecclesiastes	7	2 Timothy	3
21st	Leviticus	25	Psalms	32	Ecclesiastes	8	2 Timothy	4
22nd	Leviticus	26	Psalms	33	Ecclesiastes	9	Titus	1
23rd	Leviticus	27	Psalms	34	Ecclesiastes	10	Titus	2
24th	Numbers	1	Psalms	35	Ecclesiastes	11	Titus	3
25th	Numbers	2	Psalms	36	Ecclesiastes	12	Philemon	1
26th	Numbers	3	Psalms	37	Song of Songs	1	Hebrews	1
27th	Numbers	4	Psalms	38	Song of Songs	2	Hebrews	2
28th	Numbers	5	Psalms	39	Song of Songs	3	Hebrews	3
29th	Numbers	6	Psalms	40–41	Song of Songs	4	Hebrews	4
30th	Numbers	7	Psalms	42–43	Song of Songs	5	Hebrews	5

May

1st	Numbers	8	Psalms	44	Song of Songs	6	Hebrews	6
2nd	Numbers	9	Psalms	45	Song of Songs	7	Hebrews	7
3rd	Numbers	10	Psalms	46–47	Song of Songs	8	Hebrews	8
4th	Numbers	11	Psalms	48	Isaiah	1	Hebrews	9
5th	Numbers	12–13	Psalms	49	Isaiah	2	Hebrews	10
6th	Numbers	14	Psalms	50	Isaiah	3–4	Hebrews	11
7th	Numbers	15	Psalms	51	Isaiah	5	Hebrews	12
8th	Numbers	16	Psalms	52–54	Isaiah	6	Hebrews	13
9th	Numbers	17–18	Psalms	55	Isaiah	7	James	1
10th	Numbers	19	Psalms	56–57	Isaiah	8–9:7	James	2
11th	Numbers	20	Psalms	58–59	Isaiah	9:8–10:4	James	3
12th	Numbers	21	Psalms	60–61	Isaiah	10:5ff	James	4
13th	Numbers	22	Psalms	62–63	Isaiah	11–12	James	5
14th	Numbers	23	Psalms	64–65	Isaiah	13	1 Peter	1
15th	Numbers	24	Psalms	66–67	Isaiah	14	1 Peter	2
16th	Numbers	25	Psalms	68	Isaiah	15	1 Peter	3
17th	Numbers	26	Psalms	69	Isaiah	16	1 Peter	4
18th	Numbers	27	Psalms	70–71	Isaiah	17–18	1 Peter	5
19th	Numbers	28	Psalms	72	Isaiah	19–20	2 Peter	1
20th	Numbers	29	Psalms	73	Isaiah	21	2 Peter	2
21st	Numbers	30	Psalms	74	Isaiah	22	2 Peter	3
22nd	Numbers	31	Psalms	75–76	Isaiah	23	1 John	1
23rd	Numbers	32	Psalms	77	Isaiah	24	1 John	2
24th	Numbers	33	Psalms	78:1–37	Isaiah	25	1 John	3
25th	Numbers	34	Psalms	78:38ff	Isaiah	26	1 John	4
26th	Numbers	35	Psalms	79	Isaiah	27	1 John	5
27th	Numbers	36	Psalms	80	Isaiah	28	2 John	1
28th	Deuteronomy	1	Psalms	81–82	Isaiah	29	3 John	1
29th	Deuteronomy	2	Psalms	83–84	Isaiah	30	Jude	1
30th	Deuteronomy	3	Psalms	85	Isaiah	31	Revelation	1
31st	Deuteronomy	4	Psalms	86–87	Isaiah	32	Revelation	2

June

1st	Deuteronomy	5	Psalms	88	Isaiah	33	Revelation	3
2nd	Deuteronomy	6	Psalms	89	Isaiah	34	Revelation	4
3rd	Deuteronomy	7	Psalms	90	Isaiah	35	Revelation	5
4th	Deuteronomy	8	Psalms	91	Isaiah	36	Revelation	6
5th	Deuteronomy	9	Psalms	92–93	Isaiah	37	Revelation	7
6th	Deuteronomy	10	Psalms	94	Isaiah	38	Revelation	8
7th	Deuteronomy	11	Psalms	95–96	Isaiah	39	Revelation	9
8th	Deuteronomy	12	Psalms	97–98	Isaiah	40	Revelation	10
9th	Deuteronomy	13–14	Psalms	99–101	Isaiah	41	Revelation	11
10th	Deuteronomy	15	Psalms	102	Isaiah	42	Revelation	12
11th	Deuteronomy	16	Psalms	103	Isaiah	43	Revelation	13
12th	Deuteronomy	17	Psalms	104	Isaiah	44	Revelation	14
13th	Deuteronomy	18	Psalms	105	Isaiah	45	Revelation	15
14th	Deuteronomy	19	Psalms	106	Isaiah	46	Revelation	16
15th	Deuteronomy	20	Psalms	107	Isaiah	47	Revelation	17
16th	Deuteronomy	21	Psalms	108–109	Isaiah	48	Revelation	18
17th	Deuteronomy	22	Psalms	110–111	Isaiah	49	Revelation	19
18th	Deuteronomy	23	Psalms	112–113	Isaiah	50	Revelation	20
19th	Deuteronomy	24	Psalms	114–115	Isaiah	51	Revelation	21
20th	Deuteronomy	25	Psalms	116	Isaiah	52	Revelation	22
21st	Deuteronomy	26	Psalms	117–118	Isaiah	53	Matthew	1
22nd	Deuteronomy	27–28:19	Psalms	119:1–24	Isaiah	54	Matthew	2
23rd	Deuteronomy	28:20ff	Psalms	119:25–48	Isaiah	55	Matthew	3
24th	Deuteronomy	29	Psalms	119:49–72	Isaiah	56	Matthew	4
25th	Deuteronomy	30	Psalms	119:73–96	Isaiah	57	Matthew	5
26th	Deuteronomy	31	Psalms	119:97–120	Isaiah	58	Matthew	6
27th	Deuteronomy	32	Psalms	119:121–144	Isaiah	59	Matthew	7
28th	Deuteronomy	33–34	Psalms	119:145–176	Isaiah	60	Matthew	8
29th	Joshua	1	Psalms	120–122	Isaiah	61	Matthew	9
30th	Joshua	2	Psalms	123–125	Isaiah	62	Matthew	10

July

1st	Joshua	3	Psalms	126–128	Isaiah	63	Matthew	11
2nd	Joshua	4	Psalms	129–131	Isaiah	64	Matthew	12
3rd	Joshua	5–6:5	Psalms	132–134	Isaiah	65	Matthew	13
4th	Joshua	6:6ff	Psalms	135–136	Isaiah	66	Matthew	14
5th	Joshua	7	Psalms	137–138	Jeremiah	1	Matthew	15
6th	Joshua	8	Psalms	139	Jeremiah	2	Matthew	16
7th	Joshua	9	Psalms	140–141	Jeremiah	3	Matthew	17
8th	Joshua	10	Psalms	142–143	Jeremiah	4	Matthew	18
9th	Joshua	11	Psalms	144	Jeremiah	5	Matthew	19
10th	Joshua	12–13	Psalms	145	Jeremiah	6	Matthew	20
11th	Joshua	14–15	Psalms	146–147	Jeremiah	7	Matthew	21
12th	Joshua	16–17	Psalms	148	Jeremiah	8	Matthew	22
13th	Joshua	18–19	Psalms	149–150	Jeremiah	9	Matthew	23
14th	Joshua	20–21	Acts	1	Jeremiah	10	Matthew	24
15th	Joshua	22	Acts	2	Jeremiah	11	Matthew	25
16th	Joshua	23	Acts	3	Jeremiah	12	Matthew	26
17th	Joshua	24	Acts	4	Jeremiah	13	Matthew	27
18th	Judges	1	Acts	5	Jeremiah	14	Matthew	28
19th	Judges	2	Acts	6	Jeremiah	15	Mark	1
20th	Judges	3	Acts	7	Jeremiah	16	Mark	2
21st	Judges	4	Acts	8	Jeremiah	17	Mark	3
22nd	Judges	5	Acts	9	Jeremiah	18	Mark	4
23rd	Judges	6	Acts	10	Jeremiah	19	Mark	5
24th	Judges	7	Acts	11	Jeremiah	20	Mark	6
25th	Judges	8	Acts	12	Jeremiah	21	Mark	7
26th	Judges	9	Acts	13	Jeremiah	22	Mark	8
27th	Judges	10–11:11	Acts	14	Jeremiah	23	Mark	9
28th	Judges	11:12ff	Acts	15	Jeremiah	24	Mark	10
29th	Judges	12	Acts	16	Jeremiah	25	Mark	11
30th	Judges	13	Acts	17	Jeremiah	26	Mark	12
31st	Judges	14	Acts	18	Jeremiah	27	Mark	13

August

1st	Judges	15	Acts	19	Jeremiah	28	Mark	14
2nd	Judges	16	Acts	20	Jeremiah	29	Mark	15
3rd	Judges	17	Acts	21	Jeremiah	30–31	Mark	16
4th	Judges	18	Acts	22	Jeremiah	32	Psalms	1–2
5th	Judges	19	Acts	23	Jeremiah	33	Psalms	3–4
6th	Judges	20	Acts	24	Jeremiah	34	Psalms	5–6
7th	Judges	21	Acts	25	Jeremiah	35	Psalms	7–8
8th	Ruth	1	Acts	26	Jeremiah	36 & 45	Psalms	9
9th	Ruth	2	Acts	27	Jeremiah	37	Psalms	10
10th	Ruth	3–4	Acts	28	Jeremiah	38	Psalms	11–12
11th	1 Samuel	1	Romans	1	Jeremiah	39	Psalms	13–14
12th	1 Samuel	2	Romans	2	Jeremiah	40	Psalms	15–16
13th	1 Samuel	3	Romans	3	Jeremiah	41	Psalms	17
14th	1 Samuel	4	Romans	4	Jeremiah	42	Psalms	18
15th	1 Samuel	5–6	Romans	5	Jeremiah	43	Psalms	19
16th	1 Samuel	7–8	Romans	6	Jeremiah	44	Psalms	20–21
17th	1 Samuel	9	Romans	7	Jeremiah	46	Psalms	22
18th	1 Samuel	10	Romans	8	Jeremiah	47	Psalms	23–24
19th	1 Samuel	11	Romans	9	Jeremiah	48	Psalms	25
20th	1 Samuel	12	Romans	10	Jeremiah	49	Psalms	26–27
21st	1 Samuel	13	Romans	11	Jeremiah	50	Psalms	28–29
22nd	1 Samuel	14	Romans	12	Jeremiah	51	Psalms	30
23rd	1 Samuel	15	Romans	13	Jeremiah	52	Psalms	31
24th	1 Samuel	16	Romans	14	Lamentations	1	Psalms	32
25th	1 Samuel	17	Romans	15	Lamentations	2	Psalms	33
26th	1 Samuel	18	Romans	16	Lamentations	3	Psalms	34
27th	1 Samuel	19	1 Corinthians	1	Lamentations	4	Psalms	35
28th	1 Samuel	20	1 Corinthians	2	Lamentations	5	Psalms	36
29th	1 Samuel	21–22	1 Corinthians	3	Ezekiel	1	Psalms	37
30th	1 Samuel	23	1 Corinthians	4	Ezekiel	2	Psalms	38
31st	1 Samuel	24	1 Corinthians	5	Ezekiel	3	Psalms	39

September

1st	1 Samuel	25	1 Corinthians	6	Ezekiel	4	Psalms	40–41
2nd	1 Samuel	26	1 Corinthians	7	Ezekiel	5	Psalms	42–43
3rd	1 Samuel	27	1 Corinthians	8	Ezekiel	6	Psalms	44
4th	1 Samuel	28	1 Corinthians	9	Ezekiel	7	Psalms	45
5th	1 Samuel	29–30	1 Corinthians	10	Ezekiel	8	Psalms	46–47
6th	1 Samuel	31	1 Corinthians	11	Ezekiel	9	Psalms	48
7th	2 Samuel	1	1 Corinthians	12	Ezekiel	10	Psalms	49
8th	2 Samuel	2	1 Corinthians	13	Ezekiel	11	Psalms	50
9th	2 Samuel	3	1 Corinthians	14	Ezekiel	12	Psalms	51
10th	2 Samuel	4–5	1 Corinthians	15	Ezekiel	13	Psalms	52–54
11th	2 Samuel	6	1 Corinthians	16	Ezekiel	14	Psalms	55
12th	2 Samuel	7	2 Corinthians	1	Ezekiel	15	Psalms	56–57
13th	2 Samuel	8–9	2 Corinthians	2	Ezekiel	16	Psalms	58–59
14th	2 Samuel	10	2 Corinthians	3	Ezekiel	17	Psalms	60–61
15th	2 Samuel	11	2 Corinthians	4	Ezekiel	18	Psalms	62–63
16th	2 Samuel	12	2 Corinthians	5	Ezekiel	19	Psalms	64–65
17th	2 Samuel	13	2 Corinthians	6	Ezekiel	20	Psalms	66–67
18th	2 Samuel	14	2 Corinthians	7	Ezekiel	21	Psalms	68
19th	2 Samuel	15	2 Corinthians	8	Ezekiel	22	Psalms	69
20th	2 Samuel	16	2 Corinthians	9	Ezekiel	23	Psalms	70–71
21st	2 Samuel	17	2 Corinthians	10	Ezekiel	24	Psalms	72
22nd	2 Samuel	18	2 Corinthians	11	Ezekiel	25	Psalms	73
23rd	2 Samuel	19	2 Corinthians	12	Ezekiel	26	Psalms	74
24th	2 Samuel	20	2 Corinthians	13	Ezekiel	27	Psalms	75–76
25th	2 Samuel	21	Galatians	1	Ezekiel	28	Psalms	77
26th	2 Samuel	22	Galatians	2	Ezekiel	29	Psalms	78:1–37
27th	2 Samuel	23	Galatians	3	Ezekiel	30	Psalms	78:38ff
28th	2 Samuel	24	Galatians	4	Ezekiel	31	Psalms	79
29th	1 Kings	1	Galatians	5	Ezekiel	32	Psalms	80
30th	1 Kings	2	Galatians	6	Ezekiel	33	Psalms	81–82

October

1st	1 Kings	3	Ephesians	1	Ezekiel	34	Psalms 83–84
2nd	1 Kings	4–5	Ephesians	2	Ezekiel	35	Psalms 85
3rd	1 Kings	6	Ephesians	3	Ezekiel	36	Psalms 86
4th	1 Kings	7	Ephesians	4	Ezekiel	37	Psalms 87–88
5th	1 Kings	8	Ephesians	5	Ezekiel	38	Psalms 89
6th	1 Kings	9	Ephesians	6	Ezekiel	39	Psalms 90
7th	1 Kings	10	Philippians	1	Ezekiel	40	Psalms 91
8th	1 Kings	11	Philippians	2	Ezekiel	41	Psalms 92–93
9th	1 Kings	12	Philippians	3	Ezekiel	42	Psalms 94
10th	1 Kings	13	Philippians	4	Ezekiel	43	Psalms 95–96
11th	1 Kings	14	Colossians	1	Ezekiel	44	Psalms 97–98
12th	1 Kings	15	Colossians	2	Ezekiel	45	Psalms 99–101
13th	1 Kings	16	Colossians	3	Ezekiel	46	Psalms 102
14th	1 Kings	17	Colossians	4	Ezekiel	47	Psalms 103
15th	1 Kings	18	1 Thessalonians	1	Ezekiel	48	Psalms 104
16th	1 Kings	19	1 Thessalonians	2	Daniel	1	Psalms 105
17th	1 Kings	20	1 Thessalonians	3	Daniel	2	Psalms 106
18th	1 Kings	21	1 Thessalonians	4	Daniel	3	Psalms 107
19th	1 Kings	22	1 Thessalonians	5	Daniel	4	Psalms 108–109
20th	2 Kings	1	2 Thessalonians	1	Daniel	5	Psalms 110–111
21st	2 Kings	2	2 Thessalonians	2	Daniel	6	Psalms 112–113
22nd	2 Kings	3	2 Thessalonians	3	Daniel	7	Psalms 114–115
23rd	2 Kings	4	1 Timothy	1	Daniel	8	Psalms 116
24th	2 Kings	5	1 Timothy	2	Daniel	9	Psalms 117–118
25th	2 Kings	6	1 Timothy	3	Daniel	10	Psalms 119:1–24
26th	2 Kings	7	1 Timothy	4	Daniel	11	Psalms 119:25–48
27th	2 Kings	8	1 Timothy	5	Daniel	12	Psalms 119:49–72
28th	2 Kings	9	1 Timothy	6	Hosea	1	Psalms 119:73–96
29th	2 Kings	10	2 Timothy	1	Hosea	2	Psalms 119:97–120
30th	2 Kings	11–12	2 Timothy	2	Hosea	3–4	Psalms 119:121–144
31st	2 Kings	13	2 Timothy	3	Hosea	5–6	Psalms 119:145–176

November

1st	2 Kings	14	2 Timothy	4	Hosea	7	Psalms	120–122
2nd	2 Kings	15	Titus	1	Hosea	8	Psalms	123–125
3rd	2 Kings	16	Titus	2	Hosea	9	Psalms	126–128
4th	2 Kings	17	Titus	3	Hosea	10	Psalms	129–131
5th	2 Kings	18	Philemon	1	Hosea	11	Psalms	132–134
6th	2 Kings	19	Hebrews	1	Hosea	12	Psalms	135–136
7th	2 Kings	20	Hebrews	2	Hosea	13	Psalms	137–138
8th	2 Kings	21	Hebrews	3	Hosea	14	Psalms	139
9th	2 Kings	22	Hebrews	4	Joel	1	Psalms	140–141
10th	2 Kings	23	Hebrews	5	Joel	2	Psalms	142
11th	2 Kings	24	Hebrews	6	Joel	3	Psalms	143
12th	2 Kings	25	Hebrews	7	Amos	1	Psalms	144
13th	1 Chronicles	1–2	Hebrews	8	Amos	2	Psalms	145
14th	1 Chronicles	3–4	Hebrews	9	Amos	3	Psalms	146–147
15th	1 Chronicles	5–6	Hebrews	10	Amos	4	Psalms	148–150
16th	1 Chronicles	7–8	Hebrews	11	Amos	5	Luke	1:1–38
17th	1 Chronicles	9–10	Hebrews	12	Amos	6	Luke	1:39ff
18th	1 Chronicles	11–12	Hebrews	13	Amos	7	Luke	2
19th	1 Chronicles	13–14	James	1	Amos	8	Luke	3
20th	1 Chronicles	15	James	2	Amos	9	Luke	4
21st	1 Chronicles	16	James	3	Obadiah	1	Luke	5
22nd	1 Chronicles	17	James	4	Jonah	1	Luke	6
23rd	1 Chronicles	18	James	5	Jonah	2	Luke	7
24th	1 Chronicles	19–20	1 Peter	1	Jonah	3	Luke	8
25th	1 Chronicles	21	1 Peter	2	Jonah	4	Luke	9
26th	1 Chronicles	22	1 Peter	3	Micah	1	Luke	10
27th	1 Chronicles	23	1 Peter	4	Micah	2	Luke	11
28th	1 Chronicles	24–25	1 Peter	5	Micah	3	Luke	12
29th	1 Chronicles	26–27	2 Peter	1	Micah	4	Luke	13
30th	1 Chronicles	28	2 Peter	2	Micah	5	Luke	14

December

1st	1 Chronicles	29	2 Peter	3	Micah	6	Luke	15
2nd	2 Chronicles	1	1 John	1	Micah	7	Luke	16
3rd	2 Chronicles	2	1 John	2	Nahum	1	Luke	17
4th	2 Chronicles	3–4	1 John	3	Nahum	2	Luke	18
5th	2 Chronicles	5–6:11	1 John	4	Nahum	3	Luke	19
6th	2 Chronicles	6:12ff	1 John	5	Habakkuk	1	Luke	20
7th	2 Chronicles	7	2 John	1	Habakkuk	2	Luke	21
8th	2 Chronicles	8	3 John	1	Habakkuk	3	Luke	22
9th	2 Chronicles	9	Jude	1	Zephaniah	1	Luke	23
10th	2 Chronicles	10	Revelation	1	Zephaniah	2	Luke	24
11th	2 Chronicles	11–12	Revelation	2	Zephaniah	3	John	1
12th	2 Chronicles	13	Revelation	3	Haggai	1	John	2
13th	2 Chronicles	14–15	Revelation	4	Haggai	2	John	3
14th	2 Chronicles	16	Revelation	5	Zechariah	1	John	4
15th	2 Chronicles	17	Revelation	6	Zechariah	2	John	5
16th	2 Chronicles	18	Revelation	7	Zechariah	3	John	6
17th	2 Chronicles	19–20	Revelation	8	Zechariah	4	John	7
18th	2 Chronicles	21	Revelation	9	Zechariah	5	John	8
19th	2 Chronicles	22–23	Revelation	10	Zechariah	6	John	9
20th	2 Chronicles	24	Revelation	11	Zechariah	7	John	10
21st	2 Chronicles	25	Revelation	12	Zechariah	8	John	11
22nd	2 Chronicles	26	Revelation	13	Zechariah	9	John	12
23rd	2 Chronicles	27–28	Revelation	14	Zechariah	10	John	13
24th	2 Chronicles	29	Revelation	15	Zechariah	11	John	14
25th	2 Chronicles	30	Revelation	16	Zechariah	12–13:1	John	15
26th	2 Chronicles	31	Revelation	17	Zechariah	13:2ff	John	16
27th	2 Chronicles	32	Revelation	18	Zechariah	14	John	17
28th	2 Chronicles	33	Revelation	19	Malachi	1	John	18
29th	2 Chronicles	34	Revelation	20	Malachi	2	John	19
30th	2 Chronicles	35	Revelation	21	Malachi	3	John	20
31st	2 Chronicles	36	Revelation	22	Malachi	4	John	21